Research Design in Political Science
How to Practice What They Preach

Edited by

Thomas Gschwend
Senior Research Fellow
University of Mannheim, Germany

and

Frank Schimmelfennig
Professor of European Politics
Swiss Federal Institute of Technology, Zurich, Switzerland

First published in 2007 by
PALGRAVE MACMILLAN
Houndmills, Basingstoke, Hampshire RG21 6XS and
175 Fifth Avenue, New York, N.Y. 10010
Companies and representatives throughout the world

PALGRAVE MACMILLAN is the global academic imprint of the Palgrave
Macmillan division of St. Martin's Press, LLC and of Palgrave Macmillan Ltd.
Macmillan® is a registered trademark in the United States, United Kingdom
and other countries. Palgrave is a registered trademark in the European
Union and other countries.

ISBN-13: 978–0–230–01947–8 hardback
ISBN-10: 0–230–01947–1 hardback

This book is printed on paper suitable for recycling and made from fully
managed and sustained forest sources. Logging, pulping and manufacturing
processes are expected to conform to the environmental regulations of
the country of origin.

A catalogue record for this book is available from the British Library.

A catalog record for this book is available from the Library of Congress.

10 9 8 7 6 5 4 3 2 1
16 15 14 13 12 11 10 09 08 07

Printed and bound in Great Britain by
Antony Rowe Ltd, Chippenham and Eastbourne

Contents

Part IV   Case Selection

Part V   Control

Part VI   Theoretical Conclusions

List of Tables

List of Figures

Preface and Acknowledgments

There is no shortage in preaching of how to design research for political science. *Designing Social Inquiry* (King, Keohane and Verba, 1994) has strongly contributed to methodological awareness in the field. It has arguably become the most influential methodological work in the discipline and a standard item on the reading lists for research design courses. At the same time, and provoked by its tendency to model qualitative research on the quantitative, statistical template, it has triggered extensive controversy and reactions by qualitative scholars. *Rethinking Social Inquiry* (Brady and Collier, 2004) collects articles that provide a nuanced response to 'Designing Social Inquiry', asserting the distinctiveness and equivalence of qualitative methodology but, in the subtitle of the volume, committing themselves to 'shared standards' in spite of 'diverse tools'.

The debate, however, has generally remained at a highly abstract and meta-theoretical level. Whereas our advanced students have become more methodologically aware and willing to improve their research designs and methods, they have also experienced great difficulties in translating the abstract considerations and prescriptions in the literature into concrete advice and guidance for their own research projects.

This gap has become obvious during a series of research design seminars with PhD students at the Mannheim Center for European Social Research at the University of Mannheim in the past years and has eventually triggered our interest in producing this book. As a group of researchers coming from diverse disciplinary and methodological backgrounds, we struggled to understand what unites and divides qualitative and quantitative research, tried to keep abreast of the increasing number of methodology books and articles, and made an attempt to pay heed to the advice we received from them in our individual research projects. We found this experience so gratifying that we decided to share it with a larger readership. This book is the result of this endeavor.

The volume represents the collective effort of all contributors. We benefited from several rounds of discussions and revisions among ourselves. We thank the Mannheim Center for European Social Research for providing such an intellectually stimulating environment and its and ETH Zurich's institutional support in the final preparation of the manuscript. In addition, we owe thanks to Michael Agner for language editing, Alison Howson, Steven Kennedy, and Amy Lankester-Owen of Palgrave Macmillan for their support and smooth handling of the project, and two anonymous reviewers for their helpful and constructive comments.

Notes on Contributors

Dirk De Bièvre, Lecturer in International Politics, Department of Political Science, Universiteit Antwerpen, Belgium.

Andreas Dür, Lecturer, School of Politics and International Relations, University College Dublin, Ireland.

Thomas Gschwend, Senior Research Fellow, Mannheim Center for European Social Research (MZES), Mannheim, Germany.

Matthias Lehnert, Lecturer, Department of Social Sciences, University of Mannheim, Germany.

Dirk Leuffen, Post-Doctoral Researcher, Center for Comparative and International Studies, ETH Zurich, Switzerland.

Bernhard Miller, Research Fellow, Mannheim Center for European Social Research (MZES), Mannheim, Germany.

Julia Rathke, Lecturer, Department of Social Sciences, University of Mannheim, Germany.

Frank Schimmelfennig, Professor of European Politics, Center for Comparative and International Studies, ETH Zurich, Switzerland.

Ulrich Sieberer, Lecturer, Department of Social Sciences, University of Mannheim, Germany.

Janina Thiem, Researcher, Mannheim Center for European Social Research (MZES), Mannheim, Germany.

Arndt Wonka, Researcher, Mannheim Center for European Social Research (MZES), Mannheim, Germany.

1
Introduction: Designing Research in Political Science – A Dialogue between Theory and Data

Thomas Gschwend and Frank Schimmelfennig

Quick-and-dirty number-crunching 'quantoids' face them. Carefully describing and interpreting 'smooshes' face them (Hatch, 1985). No matter where they stand on ontological and epistemological grounds and how we stereotype the respective 'other side', all researchers face similar challenges posed to core issues of research design. How you deal with theses challenges defines the research design for your individual projects. A research design is a plan that specifies how you plan to carry out your research project and, particularly, how you expect to use your evidence to answer your research question.[1]

What is a relevant research problem? How can I improve concepts and measurements in my research? Which and how many variables and cases should I select? How can I evaluate rival explanations and which theoretical conclusions can I draw from my research? Which evidence would lead me to reject and reformulate my initial theory? These are central questions political science students inevitably face when they embark on their own research projects in a Master's or a PhD program.

This book was written to help advanced students of political science think about these issues and come up with solutions for their own research. It has emerged out of a seminar course that we directed for several semesters. As the course united researchers from both the quantitative and qualitative 'camps', mutual misunderstandings and heated debates were inevitable. Despite this, seminar discussions also shaped a number of shared beliefs that provide the common ground for this volume:

1. The methodological pluralism in our discipline is a strength rather than a weakness.
2. The basic problems of research design are the same for qualitative and quantitative political science research.
3. The methodological debate in the discipline often remains at an abstract level and does not give sufficient practical guidance for dealing with basic research design problems.
4. The distinction between qualitative and quantitative research is often inadequate. Some solutions to research design problems are common to both types of research; others cross-cut the traditional qualitative-quantitative divide.
5. At any rate, finding solutions to research design problems involves substantial trade-offs along the way. Each solution has its strengths and weaknesses.

Thus, the contributions to this volume do not start with general methodological discussions, but each focuses instead on a specific problem of research design. They explicate the problem, discuss various solutions, emphasize the typical trade-offs involved in choosing one or the other solution, present practical guidelines and illustrate the use of these guidelines in an example taken from their own research. In the remainder of the introduction, we will give an overview of the basic problems and different types of research design that will be taken up in the individual book chapters.

Core issues of research design

At a very general level, scientific research can be conceived of as a dialogue between theory and data. Researchers formulate a theory, analyze data to test it, reformulate their theory in light of the empirical evidence, and then move on to test the reformulated theory with new data. Or, starting at the other end, researchers make observations, develop a theory to explain them, use additional data to test their theory, and possibly reformulate it afterwards. Individual research projects do not necessarily go through the entire cycle. Science is a collective enterprise. Some research projects focus on testing existing hypotheses; others are more concerned with explaining specific observations and generating new hypotheses.

We claim, however, that all research projects that take part in this dialogue between theory and data face the same set of core research design issues. These are: defining the research question and problem; specifying concepts and theory; operationalization and measurement; selecting cases and observations; controlling for alternative explanations; and drawing theoretical conclusions from the empirical analysis.[2] In the following paragraphs, we will address these tasks one by one.[3]

Defining the research problem.   First of all, the researcher is faced with the question: 'What should I do research on?' The most general answer to this question is: 'Something relevant.' But relevant to whom and in which way? At this point, we can distinguish between theoretical or scientific relevance on the one hand, and social relevance on the other (see King, Keohane and Verba, 1994, p. 15). Research is relevant to the scientific community if it advances the collective dialogue between theory and data beyond the current state of the discipline – by formulating, testing and improving theory, by generating and improving data, and by describing and explaining observations. To do so, the researcher needs to identify puzzles and problems in the discipline such as a theoretical controversy; imprecise, inconsistent, incomplete or otherwise 'bad' theory; untested theories and unexplained observations; unreliable, invalid or otherwise 'bad' measurement and data. Research is socially relevant if it addresses social problems, improves citizens' and policymakers' understanding of the problem and, possibly, offers solutions. To do so, the researcher needs to clarify the social relevance of her research and demonstrate how it can be used to understand and solve social problems (Gerring and Yesnowitz, 2006). Yet the current state of the discipline leaves considerable room for improvement, and political problems abound. So researchers still have to decide (and justify) which of the numerous problems and puzzles they choose to address.

Specifying concepts.   Whether we formulate and test theories or describe and explain observations, we inevitably use concepts such as 'democracy', 'party', 'conflict', and 'peace'. In order to make research relevant, these concepts need to be theoretically and/or socially important. But they also need to be (properly) specified. It must be clear what we mean by a specific concept, that is what its defining attributes are, how attributes and concepts relate to each other, and which empirical phenomena they include and exclude. What attributes define a 'democracy'? Does 'peace' exclude 'conflict'? How do 'parties' differ from other organizations? Clear and unambiguous concepts are not only required for formulating testable theories in the first place. When engaging in a theoretical controversy, the researcher needs to examine the concepts of the competing theories – especially when the theories use the same terms. Starting from the data, descriptive inference requires no less careful concept specification – for instance, if you make statements like 'The majority of states are democracies' or 'The occurrence of war is decreasing'.

Specifying theory. Causal theories formulate cause-effect relationships between concepts. Thus, researchers not only need to specify the concepts themselves but also their relationship. Most basically, theories specify the order of the causal relationship between the concepts: what is the cause, what is the effect? Further specification may concern the form of the relationship (linear or non-linear) and the direction (positive or negative). Theories also need to specify the relationship among various assumed causes. Is it additive, as commonly assumed in linear regression models, or multiplicative, as is the case for interaction effects? Alternatively, causes can be characterized as necessary and/or sufficient conditions of the outcome. For instance, democratic peace theory holds that 'joint democracy', the fact that two countries are both democratic, is a sufficient (but not a necessary) condition for durable peace between them.

Furthermore, theories should specify the causal mechanisms that link cause and effect and theorize on the process through which the cause produces the effect. For example, the democratic peace has been explained by the transparency and inertia of political decision-making in democracies, which prevents secret preparations to war, slows down military escalation and gives democracies sufficient time to negotiate and find peaceful solutions to their conflicts (Russett, 1993, pp. 38–40). Advocates of causal mechanism analysis also generally demand that social science theories must specify their 'microfoundations' (Coleman, 1990; Hedström and Swedberg, 1998). That is, they must show how social structures and environments translate into individual desires and beliefs (macro-micro), how the actor produces preferences and actions on the basis of these desires and beliefs (micro-micro), and how the actions of many individuals are transformed into a collective, social outcome (micro-macro). The more fully a theory is specified, the more fully it potentially explains observations and the better it can be tested.

Measuring concepts. By specifying concepts and theory, we arrive at testable theoretical propositions. In order to conduct the empirical test, however, the concepts need to be operationalized and measured. Obviously, democracy – even if clearly specified as a concept – cannot be observed directly. This is often also true for the defining attributes. Alvarez and colleagues (1996), for instance, define democracy as a political regime in which offices are filled by contested elections. They then go on to provide 'operational rules', which specify the offices that need to be included (the chief executive and the legislature) and indicators of 'contestation' (above all that there has to be more than one party). Furthermore, the operationalization would have to include indicators for determining the 'chief executive', the 'legislature' and 'parties'. Even after such a fine-grained operationalization, researchers still have to choose the instruments for measurement, for example expert assessments or legal documents. At any rate, the measurement needs to be both valid (the data needs to correspond to the specifications of the concept) and reliable (repeated measurement of the same phenomenon must produce the same values of the indicator).

Selecting cases.   Problems of case selection and selection bias are core issues in both quantitative and qualitative methods textbooks. To be precise, we need to distinguish between units of analysis, cases, and observations. The unit of analysis is the abstract entity that we study (e.g., states, institutions, decisions) which is often given by the theory. 'Case' refers to the specific units of analysis that we choose to analyze. If the unit is 'state', this could be a single-case study of Sweden or a comparative case study of Sweden and Norway. Finally, one case may be equal to one observation if it consists in a single set of values of the independent and dependent variables. A single case, however, can also yield multiple observations. Research on the accession of Scandinavian countries to the European Union might be based on a single set of values for independent variables such as GDP per capita, growth, and export dependency for each Scandinavian state. Alternatively, we can make multiple 'data-set observations' (Collier, Brady and Seawright, 2004b, p. 252) for each case, for instance by observing the values of these economic variables at different points in time. Or we can turn to a series of 'causal-process observations' (Brady, Collier and Seawright, 2004, p. 11) in order to see how structural economic conditions were transformed into decisions on EU accession (such as lobbying by interest groups and election or referendum outcomes).

For theory testing, the question is how observations can be selected so that the results of the analysis are unbiased and provide a valid assessment of the theory. For the description and explanation of social phenomena, the question arises as to whether the selected observations represent the class of phenomena adequately. Is '9/11' representative of transnational terrorism? Does an analysis of 'Blairism' allow for general conclusions on the tendency toward personalization in current parliamentary democracies? Sometimes random selection is possible (as in studies of electoral behavior) but even here the selection procedure may privilege one group of respondents over another – for instance, those people spending a lot of time at home and thus more likely to respond to calls by the polling institute. Sometimes we know the entire population of cases – such as democracies or post-communist revolutions – but empirical analysis of more than a few cases would be too demanding, and the random selection of those cases would most likely lead to bias. Finally, we may not even know the universe of cases. Generally, researchers are therefore confronted with either unintended or intentional non-random selection which must be taken into account in order to arrive at valid generalizations and theoretical conclusions.

Controlling for alternative explanations.   In the dialogue between theory and data, we specify a theory in order to test it on the basis of the selected cases and measurements. Alternatively, we draw on or construct a theory in order to explain a set of observations or a specific outcome. Yet even if we find a strong relationship between the theorized causes and the observed effects, how can we be sure that this relationship is not spurious and that other causal factors would not explain the observations just as well if not better? For instance, the 'democratic peace' might be attributed to the hegemony of liberal great powers or to high economic interdependence between democratic countries. In other words, we have to address, and control for, alternative causal factors and explanations in our research. But how many and which alternative factors or variables should be included in the analysis, and how do we decide on which of these rival theories or causes provide the best explanation?

Drawing theoretical conclusions.   Let us assume we have successfully tested a well-specified theory with valid and reliable measurements on an unbiased selection of cases and that we have been able to reject alternative explanations. In this case, the theory is corroborated and does not need to be revised or rejected. Often, however, we will encounter anomalies such as deviant cases or statistically insignificant relationships. What if, for instance, we find a single instance of two democratic countries waging war against each other? Could one deviant case simply be ignored or would this mean the democratic peace theory is flawed and should be dumped in the junkyard of falsified hypotheses? Could the theory be saved by respecification or by limiting its scope? At any rate, empirical research results do not speak for themselves. The conclusions we draw from them need to be well considered so that knowledge is improved rather than prematurely destroyed or falsely preserved. At

Table 1.1   Research design tasks and problems

Research design issue	Challenge
Research problem	Relevance
Concepts and theory	Clear specification
Measurement	Validity and reliability
Case selection	Valid and general inferences
Control	Valid and best explanation
Theoretical conclusions	Scientific progress

first glance, these considerations do not seem to be part of the research design, because they only come up after research has been concluded. However, research should be designed from the start in a way that allows us to draw the right conclusions for theory.

Table 1.1 sums up the main challenges posed by the various issues of research design. We need to define a relevant research problem, clearly specify our concepts and theory, provide for valid and reliable measurement, select cases that allow for the formulation of valid inferences and generalizing our results, control for alternative explanations to demonstrate the validity and superiority of the proposed theory, and advance scientific progress in drawing our theoretical conclusions from the findings. How we get there or, more modestly, how we get closer to meeting these challenges, will be the subject of the chapters in this volume.

Basic types of research design

In general, research designs can be individually tailored to the concrete research problem at hand. However, the literature suggests that there are a few basic types of research design that researchers can opt for and that differ with regard to, for instance, the selection of variables and cases, the choice of data and methods, and their implications for theory. In the following, we will provide an overview of the different types that will be taken up in the individual chapters. The one basic dichotomy is that of factor-centric vesus outcome-centric research designs; the other one is large-n versus small-n designs.

Factor-centric versus outcome-centric research design.   George and Bennett (1997) originally introduced the difference between factor-centric and outcome-centric research to describe alternative inference processes in case studies. There is no need, however, to restrict this terminology merely to case study research. In fact, we find it very helpful when evaluating potential research designs more broadly.[4] Research designs can be distinguished by the type of causal inference a researcher is trying to make in order to answer a research question. In planning to make a causal inference a researcher might be either interested in providing evidence for one or more particular causal mechanisms and effects or, instead, wants to account for specific outcomes as completely as possible. For instance, you could be interested in the mechanisms of how voters' preferences for particular parties facilitate their decision in the voting booth or, instead, try to predict their voting behavior.

We call a research-design *factor-centric* if one is primarily interested in the explanatory power of causal factors. The goal is to estimate the direction and size of a particular causal effect of one or a few independent variables, X_i ($i = 1, \ldots , n$), on a dependent variable, Y, and to assess their robustness. Independent variables are either explanatory or test variables, which are of key interest for the causal effects and mechanisms you are after, or mere control variables, which are included to make sure that the causal effects can really be attributed to the explanatory or test variable rather than to alternative causal factors. Typical research questions of factor-centric research designs are: Does X_i cause Y or what effect does a X_i have on Y and how much? Thus if you are interested in how partisan preferences anchor a voter's decision-formation process, you might want to allow for alternative ways in which vote-choice decisions can be rooted – such as ideological or candidate preferences – in order to disentangle their potential impact from that of your major explanatory variable of interest.

A research design is *outcome-centric*, however, if one is primarily interested in explaining outcomes. The goal is to comprehensively assess potential and alternative explanations by considering many independent variables, X_i, that *in toto* try to account for variance in the dependent variable, Y, as completely as possible. Examples are explanations of the varying success of UN peacekeeping operations or the differential impact of EU law on the member states. Outcome-centric research might also be interested in explaining specific single events (the Iranian revolution or the end of the Cold War – in other words, a dependent variable without variance). The typical research question of outcome-centric research designs is: What causes Y or why Y? Thus if you are interested in predicting individual voting behavior you might want to choose an outcome-centric research design and consequently include additional independent variables (e.g., contextual or media effects) that help you better predict behavior in the voting booth, even though the omission of those variables does not have the potentional to distort the individual-level relationships that factor-centric researchers might focus on.

What reasons might there be to choose one design rather than the other? We suggest that the choice is mainly up to the researcher's interest and considerations of relevance. If you are mainly interested in explaining important events in politics (such as wars or revolutions) or predicting the outcomes of specific political decisions (such as the formation of a government coalition), the obvious choice is an outcome-centric design. This often requires an in-depth knowledge of phenomena in which you are interested.

If, however, your research is driven by a theoretical interest in causal factors (such as resources or institutions) or mechanisms (such as political socialization or political dilemmas), factor-centric designs are the most suitable. Researchers opting for a factor-centric research design have to 'control for', 'account for' or 'hold constant' the influence of all potential confounding factors in order to separate out those effects from the causal relationship in which they are primarily interested. This is the central aspect for making valid inferences based on factor-centric research designs. There are various strategies that facilitate researchers in disentangling the causal net. Including control variables in regression equations, matching methods or laboratory and field experiments are potential solutions that require many observations. Yet there also exist strategies that allow for distinguishing the hypothesized from confounding effects without leveraging many observations. One strategy is to systematically compare only a few carefully matched cases. Another strategy is the quasi-experiment, where one compares the very same case before and after the 'treatment' such as an institutional change or a policy intervention (George and Bennett, 2005, ch. 8).

The choice between factor-centric and outcome-centric research designs is not necessarily tied to the state of theory development in a given field, although in theoretically less advanced fields researchers often opt for an outcome-centric research design. Such researchers try to explore new phenomena by focusing directly on the variance of the dependent variable. Nevertheless, good arguments have been made that focusing on a comprehensive explanation of a phenomenon by maximizing the accounted variance of a dependent variable may not be the most promising first step to develop new theoretical and empirical insights (e.g., Geddes, 2003, ch. 2, King, Keohane and Verba, 1994, p. 169, note 8). Such a strategy may simply not be feasible due to data collection problems, may make estimates of all causal effects more uncertain, or may be a hindrance to the accumulation of knowledge based on a common theoretical framework.

Alternatively, following a factor-centric research design strategy, one could break up a comprehensive explanation into more manageable building blocks of a theory, identify relevant variables to describe the causal mechanisms involved in these blocks, and afterwards, piece those building blocks together. There is, however, considerable skepticism as to whether such a 'lego' strategy (Pierson and Skocpol, 2002, p. 717) actually facilitates the accumulation of knowledge. Critics of this approach point out that, rather than answering big relevant questions in broad contexts, this strategy leads to robust answers of small and potentially trivial questions (Pierson and Skocpol, 2002, pp. 713–18).

While theory development of a given field might predispose researchers to employ a particular research design, it in no way determines the choice between factor-centric or outcome-centric research designs. Even in theoretically more advanced fields, researchers do not only opt for a factor-centric research design, although it might be easier to isolate a particular causal factor and focus on the direction and size of its effect, given the advanced state of theory development. For instance, researchers may be primarily interested in forecasting future outcomes such as elections or state failures. Then, of course, outcome-centric research designs are essentially required to answer this kind of research question.

Large-n versus small-n research design. What's your 'n'? One of the most often applied dichotomies to classify research designs refers to the number of cases and observations you study. Large-n and small-n research designs differ in the way in which they leverage available empirical information. Large-n studies are commonly associated with statistical tests of correlation-based inferences following a probabilistic model of causation and leveraging 'data-set observations', that is, 'observations [that] are collected as an array of scores on specific variables for a designated sample of cases ...' (Brady, Collier and Seawright, 2004, p. 12).

Small-n studies, however, are commonly associated with either within-case analysis or cross-case comparisons (George and Bennett, 2005) and with leveraging multiple 'causal-process observations' for a single case (Brady, Collier and Seawright, 2004, p. 252). Case studies rely on process-tracing in order to better understand the causal mechanisms of the relationships and phenomena of interest (e.g., see George and Bennett, 2005, pp. 147–9). Such inferences can be made by closely tracing hypothesized causal processes either within a particular case or by a systematic (controlled) comparison across a small number of cases (such as George and Bennett, 2005, ch. 8).

In other words, large-n studies seek to achieve and increase the validity of causal inferences by increasing the number of cases and data-set observations, whereas small-n studies seek to attain the same goal by carefully matching a limited number of cases and increasing the number of causal-process observations. Small-n research prefers depth to breadth, whereas large-n research prioritizes breadth. As a result, small-n research potentially leads to very precise causal stories for one or a few cases at the expense of generality, whereas large-n research strengthens our belief in the generality and average strength of causal effects at the expense of rendering individual cases largely 'invisible' (Ragin, 2000, p. 31) and by being unable to explain any single case precisely.

How should one choose between a small-n and a large-n research design? A fundamental principle is that better data collection methods are preferable to better data analytical methods. Thus, it is the art-part of designing your research in cleverly using available information, or gathering new information, and thinking hard about alternative sources of information and how they can be leveraged. Whenever sufficiently quantifiable and comparable information is available, large-n research designs are typically used. But buyer beware! Increasing the number of observations, even if potentially available, is no free lunch. Is the new information really comparable to the original? Do I have to stretch concepts in order to derive comparability? Do the indicators fit the new cases? The leverage obtained by adding observations might be reduced. Alternatively, no harm is done in adding causal process information to bolster causal claims based on the original data set. In fact, this perception is also shared by hard-core large-n statistical wizards (for instance, see Beck, 2006; Goldthorpe, 2001).

The division of published research into small-n and large-n is not only conceptual but shows up in actual research practice as well (see Bollen *et al.*, 1993, p. 327; Ragin, 2000, p. 25). Apparently there is a divide between small-n and large-n research designs, but what is small and what is large in that regard? On the lower end there are many single-case studies or studies with a handful of cases, while on the upper end there are also many studies that employ 50 and more, and in case of survey data, thousands of observations. Given that we all have finite time horizons and eventually need to produce some research output, researchers typically focus on the depth of their case knowledge when employing a small-n research design while they focus on the breadth of their findings when employing a large-n research design. Studies between those two poles have 10 to 50 observations. For such a study, it becomes less clear whether it should leverage on in-depth knowledge or on its breadth. On the one hand, there are quantitative electoral forecasting models containing less than 15 observations which nevertheless employ the method of statistical control common in large-n research designs (e.g., Bartels and Zaller 2001; Lewis-Beck and Rice, 1992; Norpoth and Gschwend, 2003). On the other hand, qualitative comparative methods such as QCA or fuzzy-set analysis (Ragin, 1987; Ragin, 2000) can accommodate dozens of observations.

At the end of the day, we are interested in why stuff happens in order to provide explanations and improve our understanding of cause-effect relations in the social world. There is, however, a considerable controversy in the literature about how to conceptualize causality. Small-n research tends to be framed as the analysis of necessary and sufficient causal conditions. This entails at least implicitly a rather deterministic (and nonlinear) view of causality. Large-n (but also some small-n) research, however, has it the opposite way around and adopts a probabilistic view of causality, according to which '..."causes" are factors that raise the (prior) probabilities of an event occurring ...' (Gerring, 2001, p. 129). In general, deterministic causes are helpful if we can assume that the relationship between independent variables and our dependent variable is in fact deterministic. They can give us clear guidelines as to what we should be seeing empirically, if they were really true, and help us disentangle the causal net. But when can we really be sure about deterministic causes in political science? On the one hand, nature might be random to some extent. Thus, even if we were able to measure our concepts precisely, we would never be able to completely explain variation in our dependent variables. This is still true even if we were to include all the variables we can ever dream of and specify the potentially non-linear model correctly. In other words, we not only assume that we included, but also modeled, all contingent causal factors correctly. On the other hand there is also the problem that all measures are imperfect. Thus the very act of measuring a theoretical concept, even if we tend to believe in a deterministic causal world, does always introduce some randomness in the analysis.

This controversy is not only relevant from a philosophy of science perspective. It also has important implications for your research design and the interpretation of your results. Think about it this way: How do we deal with a single case or observation that deviates considerably from an otherwise nice causal pattern? If you believe in a deterministic causal world with perfect measures and correctly specified models of relationships, you will have a serious problem. The single deviant case is evidence against your theory and must lead to its reconsideration. For believers in probabilistic causes, be they small-n as well as large-n researchers, a deviant case is simply an outlier. However, even if you believe in deterministic causes and perfectly specified theoretical explanations, outlying observations can happen and do not by themselves invalidate your hypothesis simply due to less-than-perfect conceptualizations of your theoretical building blocks and measurement error.

There are several ways to deal with outlying observations independent from the number of observations available. One strategy is to argue that the model is correctly specified and observations deviate from the general pattern because of noisy measures. Another way is to account for outlying observations directly by rethinking your theory. Following this strategy, the deviations from an expected general pattern are of substantive interest rather than produced by our inability to measure precisely. When rethinking your theory, one conceivable strategy would be to try specifying 'scope conditions' (Ragin, 2000, pp. 61–2; Walker and Cohen, 1985) and make explicit under what circumstances we expect certain relationships to hold. Maybe the theorized causal structure does really only hold for a sub-sample of all available observations – given the unit homogeneity assumption (Achen, 2002, pp. 446–7). Another strategy would be to keep all observations but reformulate the expected universal causal relationships by considering interaction effects or non-linear transformations among independent variables. This would allow you to stipulate conditional or non-linear effects of several explanatory or test variables on your dependent variable. In addition, including new independent variables might prove helpful to better account for outlying observations. Probably due to the economy of scale – that is, a single outlier does seem to matter more for a proposed explanation if the number of observations is five rather than 5000 – small-n researchers are likely to jump at deviant cases while large-n researchers look rather for a quick statistical fix if they care at all about a few outlying observations (e.g., Western, 1995).

Nevertheless, many important theories are framed in terms of necessary and sufficient conditions (see, for example, Dion, 1998; Goertz and Starr, 2003; Seawright, 2002). In trying to bridge the gap between deterministic and probabilistic causal worlds, new methodological approaches develop tests and estimate models of necessary and sufficient conditions, partly within a Bayesian framework in order to avoid falling into a small-n trap (Braumoeller, 2003; Braumoeller and Goertz, 2000; Clark, Gilligan and Golder, 2006; Seawright, 2002). Thus the

Table 1.2   Typology of research designs

		Type of causal inference	
		Factor-centric	Outcome-centric
Number of observations	Large n	Statistical control, (field) experiments	Forecasting, qualitative comparative analysis
	Small n	Cross-case comparisons, quasi-experiments	Case studies

choice between small-n and large-n research designs is partially independent of whether statistical tests are used, whether correlation- or process-based inferences with data-set or causal-process observations are employed, and of whether one believes in probabilistic or deterministic models of causation.

We thus arrive at a two-dimensional conceptualization of research designs represented by the cells on the main diagonal in Table 1.2 that goes beyond the widely used dichotomy of qualitative and quantitative research. Factor-centric research designs employ the method of statistical control or (field) experiments to disentangle a key causal factor in the causal net if many observations can be leveraged for inferential purposes. Outcome-centric small-n researchers provide an in-depth, within-case study of potential factors and causal processes that explain the occurrence of single events as comprehensively as possible. The off-diagonal cells are not empty, however. On the one hand, focused cross-case comparisons or quasi-experiments can be used in factor-centric research designs if only a few observations are available. On the other hand, there are large-n outcome-centric research designs, which have the potential to describe a phenomenon and forecast future occurrences of this phenomenon using statistical as well as qualitative comparative methods.

An overview of the chapters

In the previous sections we gave an overview of the core problems and different types of research design. In order to get to know our tool-box for developing a well-designed research project, we need to know to what extent the core problems of research design are the same for all of them. The literature is spread along two extremes here. On the one hand, some argue that qualitative research should merely follow a quantitative template of how to do good research as closely as possible and everything will be all right (King, Keohane and Verba, 1994). This is 'quantitative imperialism'. At the other extreme, there are scholars who portray qualitative and quantitative research as having entirely different logics (see, for instance, McKeown, 1999; Thomas, 2005). Consequently, qualitative and quantitative research designs – be they factor-centric or outcome-centric, small-n or large-n – cannot talk to or learn from one another. This is 'qualitative separatism'. (One could imagine qualitative imperialism as well as quantitative separatism, but these positions are rather rare in contemporary political science.)

In this book, we start from the assumption that research generally consists of a dialogue between theory and data and that all types of research at least face the same problems and challenges. Whether they also lend themselves to the same solutions, however, is an open question that will be taken up in the individual chapters, each of which focuses on one research design issue. The chapters follow a common template. They first start with a specific problem of research design in political science. Second, they explicate the problem, discuss various solutions, and emphasize the typical trade-offs involved in choosing one or another solution. Third, each chapter presents practical guidelines on how to deal with this particular research design issue in actual research. Fourth, they illustrate the use of these guidelines in an example taken from the authors' own research.

In Chapter 2 on 'Increasing the Relevance of Research Questions', *Matthias Lehnert, Bernhard Miller*, and *Arndt Wonka* define and distinguish theoretical and social relevance. The chapter then focuses on the widely neglected social relevance of research designs. Lehnert, Miller and Wonka deny that there is an inherent trade-off between theoretical and social relevance and show how researchers can generally improve the relevance of their research projects by responding to three questions. Who is affected by what? How can the results be evaluated? Which advice can be offered?

Do you really know what you are talking about? This is *Arndt Wonka*'s central question in Chapter 3 on concept specification as a central issue for research design in political science. Although it is not uncommon in the literature that different defining attributes are used to refer to the same concept, Wonka maintains that ambiguous concepts are not helpful in generating research which is expected to yield relevant results. After formulating some hands-on advice on how to avoid conceptual ambiguity, Wonka puts these suggestions to work and applies them to the concept of 'supranationality' as is used in his and other scholars' research on the European Union.

In Chapter 4 on 'Typologies in Social Inquiry', *Mathias Lehnert* deals with a special case of concept specification. He critically evaluates whether and how typologies can be used for either description or explanation of social phenomena. He thereby develops three criteria by which different 'types of typologies' can be distinguished in order to confine the use of typologies to particular purposes. Typologies provide simplified accounts of complex phenomena and can help establish unit homogeneity in both factor-centric and outcome-centric research designs. In addition to providing advice on when and how to use typologies in political science, Lehnert illustrates how typologies can be used fruitfully by referring to his own and other scholars' work on political institutions and their effects on political outcomes.

Measurement, *Bernhard Miller*'s topic in Chapter 5, is the next logical step following concept specification. Miller highlights both the challenges when devising measures, couched in issues of reliability and validity, as well as the tools that can be employed to address those challenges; here, he focuses particularly on the efficient use of indices as composite measures. He emphasizes the universal role of theory and concepts in any measurement process for any research design. Besides explicitly considering typical trade-offs one faces in everyday research practice, Miller also provides clear advice on how to devise new measures and illustrates them using his research on coalition committees.

In Chapter 6 *Julia Rathke* deals with the problem of comparability and equivalence of measurements when relying on secondary data sources. She argues that increasing the number of observations is no free lunch but requires at least conceptually equivalent measures. Rathke distinguishes between two different strategies in the measurement process to make sure that we arrive at conceptually equivalent measures: increasing the level of abstraction and establishing functional equivalence. After providing some practical advice on how to make data and indicators comparable, Rathke draws on her research on the effects of social capital on political orientations in Germany to demonstrate the practicability of her advice.

Two chapters deal with selection and selection bias – one in quantitative research, the other in qualitative research. In her discussion of selection bias in large-n research, *Janina Thiem* in Chapter 7 deals with challenges that quantitative research often encounters: the universe of cases – that is, the population of interest – is quite large and theoretically well-defined but only partly observable. If those unobservable observations of the realized sample are not randomly distributed, every inference drawn from this sample will be biased. While well-known statistical fixes – which may or may not be helpful for a given research problem – exist for such situations, Thiem argues that successfully dealing with selection bias is foremost a theoretical problem. She then provides practical guidelines on how to identify and deal with potential selection biases theoretically as well as statistically and finally applies these guidelines to potential selection effects in the analyses of roll call votes in the European Parliament.

In his discussion of case selection and selection bias in small-n research, *Dirk Leuffen* in Chapter 8 focuses on a situation that qualitative research often encounters: the universe of cases is quite large but not well-known or not well-defined. After reviewing Mill's classical methods of agreement and difference and the equally well-known most-similar systems or most-dissimilar systems designs, Leuffen presents theory-guided typologies as a strategy for case selection. He specifically argues that leverage can be increased by narrowing down the domain, focusing on a small set of theoretically interesting cells of the typology, and concentrating on 'hard cases'. He illustrates this strategy with an example from his research on French divided government.

Chapter 9 by *Ulrich Sieberer* focuses on the research design issue of control and discusses some basic theoretical and methodological choices when selecting independent variables and the trade-offs that come with them. He argues that the status of independent variables to control for the influence of alternative factors differs greatly depending on whether factor-centric or outcome-centric research designs are employed, while it makes no difference whether you employ small-n or large-n designs. Sieberer derives a number of practical guidelines and illustrates them using his own work on explaining party unity in legislative voting behavior.

Andreas Dür tackles the challenge of discriminating between rival explanations in outcome-centric qualitative research. In Chapter 10 Dür distinguishes three problems – omitted variable bias, explanatory overdeterminacy, and indeterminacy – and suggests various strategies to meet this challenge successfully: uncovering logical inconsistencies in alternative explanations, increasing the number of observable implications of one's own and rival theories, examining causal mechanisms through process tracing, and selecting additional 'most likely' or 'least likely' cases. After discussing their strengths and weaknesses, he illustrates the use of these strategies in his own research area: the analysis of trade liberalization.

Dirk De Bièvre in Chapter 11 is concerned with the final phase of the research process: what to do with a theory after it has been tested

empirically and found wanting? He puts forward a theoretical understanding of falsification – entailing the replacement of faulty hypotheses with new, presumably better ones – and presents guidelines for
formulating hypotheses and conducting research so that researchers
can make the most of theoretical falsification. De Bièvre draws on a
current research project on the effects of judicialization in the WTO to
illustrate the use of these guidelines.

Finally, in the concluding chapter we are concerned with the lessons
that can be learned for improving the dialogue between theory and
data. While all types of research face the same challenges there is no
cookie-cutter approach to help us dealing with them. Instead different
research designs offer and require different solutions, each of which produces specific trade-offs. How you evaluate these trade-offs should determine how you carry out your research project and, consequently, the
type of research design you choose.

Notes

1. For similar definitions, see Brady, Collier and Seawright (2004, p. 302); de Vaus
   (2001, p. 9); or King, Keohane and Verba (1994, p. 118).
2. For a similar list drawn from King, Keohane and Verba (1994), see Collier,
   Mahoney and Seawright (2004, pp. 36–7).
3. In reality, however, designing research is rarely so neatly ordered. It does not
   always start at the beginning of the process or finish at its end, and it involves
   a lot of going back and forth between the design problems.
4. For similar distinctions see Ganghof (2005a); Gerring (2001, p. 137); Scharpf
   (1997, pp. 24–7).

Part I
Research Problem

2
Increasing the Relevance of Research Questions: Considerations on Theoretical and Social Relevance in Political Science

*Matthias Lehnert, Bernhard Miller and Arndt Wonka**

> The trick is to make social science speak to problems that we care about without sacrificing the rigor that qualifies it as a science. (Gerring, 2001, p. 257)

Introduction

Most introductions to the methodology of social inquiry start somewhere in the middle of the research process. They do not, however, shed light on the first stage of a research project (e.g., Brady and Collier, 2004; George and Bennett, 2005; Pennings, Keman and Kleinnijenhuis, 1999). Others touch upon the issue – but in some rather vague way (Geddes, 2003; Gerring, 2001; King, Keohane and Verba, 1994). Most importantly, such companions do not say anything about how to find appropriate research questions. Experience tells us that determining the question one sets out to answer is by no means an easy task. In this chapter, we offer some guidance in this respect. The concept of relevance which we use builds on three pillars: methodological appropriateness, theoretical relevance and social relevance. Methodological appropriateness is the subject of the chapters which follow in this book. We will therefore only briefly discuss it here. Theoretical relevance refers to the analytical value

---

* This chapter represents a collective endeavor; the ordering of the authors is alphabetical.

a research question adds to the scientific discourse of the subdiscipline – such as international relations, comparative political science, political sociology – it addresses. Socially relevant research furthers the understanding of social and political phenomena which affect people and make a difference with regard to an explicitly specified evaluative standard.

In this chapter, we will focus on social relevance for three reasons. First, except for superficial discussion, the topic is absent in the literature on research design while other aspects of relevance are treated in more detail. The second reason is that the scientific community provides multiple incentives for scholars to contribute theoretically relevant work, but there is little encouragement for socially relevant contributions. This, in our eyes, is all the more pressing since – our third reason for stressing social relevance – political scientists have repeatedly been urged to take social relevance more seriously (Gerring and Yesnowitz, 2006; Graf Kielmansegg, 2001; Hennis, 1963). Since political science has, it is argued, a competitive advantage with respect to politics, it is obliged to contribute substantially to public discourse. We do not discuss the value of such appeals addressing the whole discipline. Ours is not an argument for a collective reorientation of political science. Neither do we urge individual scholars to focus exclusively on social relevance. From our point of view it is perfectly legitimate for a social scientist to answer questions and solve problems irrespective of whether anyone outside the field considers her research relevant. We acknowledge, however, that there is a search for increased social relevance and want to offer some advice for how to increase the social relevance of any given research project. While our main focus is on finding socially relevant research questions, our advice will prove helpful for all scholars interested in increasing the relevance of their research. We hold that any project's social relevance can be increased, irrespective of the stage to which it has already progressed.

So far, practical guidelines on how to contribute socially relevant research questions have been rare and usually restricted to rather general hints (e.g. King, Keohane and Verba, 1994, p. 15). To be sure, we do not offer a coherent method for attaining social relevance. Such a method is inconceivable. We do offer, however, three questions which might help to orient researchers to those aspects of their subjects which are more likely than others to be considered socially relevant. We proceed in four steps. First, we define three standards with which social science research is customarily evaluated (though often implicitly). Second, we define what we mean by social relevance. Third, we present three questions for increasing the social relevance of a research project. We then turn to some practical examples of what we consider socially relevant political science.

The relevance of research questions

Two dimensions of relevance

The concept of 'relevance' which constitutes the analytical foundation of this chapter comprises two dimensions, a theoretical and a social dimension. The analytical separation of these two dimensions is important because weaknesses on each dimension ask for different considerations and cures. Instead of questioning the relevance of her research project 'in general', our separation allows the researcher to scrutinize her research question in a differentiated way. The theoretical dimension of relevance relates to a project's contribution to a given theoretical discourse and represents social scientists' 'inside' or 'peer perspective', whereas social relevance relates to the value which the findings of a research project have for non-peers. The social dimension thus represents a project's 'outside' perspective and ideally increases citizens' political knowledge and awareness. In the subsequent paragraphs we discuss both dimensions in more detail, though with varying emphasis. Although the relevance of individual work can and should be carried out along both dimensions, we will focus on the social dimension. Let us stress here that there is, in our mind, no trade-off inherent to this conception of relevance. While each researcher can decide how much her contribution should address issues of theoretical or social relevance opting for high social relevance does *not* mean that the contribution need be any less relevant theoretically. The same, of course, holds true vice versa.

A final note is in order. The methodological appropriateness of an empirical research project is a necessary pre-condition for the persuasiveness of any empirical research result and thus has a bearing on both the theoretical and social relevance. In contrast to the other chapters in this volume, we do not discuss ways and means to produce methodologically appropriate work. Rather we assume that a project meets the methodological standards of the discipline.

Defining theoretical relevance

A theoretically relevant contribution increases the analytic leverage political scientists have at their disposal when describing and explaining political phenomena (King, Keohane and Verba, 1994). In other words: theoretically relevant work helps us to arrive at a better understanding of the phenomena that we study theoretically or empirically. The theoretical relevance of a research question can only be assessed with regard to the scientific discourse which deals with the subject to be studied. This discourse mainly takes place in the scientific literature. The researchers participating in a theoretical discourse argue about the analytical usefulness of the theoretical concepts which are conventionally employed and, if the goal of the research is explanatory, formulate competing hypotheses with respect to the object under study. Thus, while we lack uniform standards across political science the scientific standards which every social science (sub-) community adopts are amply evident for any researcher interested in the topic from the respective literature.

How then can theoretical relevance defined in this manner be achieved? The pertinent literature is almost uniformly mute on this point. While King and colleagues (1994, pp. 15–17) offer some advice, Geddes (2003, pp. 28–30) considers their recommendations to be overly specific and not applicable to all subfields of the discipline. Geddes herself provides helpful clues on how a given research question can be successfully turned into a research design but says little more than King and colleagues (1994) about theoretical relevance (2003, pp. 28–30). In this chapter we provide a more complete listing of criteria for achieving theoretical relevance. We claim that first and foremost it is of fundamental importance that the researcher explicitly tie her contribution to the pertinent body of literature. This not only helps avoid the production of theoretically redundant work, that is, the explication of ideas which have already been stated. An explicit tie to the relevant scientific literature also supports the cumulative character of research, in other words the fundamental scientific idea that the work of different researchers builds on each other. This contributes to the improvement of our overall understanding of particular phenomena. Thus, after having explicated her theoretical approach and linked it to the relevant literature, a researcher who wants to formulate a theoretically relevant research question can do so by:

- empirically testing so far untested theoretical hypotheses. Such an endeavor not only helps to increase our empirical knowledge about social phenomena; it also allows us to reject empirically unconfirmed hypotheses, thus eventually leading either to theoretical refinement or empirical rejection.
- identifying logical inconsistencies within a theory (Dür, Chapter 10). Raising a research question which addresses and eventually overcomes such theoretical inconsistencies by (re-) formulating the theory is theoretically relevant.
- identifying empirical cases for which a theory cannot account. Research questions which address deviating cases can eventually lead

to reformulated theory with increased empirical applicability and greater leverage.

- developing theoretical concepts (Wonka, Chapter 3). Better specified concepts help both in theory formulation and in empirical testing and therefore contribute to increasing a subdiscipline's analytical leverage.
- formulating alternative explanations (Dür, Chapter 10). Alternative explanations explicate causal mechanisms which have not been discussed in the literature thus far, but which might better take account of the observed empirical pattern.
- providing alternative explanations integrating (or eliminating) existing theoretical approaches. The resulting theoretical framework will be superior to these existing accounts.
- applying a theory to a new empirical domain. If an existing theory can be meaningfully applied (see Wonka, Chapter 3) to empirical phenomena not covered by the respective theory up to this point, the author contributes to a research community's knowledge about the degree of a theory's general character.
- synthesizing different theories. Contributions which identify common assumptions and potential complementary arguments consolidate theoretical knowledge and should therefore be considered theoretically relevant.

Thus, when dealing with the theoretical relevance of our research questions we take an inside perspective which is exclusively directed at the discipline's efforts to advance the knowledge in a specific subfield. If a project's research question can contribute to the specific scientific discourse and to the advancement of the knowledge produced by it,[1] it scores high on one of our relevance dimensions, *theoretical* relevance. In the next section we will introduce a second dimension, *social* relevance.

Defining social relevance

How can social relevance be defined so that it can serve as a goal and measuring rod for social research? Probably the most popular definition of social relevance centres on the question of whether people *care*. Brian Barry and Douglas Rae ask why the public should '*care* to know (and pay for knowing) what we have to say about politics?' (1975, p. 338, emphasis added). Having an answer to this question can then be seen as a sign of relevance. Accordingly, Gerring and Yesnowitz argue that the social sciences should focus on 'something that citizens and policymakers *care* about or might *care* about' (2006, p. 114, emphasis added). This suggestion, however, points to the problems that bedevil the definition of relevance as 'caring': Do people actually have to care? Or does it suffice to argue that people might care? Obviously the latter is less strict a crite- rion than the former. We opt for as precise a criterion as possible and therefore differentiate the ambiguous standard of 'relevance as caring' into two elements: First, what matters is that somebody is affected by a social phenomenon. Second, one must be able to argue that this impact makes a difference with regard to an evaluative standard; in other words, one possible outcome or state of a social phenomenon is better – or worse, for that matter – than another.

'Being affected' is less ambiguous a standard than 'caring for some- thing': Whether people care is often hard to say. Whether somebody is affected by a social phenomenon is much easier to judge. It has been argued for being socially relevant a subject 'should be consequential for political, social or economic life, for understanding something that affects many peoples' lives' (King, Keohane and Verba, 1994, p. 15). While we do stress the aspect of 'somebody being affected', we do not consider the sheer number of people affected by some phenomenon a criterion for social relevance. Research does not become more relevant simply because the subject studied affects more people. Moreover, we argue that social relevance must not be equated with the rule that 'some- body must be affected by something somehow'. Everybody is affected by a myriad of factors, some of which are known but most of which are unknown to us. While all consequences by definition make a difference in a descriptive sense, probably not all are evaluated differently: Many consequences do not interfere with our welfare, utility, or happiness. The criterion of 'being affected' therefore seems to be lacking elements the 'caring for' standard had included. This, we argue, is evaluation or *values*. Social relevance not only means that people are affected by some phe- nomenon but also that they evaluate the various possible consequences differently. We argue that social relevance presupposes some variance in evaluation. For attaining social relevance, it does not suffice to show that a phenomenon leads to different outcomes as long as no argument can be made that one outcome is better or worse than another. This, how- ever, makes an evaluative standard necessary according to which some things can be said to score better than others. To be sure, a social scientist who finds out that some value on an independent variable leads to A and another leads to B produces theoretically relevant work. Yet, if she cannot point to any standard of evaluation according to which the two options score differently, her findings are socially irrelevant.

Two implications follow from this argument: First, it is impossible to assess the social relevance of political science research without referring to *some* evaluative standard, be it effectiveness, legitimacy, unemployment, stability or some other criterion. Second, once we have established a standard with which we set out to evaluate social phenomena, in order for our work to attain social relevance we must explicate that different possible outcomes under study score differently on the particular evaluative scale applied. Barry and Rae (1975, p. 339) explicate this close relationship between relevance and evaluation. People acknowledge the relevance of research if 'they find the moral, ethical, evaluative problems raised by political choice puzzling and would like to think more clearly about the difference between good policies and bad ones'. Note that we do not take a stance either on which *particular* standard to apply or on where the criterion should be taken from.[2]

While we now have acquired a differentiated understanding of social relevance, one element is still missing: practical advice. One might question the value of knowing about a phenomenon as long as one is unable to deliberately change the order of things. The question then is whether social relevance presupposes that researchers offer practical advice. Wilhelm Hennis has repeatedly argued that political science is a practical science, a medical science for the body politic (Rosa and Kaiser, 2004). Gerring and Yesnowitz agree: 'Social science, in all its guises, is *practical* knowledge' (2006, p. 111; emphasis in original). While we wholeheartedly acknowledge the added value of recommendations deduced from social science research, we do not think that it is imperative for social research to offer practical advice in order to be socially relevant. Our position is two-fold: On the one hand, we do believe that practical advice actually increases a research project's social relevance. We do not, on the other hand, argue that work from which no practical implications follow is socially irrelevant. Understanding events, phenomena, processes and causal relationships is a precondition to formulate practical advice. And as social scientists, we have the analytical tools to identify and analyze these aspects of social life. This again can help politicians as well as citizens to make up their minds. Practical advice is always welcome but it is not a *sine qua non* for attaining social relevance.

To sum up the above discussion in a condensed definition of social relevance to which we will refer throughout this chapter: Socially relevant research furthers the understanding of social and political phenomena which affect people and make a difference with regard to explicitly specified evaluative standards. Given this definition we will now turn to the crucial question of how to increase the social relevance of a given research project.

Theoretical and social relevance: a question of trade-offs?

It is occasionally taken for granted that there is a trade-off between theoretical and social relevance in political science. Contributions – according to this view – can thus be either theoretically or socially relevant. An increase in one dimension necessarily implies a decrease in the other. We could not differ more. We do not think that a researcher is confronted with a zero-sum trade-off when aiming at increasing her research project's social *and* theoretical relevance. Research questions derived from the scientific literature and found to be theoretically relevant *can* very well be of high social relevance. Theoretically relevant research questions are thus not inherently socially irrelevant. Likewise, just by choosing a socially relevant research question, a researcher *does not* opt for a theoretically irrelevant question. When approaching a political phenomenon, a researcher is free to choose any theoretical approach. Thus, she can pose a socially relevant question and do this by applying a theory hitherto not applied to such a topic. Or she could formulate a hypothesis which runs counter to existing and established theoretical wisdom, thereby theoretically explaining a socially highly relevant phenomenon.

In principle, therefore, there is no zero-sum trade-off between social and theoretical relevance. In reality, however, a researcher might very well get struck by the above sketched insufficiencies of a theoretical discourse, which is of no social relevance. Thus, she might set out to add to the elimination of these insufficiencies and provide theoretically highly relevant work to her research community. Under these circumstances her work might be of no interest to any audience outside academia and therefore not be socially relevant.[3] Thus a researcher can aim at scoring high on the dimension of theoretical relevance, while not caring the least about her project's social relevance. This may not only earn her publications in the most renowned peer reviewed journals of our discipline or monographs published by outstanding publishers and the consequent recognition by peer researchers. It may also earn her a materially safe livelihood as a full professor. This is a perfectly fine life for a social scientist! However, since we do not think that aiming at social and/or theoretical relevance involves a trade-off, we encourage researchers to aim at both a high level of theoretical *and* social relevance. In the next section, we will provide some practical advice on how to increase the social relevance of one's work.

Practical recommendations

There is not one way to produce socially relevant work and most authors will rightly argue that each topic is unique with regard to its relevance. Yet, we think that there are substantial aspects which are common to all topics and which can be used to underscore and stress the social relevance of the respective research. In what follows we present three questions which help the researcher improve the social relevance of her contribution.

Who is affected?

King, Keohane and Verba argue that for a topic to be relevant it needs to affect many people's lives (1994, p. 15). This suggests that a linear relationship exists between the number of people affected and the social relevance of the research question. It follows that we should conduct research only when large numbers of people are concerned. We beg to differ. The question really is: who is *potentially* affected? In addressing this question the researcher should attempt to find out what effect the answer to her research question might have on the affected. Since we wish to gain analytical leverage to broaden our understanding of the object to be studied, a second and related question has to be asked: What is it that people are affected by? In order to find an answer we need to specify the mechanisms at work. This in turn will help the reader understand in which way the people are affected. The two questions help to separate the 'who' and the 'by what' aspects which in turn aids in making the argument more accessible to people outside political science.

Asking these simple questions will make a difference to any research project in several ways. They will render the contribution more focused on those aspects of a problem that really matter rather than on some arcane mind games or truisms like 'generally important to the functioning of a democracy'. In addition, they will result in more precise arguments because they focus attention on real people rather than abstract entities (citizens instead of states, democracies, institutions). Asking the questions might also help us to identify questions that are of interest: If we cannot make a claim why anybody is affected by a phenomenon, why should we care about it? Most social science contributions do address a constituency. So why not flesh out which implications a research contribution has – and how the impact might come about?

There is another twist to be considered here. Some topics might feature prominently in a current debate. The number of addressees is certainly larger if the contribution tackles a topic currently enjoying broad attention, and people are more likely to listen. To avoid any misunderstanding: it is not our intention to suggest that researchers become intellectual ambulance chasers – as our insistence on clear criteria for defining social relevance demonstrates. At the same time, however, the topical agenda shapes people's perceptions and makes a broader audience more ready to receive new information. Topics are then perceived to be more relevant. Forecasting models become relevant when there are elections coming up, and the analysis of Islam has found a larger audience after 9/11. Understanding the mechanisms tied to a social phenomenon affecting people will improve their political knowledge and awareness and help in forming some justifiable opinion on the subject matter.

Defining the audience will lead to other questions that might further our research: Affected by what? How? It is here where we are pushed to systematically describe the phenomenon we hold to be relevant. This information can subsequently serve to explicate causal mechanisms. This step is important to check how direct the impact of the phenomenon of interest on the lives of people is.

How can the results be evaluated?

The first question assumes a positivist perspective, yet every author will also need to evaluate her findings. In other words, state in which way people are affected and why they should care. In contrast to economics, the (other) social sciences do not have an agreed upon standard to turn to for evaluating results (efficiency, pareto-optimality). It is therefore hard to judge whether something is beneficial or detrimental. While political decisions or outcomes *can* be judged in terms of their efficiency, this will be insufficient or unsatisfactory in many cases. Most research, particularly in the rational-choice tradition, *implicitly* makes evaluative judgments. Gerring and Yesnowitz (2006) have convincingly argued that normative standards are vastly more important in political and social science in general than they are in economics.

Therefore, a central criterion for social relevance is to establish standards which help the people affected gauge the implications of the research. Political processes and outcomes might be evaluated along standards like legitimacy, accountability, stability, or transparency – to name just a few. Often, criteria like unemployment or inflation are taken to be universally accepted standards for good policy. But they need not be![4] Standards are important, because they might alter the perception of an issue and thus the reason why we consider an issue relevant. For every research project intended to be socially relevant, a researcher needs to consciously search for a suitable evaluative standard, and, if there is more than one, consciously make a choice. This standard needs to be made explicit. It is beyond an empirical research project to justify it theoretically, a task which – in most cases at least – is best left to political theory. One further question which can help structure this process is: Why should we consider research findings one way *rather* than another? If for example economic standards are usually applied to a research area, the addressees would certainly profit from an answer to this question.

What advice can be offered?

Any contribution becomes more valuable when there is something practical to learn from it; social scientific contributions are no exception. If things are going badly, knowing this is better than not knowing it. It is even more helpful, however, to tell people how they can make things better. The researcher will increase the social relevance of her work by pointing out the practical implications of the research. This question is tied closely to the evaluation of social phenomena, outcomes, policies or the like. If results are found to be unsatisfactory, a potential demand for change exists. On the basis of the results and the evaluation, we can provide expert knowledge of what might happen if changes were made to specific aspects of the status quo. Since any prognosis necessarily exceeds the universe of cases in our initial study, we need to argue why changes would be beneficial. If studies are based on comparative knowledge it is easier to argue for policy transfer and justify certain options of policy change. Again, however, any policy recommendation is based on a set of values we promote. We argue for a certain idea of good society or good governance. Answering the question entails telling the addressees what we hold to be either desirable ends or regrettable states of affairs and then how they either achieve or avoid them.

Application

This section has two objectives. We first want to show how selected contributions stress theoretical and/or social relevance to different degrees. In the second part we illustrate how we attempt to increase social relevance of our own work. We have argued that the relevance of research questions in political science can be assessed along the two dimensions of theoretical and social relevance. The degree to which each dimension is incorporated into the research design is a decision each researcher has to make. By demonstrating how well-known contributions in our field have put different emphasis on these aspects, we wish to convey a more concrete idea of how theoretical and social relevance are put into practice. In order to accomplish this, let us briefly back up the criteria on which the dimensions are based. Theoretically relevant work increases the analytical leverage over a given topic and thus enhances political scientists' ability to describe or explain a political phenomenon. Socially relevant work focuses on phenomena which affect people, and discusses their impact with regard to specified evaluative standards.

We rely on the typology below to choose work for our discussion which scores high on the dimension of social relevance (2), with regard to theoretical relevance (3), or stresses both dimensions (4) (Figure 2.1). Figure 2.1 does not suggest that work in Cell 2 has nothing at all to offer theoretically or that contributions in Cell 3 have no social relevance. What it does say is that an author has decided to particularly emphasize some aspect rather than another (2 and 3) – or pays attention to both (4).

We base our selection of the works on the following considerations. As theoretically relevant examples, we choose work which incited intensive discussions in the respective communities. We take this to indicate that a work indeed did make a contribution to the discipline's analytical arsenal. Thus we classify contributions as theoretically relevant which contributed significantly to the improvement of the existing scientific discourse. As for social relevance our criterion for a high score is that an author pays explicit attention to how her research affects peoples' lives and evaluates her finding against an explicated evaluative standard.

Let us begin the discussion with Cell 1. There are contributions in each subdiscipline which do not attract special attention as they neither

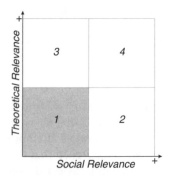

Figure 2.1   Types of examples of relevant research questions

improve our theoretical or empirical understanding of a given problem nor speak to problems of social relevance. We do not think it serves anyone to provide examples in this category. As an exemplary work for Cell 2 we suggest Samuel Huntington's *Clash of Civilizations* (1996). The social relevance of the book hardly needs discussion. Countless references in speeches by policymakers and newspaper contributions speak for themselves. The book's interest lies in whether cultural differences between 'civilizations' will spark violent conflict in the future. It is this aspect of the book which addresses all of us as a potentially affected audience. The evaluative standard – quite starkly – is the difference between war and peace, an evaluative standard which directly connects with many people's lives. While Huntington's contribution is theoretically relevant to some extent (Jervis, 1997), the book is 'admittedly not a work of social science' (Rosecrance, 1998, p. 979). Huntington deliberately decided not to dwell on the intricacies of IR theory and does not ask what might be wrong with state- or institution-centered explanations. Instead he primarily addresses the more practical implications raised by his topic. Social relevance, however, is not inherent in any discussion about war and peace. In the wake of its publication, it is important to point out that *Clash of Civilizations* has drawn a plethora of contributions which aim primarily at being theoretically relevant (e.g. Henderson, 2004; Reynal-Querol, 2002).

George Tsebelis's *Veto Players* (2002) also has received much attention – but of a different kind. A candidate for Cell 3, Tsebelis presents a theory of how political change occurs given a set of institutions or actors with the formal power to veto decisions. While much depends on the preferences of these veto players, a central claim of his theory is that political systems with many veto players exhibit more policy stability than do systems with few veto players. Tsebelis himself uses his theory to inform or confront a number of literatures – from the classical parliamentary-presidential dichotomy to law production in democratic systems to EU decision-making. This way, his contribution has provided an analytical perspective which not only has made possible numerous clarifications and improvements, but has also encouraged cross-fertilization of various political science subdisciplines. While Tsebelis mentions concepts like regime stability and analyzes veto players' effect on macroeconomic output, he has, however, opted not to discuss whether blockade is good or bad – and for whom. Likewise, in his chapter on macroeconomic output, there is no discussion of if and when a slower or more rapid change from one national budget to the next has positive or negative outcomes. To be socially relevant as we argued above, it would have been necessary to explicate on the evaluative standard and show why and how it can make a difference on the people affected.

Cell 4 underlines our argument that there is no trade-off inherent in the two dimensions of relevance, but that it is rather a matter of research design whether to address only one dimension of relevance or both. A good example of a theoretically and socially relevant work is Arend Lijphart's *Patterns of Democracy* (1999). Lijphart argues that a certain institutional configuration facilitates consensus and, so Lijphart claims, leads to better social and economic performance. He attracted attention to institutional configurations which had previously been disregarded in the literature and thus provided an analytical framework which increased political scientists' empirical leverage over all existing democratic political systems. Not least, Lijphart's analysis constitutes the reference point against which Tsebelis and other comparativists have developed their theoretical frameworks. Its constructive adoption has increased the analytical leverage of many ensuing contributions and is the major reason for the theoretical relevance of his work. Lijphart explicitly argues that consensus democracies increase democratic quality as they fare better in providing economic well-being, social peace, and environmentally friendly politics to their citizens (1999, p. 275). Thus, evaluative standards are clearly specified. The institutions which make up this 'kinder and gentler' form of democracy, Lijphart goes on to argue, can be exported to other countries to have similar effects on the well-being of citizens there. His advice accordingly is to emulate the institutional configurations of consensus democracies. Lijphart's is thus a book which builds a powerful theoretical arsenal and shows how and to whom the theoretical findings actually matter. In Lijphart's case, the audience is easily determined. It is the (potential) institutional designers but also the broader democratic public who are affected by the diagnosis that their polities might in some way be improved.

This application part would be incomplete if we did not address the design process. Since our own work could not have been as illustrative as established contributions for the purposes above, we will only now use it to show how we have aimed to increase the social relevance of our research.

Lehnert focuses on the German Conference Committee (*Vermittlungsausschuss*) and its impact on German legislation. Mostly, this committee is perceived as an efficient institution (Tsebelis, 1990) which helps to dissolve legislative gridlock. Lehnert points out that despite these alleged qualities, the Conference Committee hardly plays any role in research contributions which concentrate on gridlock in the German bicameral system. He thus faces the theoretically challenging task of incorporating the Conference Committee into the spatial models which are dominant in the incisive literature. However, rather than indulging in abstract formal modeling, Lehnert sets out to search for such committee effects which affect the well-being of a broader audience. This approach has led him to scrutinize the distributive capacity of the German Conference Committee. Lehnert argues that the Conference Committee must not be considered an innocuous, efficient institution. Rather, it might have considerable distributive effects which Lehnert relates to evaluative standards such as the quality of policy solutions, the capacity of an elected government to act, and the clarity of responsibility. The search for a socially relevant perspective on the German Conference Committee, however, has not led the project away from theoretical problems. Lehnert employs formal concepts in order to address substantive questions. What is more, he argues that only if the Conference Committee's distributive effects are explicitly taken into consideration does it make sense to incorporate the committee into formal models of bicameral decision making.

Miller's research explores coalition committees (CoC) in Western European democracies, with a particular focus on Germany.[5] His interest in the topic was stipulated by the fact that while CoCs have existed in a number of countries (see the contributions to Müller and Strøm, 2000), we know very little about why they exist and close to nothing about how they work. To this lack of empirical knowledge came the theoretical puzzle that, according to classical coalition theory, governments once formed should be stable and have no need for coordination or conflict resolution. In the search for an adequate theoretical framework, the literature on informal institutions offered useful analytical tools but also highlighted a normative aspect of the research topic. The informal nature of CoCs raised the question of whether this arena impeded its legitimated formal equivalents. Miller thus opted to include a discussion highlighting potential and actual conflicts over competencies and policy decisions between informal and formal institutions. Another charge against informal areas is that they are not transparent and therefore potentially undemocratic. The author decided to include in his design a section which discusses – in light of the empirical findings – how opaque CoCs really are. While it is possible to argue that all citizens are in some respect affected by coalition policy-making – and thus by the CoC – the connection remains indirect. Still, it is worth spelling it out, as it might create awareness of the institution and its effects. Social relevance was not a part of this research design from the beginning onwards, but as it turned out, socially relevant elements could be integrated without extensive effort.

Wonka's research aims at a better understanding of the European Commission as an influential actor in European Union politics. The Commission's powers rest on its monopoly to initiate legislative decision-making processes by introducing its proposals. In addition, the Commission is the guardian of the European Union treaties, having the obligation to penalize member states' non-compliance with these treaties. Relying on principal-agent theory, Wonka theoretically and empirically analyses EU member states' selection and appointment of European Commissioners in order to arrive at an assessment of European Commissioners' political characteristics as the basic policy preferences of the Commission's collective political leadership. In addition, the European Commission is conceptualized as a collective actor, and decision-making processes inside it are analyzed to assess the relative influence of the Commission President and European Commissioners on the quality of Commission policy outcomes. The study thereby addresses questions of theoretical relevance to scholars interested in the political dynamics of the EU, be it from the perspective of European integration, EU regulatory dynamics and EU policy-making, or with an interest in the functioning of EU institutions. Social relevance has played a minor role in the research design. Not least this is due to the fact that peoples' affectedness by the Commission can – at best – be assessed only indirectly. Although the design of the study aims at theoretical relevance, social relevance could be attained first of all by discussing whether the European Commission is indeed an unaccountable Brussels bureaucracy, able and willing to realize its own bureaucratic interests vis-à-vis member state governments and European citizens alike. If the theoretical and empirical analysis supports this view, then ways of realigning the European Commission with European citizens' policy preferences can be discussed. Different institutional models of selecting the EU's political leaders and their likely effect on EU policy outcomes could be debated. The discussion could range from a direct election of the European Commission president by the European citizenry, to a full-blown parliamentarization of the EU, where a directly elected European Parliament is in full command of selecting and electing Commissioners and the Commission President. This could inform the debate on the accountability of EU institutions, a topic related to the discussions on the EU's supposed democratic deficit. The likely policy consequences of implementing different mechanisms of political elite selection in the EU could then be evaluated with respect to how effective they are at aligning the Commission's policy preferences with those of the European citizenry.

This concludes our discussion of how social relevance can be incorporated into political science research designs. Our message is clear: It does not take too much to address issues that 'people' care about.

Conclusion

Repeatedly, social scientists have been urged to produce work which is more socially relevant. Practical advice for how to meet this criterion, however, is rare. This is regrettable given our conviction that any research project's social relevance can be increased by addressing the subject studied from a certain angle. In this contribution, we have shown how such a perspective can be developed by addressing three simple questions: *Who is affected? How can the results be evaluated? Which advice can be offered?* We think that taking these questions seriously fosters the social relevance of any particular research project. Working with these questions will prove especially commendable for finding a research question, since it leads the scholar to the consequential and problematic aspects of a social phenomenon. To be sure, there is no coherent method with which social relevance can be attained. The advice we offer, however, helps to develop such a perspective on any given phenomenon, which is then likely to lead to socially relevant findings.

We do not wish to suggest that political science as a whole must strive for social relevance. Neither do we wish to imply that any individual scholar needs to produce socially relevant work. For those choosing to do so, the existing literature has provided little guidance – despite the fact that social relevance is increasingly considered pertinent. We have argued that some advice can and should be given to scientists who want to increase the social relevance of their work. In this chapter, we provided such advice.

Notes

1. The exact forms which scientific progress takes, i.e., by the revolutionary replacement of one paradigm by another (Kuhn, 1969) or by contributing to the development of an alternative research program (Lakatos, 1979) need not interest us here. Crucial in our context is that scientific progress can only be attained by directly addressing the theoretical and empirical status quo of a given area.

2. In this chapter, we deal with the question of how to increase the social relevance of *empirical* research projects. Obviously, the criterion of relevance can be extended to the evaluation of values. This, however, by far exceeds the confines of empirical research. It is at this point where the normative reasoning of social philosophy and empirical social science meet. Empirical researches can profit a lot from taking into consideration the debates on values and evaluation (Barry and Rae, 1975). We are well advised to question the relevance of our evaluative standards and to be aware of relationships between values. However, given our focus on empirical research we do not go any further into social philosophy.

3 Of course, the opposite might as well be the case: Someone addresses a socially relevant question by applying well-established theoretical tools.

4. High inflation, for example, devalues debt and thus stands to help more people than it might hurt in most societies.

5. Coalition committees are informal conflict resolution mechanisms where cabinet members, representatives of the parliamentary party groups and party leaders attend.

Part II

Concepts and Theory

3
Concept Specification in Political Science Research

Arndt Wonka

The need for *reconstruction* results from *destruction*, from the fact that our disciplines have increasingly lost all 'discipline'. Amidst the resulting state of noncumulability, collective ambiguity, and increasing incommunicability, it is imperative to restore or attempt to restore the conceptual foundations of the edifice. This is not to say that an exercise in conceptual reconstruction will restore consensus – we are far too disbanded for that. However, if the exercise succeeds, it will restore intelligibility – and, with intelligibility, an awareness of the enormous intellectual waste brought about by our present-day indiscipline (and methodological unawareness). (Sartori, 1984, p. 50)

Introduction

Political scientists seek to derive general statements from their empirical observations. For that purpose they make causal and descriptive inferences. The goal of inference is to produce reliable descriptive information, to test existing theories, and to formulate new theories (King, Keohane and Verba, 1994). The validity of empirical and causal inference, however, depends crucially on properly specified concepts. First of all, the clear definition of a concept allows others to understand the meaning of what we write. In addition, the content of concepts determines the content as well as the explanatory and the empirical scope of our theoretical hypotheses. For other steps in the process of designing research, unambiguous concepts are most obviously important in the design of an empirical strategy and the subsequent development of adequate measures (for a discussion of measurement, see Miller, Chapter 5). The reason for this is obvious: How are we to evaluate a measure's adequacy if we are not sure what to measure in the first place?

A number of articles and book chapters have been devoted to theoretical discussions of concepts and concept specification (Collier and Mahon, 1993; Gerring, 2001; Sartori, 1970, 1984). My aim in this chapter is much more modest and instrumental: I would first of all like to draw the reader's attention to the centrality of concepts in political science research, by discussing how the quality of concepts affects the clarity of theoretical arguments and the empirical scope of theories. In line with the other chapters of this volume, in section three, I will then provide practical guidelines for how to get most out of the concepts we wish to apply in our research projects. The fourth section applies this chapter's recommendations to the concept of 'supranationality' which I frequently struggle with in my own research on the European Union (EU). A brief discussion concludes this chapter.

Design problem: concepts and concept specification in political science research

There are three components which make up a concept and have to be distinguished analytically (Gerring, 2001; Sartori, 1984): a *term* assigns a name to a concept. Attributes which define a concept's meaning fill the term with substance. All attributes taken together constitute a concept's *intension*. A concept's intension is not only important because it defines its meaning. The intension of a concept should demarcate this concept from other concepts. Otherwise overlaps in meaning will lead to confusion. Finally, a concept's defining attributes relate the concept to real world phenomena. The empirical scope of a concept is regularly referred to as its *extension*. Analytically useful concepts draw distinct boundaries between the real world phenomena denoted by themselves and those denoted by other theoretical concepts. Figure 3.1 summarizes the above and puts it into the broader research design context: We start with a theoretical statement, that is, a hypothesis (see De Bièvre, Chapter 11; Dür, Chapter 10). To make sure that anyone is able to understand the statement's meaning, we specify the concepts contained in the statement. This is done by explicating the concepts' defining attributes. Finally, the concept has to be operationalized in order to systematically relate it to real world phenomena (Miller, Chapter 5) – and to test the empirical plausibility of our theoretical statements.

Concept specification then is the process by which a researcher defines and explicates the attributes of the concepts she uses in her

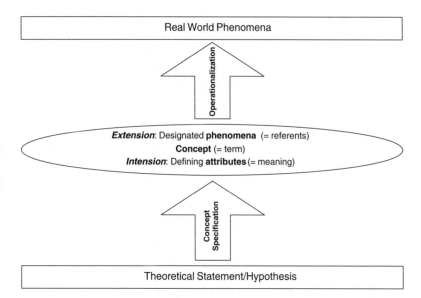

Figure 3.1   Concepts and concept specification in the broader research design context

research. As such, concept specification can mean both the adaptation of an existing concept to actual theoretical or empirical needs and the formation of a completely new concept, which has to be specified from scratch. The (instrumental) goal of both kinds of concept specification is the same: We want to have analytical instruments at our disposal, which allow us an unambiguous theoretical discourse as well as the clear denotation of the empirical phenomena relevant for our research project. Therefore we have to be clear about what the terms mean with which we operate and confront other researchers. In political science the term 'democracy', for example, refers to a specific form of organizing the relationship between those that govern and those governed in a given territory. The term could be specified by the following defining attributes: (1) the guarantee of citizens' basic rights; (2) the rule of law; and (3) regular competing elections for political offices. This specification of the concept of democracy then extends to all states whose organization of political power exhibits these attributes.

Some political scientists may oppose this chapter's postulate that unambiguous concepts are a prerequisite for meaningful (empirical) research. They take vague concepts and associative discussions as an inspiration and thus deliberately operate with vague concepts. They mistake conceptual vagueness for creativity. I hope that the arguments in this chapter convince the reader that, rather than promoting inventive political science research, vague concepts inhibit it.

Another reason why concepts often have an ambiguous meaning is that the same term is used with different defining attributes. As a consequence, many concepts lurk under the same term. In 1942, Baudin made this observation with respect to corporatism: 'The army of corporatists is so disparate that one is led to think that the word, corporation, itself is like a label placed on a whole batch of bottles which are then distributed among diverse producers each of whom fills them with the drink of his choice. The consumer has to look carefully' (Baudin, quoted in Schmitter, 1979, p. 10).[1] As this example makes clear, scientific discourse based on ambiguous concepts is at least confusing, more likely unproductive and definitely not cumulative.

Yet another reason for conceptual ambiguity is that political science concepts often originate outside the academic discourse. Researchers might take them from politicians' discourse or from everyday speech. The already discussed concept of 'democracy' is an appropriate example, as is 'freedom', 'justice', or 'happiness'. Such concepts are regularly laden with historical and political connotations and carry a backpack of meanings. As a result, they are often highly ambiguous.

To avoid such ambiguity, one could argue that only 'scientific' concepts should be employed in research. In the extreme case, such advice would amount to the exclusive reliance on a strictly formalized artificial language, out of touch with popular discourse. Is such advice reasonable when taking into account the costs of such a proceeding? I do not think so. Relying on formalization will definitely exclude problems which arise from a concept's popular use. In addition, it is unlikely that an artificial concept created for a specific scientific purpose will acquire different meanings over time. At least that is what we know from other scientific disciplines. Think, for example, about chemistry's table of elements. Yet, the costs of proceeding in this manner are considerable: Anyone who wants to use such concepts or interact with researchers using them will have to resort to the formalized language. Existing concepts would eventually have to be translated. It is unrealistic that political scientists in general will acquire these skills and that formalization therefore will be the cure for conceptual ambiguity in our discipline. In addition, concepts which originated in popular discourse might be the most interesting and socially relevant. Political scientists have the professional skills to inform public discourse on popular concepts such as, for example, 'democracy'. Yet, the exclusive reliance on an artificial language would severely limit our ability to communicate our results to a non-academic audience and to contribute productively to public discourse (see Lehnert, Miller, Wonka, Chapter 2). The most important reason, which speaks against the reliance on using artificial language to arrive at unambiguous concepts, is much simpler, however: The *sine qua non* for a concept's unambiguity is the explication of its defining attributes. Our natural languages are sufficient for this purpose, as the example of 'democracy' above shows.[2]

The definition of concepts must take place in the early phases of designing a research project. The effort that has to be invested in this step of designing a research project might vary. If no specification of a concept is available in the literature, we have to come up with our own definition. This definition should not contradict the meaning usually associated with the term, because such a proceeding would give away the 'everyday-analytical' leverage of the term which it owes to its non-scientific use. In most instances, however, we will be able to rely on a concept's specification in the literature. This is not least because we usually choose to embed our research projects in specific scientific discourses. The choice of the scientific discourse will most likely be based on the fact that we deem the concepts it deals with appropriate for our research purposes. In case we can rely on already specified concepts, our task is to make the respective concepts' definition explicit. If, for example, one plans to work with the concept of 'corporatism', one should be explicit about which of the many variants of the concept (Siaroff, 1999) one is working with.

(Re-)specification of a concept has to be considered if the original concept does not fully cover a researcher's theoretical interest, or if the concept will be applied to a different spatial or temporal context. If the concept is applied to a different context, the fit between the cases investigated and the original concept might be lost. Thus, to make the concept fit for traveling to a new empirical context, it might be necessary to respecify it (see Rathke, Chapter 6). Otherwise, concepts are stretched to empirical cases which the concept does not cover due to a misfit between the latter's defining attributes and the former's empirical characteristics. This might eventually lead to an erroneous theoretical classification of empirical cases. Descriptive as well as causal inferences drawn from such a basis would then be erroneous as well.

Reducing the number of defining attributes is one way to re-specify a concept to adapt it to a different empirical context: 'The rules of climbing and descending along a ladder of abstraction are thus very simple rules – in principle. We make a concept more abstract and more general by lessening its properties or attributes. Conversely, a concept is specified ... by augmenting its attributes or properties' (Sartori, 1970, p. 1041). Making a concept more abstract might allow for a valid application to a wider empirical context. Yet, it does not come without costs, because such a strategy is very likely to reduce a concept's analytical leverage. An abstract concept of corporatism defined as 'a political system in which private interest groups and public actors interact on a regular basis' is applicable to a large number of political systems. At the same time it offers little analytical leverage, because it does not allow us to empirically discriminate between systems of interest intermediation with different structural and behavioral properties. Theoretically, such a definition is nonsense since it blurs the differences between the theoretical concepts of 'pluralism' and 'corporatism' and thereby causes ambiguity. As an alternative to decreasing the theoretical distinctiveness and the analytical leverage of 'corporatism' by increasing the level of abstraction, one could revert to a different, even more abstract concept, which satisfies the theoretical as well as the empirical needs. To capture interest intermediation between private and public actors, one could for example revert to 'governance'. Now, whether such a strategy is reasonable depends first of all on the theoretical interests pursued. If one is interested in studying 'corporatism', operating with 'governance' is no viable option. If the application of a more abstract concept is not precluded for substantive reasons and if the abstract theoretical concept gives the researcher analytical leverage nothing speaks against using it.

Another strategy for adapting concepts to different empirical contexts is based on the premise that a concept consists of one or a few central attributes and a number of non-central attributes. Collier and Mahon call such concepts 'radial concepts' (Collier and Mahon, 1993). While the 'prototype' radial concept contains all defining (central and non-central) attributes, variants of the concept may contain only the central attribute and one of the prototype concept's non-central attributes. To designate the different meanings of the respective variant terminologically, an adjective is added to the prototype concept (Collier and Mahon, 1993, p. 848). Consequently, not all cases covered by one of the concept's variants have to exhibit all of the prototype concept's attributes. All variants nevertheless share some of the prototype concept's attributes. Thus, to allow for empirical variations of the prototype of 'corporatism', many variants have been formulated by adding an adjective. 'Sectoral' corporatism, for example, has been introduced to apply the concept to countries in which the structure of interest representation in some economic sectors is corporatist while in others pluralist patterns might prevail. Theoretically such a refinement might be of interest to reflect on how such 'mixed' systems perform macroeconomically. Empirically the refinement of the concept is instrumental to avoid overgeneralizations in describing countries' structures of interest representation. This strategy might preserve the basic meaning of the (prototype) concept, while its substantial and terminological qualification as a variant of the concept guarantees its valid empirical application. Thus, radial concepts allow the flexible adaptation of a concept to a wider context without necessarily having to make it more abstract or eventually having to resort to the use of a different concept. Yet the formulation of ever more variants of the prototype concept might negatively affect this concept's original appeal by reducing its distinctiveness and its analytical leverage by blurring clear demarcations between the different variants. Another lesson learnt from the dazzling conceptual history of 'corporatism'.

Which of the above discussed strategies one applies to adapt a concept to its research employment very much depends on the researcher's theoretical goals and the theoretical state in the respective field. In a conceptually highly fragmented context, the researcher might not only strive for more abstract concepts for empirical reasons, but also to achieve theoretical integration by cutting through the conceptual jungle. A researcher with such an interest should follow Sartori's advice and define abstract concepts with relatively little properties or attributes. In the opposite case – that is, if the concepts in a given field are highly abstract and ambiguously employed – the researcher will very likely opt for a radial concept, because increasing the level of abstraction would run counter to the researcher's intention. In addition, one might want to preserve the original concept to the largest extent possible and simply qualify it for an extended application, because it has thus far been meaningfully applied in the literature and has gained considerable prominence.

Finally, instead of respecifying existing concepts, there is always the option of forming completely new concepts. However, the benefits of forming new concepts should always be carefully weighed against potential costs. If well-specified concepts exist which already serve our theoretical interests, the temptation to form a new concept should be resisted. A pragmatic reason for this is to save energy affiliated with promoting a new concept and arguing for its usefulness. A substantive reason is that the creation of ever new concepts bears the risk of ever smaller research communities developing their own conceptual languages. This inhibits intelligible discourse across those communities and risks making intellectual cross-fertilizations among sub-disciplines increasingly difficult to achieve. If the goal of a research project is the innovation of a completely new theory, however, then concept formation will be one of its central tasks. The same holds if one aims at replacing a highly fragmented and ambiguous concept with a new one. This is what Siaroff (Siaroff, 1999) did with his proposal to capture countries' differences in their systems of interest intermediation through his concept of 'integration' instead of the established concept of corporatism. If none of the above is the goal of a research project, the formation of new concepts should be treated with care.

To this point this chapter has made clear that in order to validly apply a theoretical concept it must be properly defined in the first place, must have an unambiguous meaning and, moreover, the empirical domain it covers should correspond to the concept's defining attributes. What has not yet been addressed, though, is how to handle a concept validly in heterogeneous empirical contexts (van Deth, 1998, Rathke, Chapter 6). An extreme position would be to argue that no concept can be meaningfully applied across different contexts. One could arrive at such a position by arguing that real world objects designated by a concept relate to and affect their social, political and economic environment differently in different empirical contexts.[3] Thus, they play different roles in different contexts. For instance, the concept of parties designates reasonably similar organizations in democratic political systems. Yet, with respect to the role they play in democratic and autocratic political systems, respectively, parties differ considerably. For empirical inferences, this is not a problem, since the aim then is not to relate a concept to others, but to describe its occurrence across contexts. Yet, for causal inference it might be a problem. Thus, we may use the concept 'party' to denote equivalent (in terms of their attributes) organizations across democratic and autocratic political systems. We should not, however, automatically make causal inferences on the equivalence of the role parties play in all these contexts based on the label itself.

I will finish this section with a short remark on concepts which cannot be directly observed. It is a truism that something which cannot be observed constitutes a particular challenge in empirical research. Should political scientists therefore stop using concepts such as power, influence or legitimacy? Of course every empirical researcher wishes to operate with observable concepts, which can be validly and reliably measured. If we have the choice between a concept which is directly observable and one which is not and both fit our purpose, we should definitely go with the former. In addition, if a particular specification of a concept allows us to observe it directly, we should specify the concept accordingly. This greatly facilitates the operationalization and valid measurement of the respective concept and allows for a straightforward decision whether a particular case can be subsumed under a concept. If our theoretical and substantive interests lead us to use concepts which are not directly observable, everything which has been said so far applies as well: Specifying a (unobservable) concept properly prevents unobservability equaling unintelligibility. Particular effort must then be spent in arguing for the adequacy of a particular way of measuring a given concept (Miller, Chapter 5).

To summarize: Concepts are the building blocks of our theories. For a productive and cumulative scientific discourse among the participants of a research community it is necessary for the meaning of concepts to be clearly understood. The whole purpose of concept specification is to define and explicate a concept's meaning to avoid ambiguity with respect to a concept's (theoretical) meaning. At the same time, a concept's specification analytically demarcates it from other concepts. In addition, a properly specified concept allows the researcher to deal with the empirical vagueness inherent in any theoretical concept and constitutes a proper base on which empirical operationalization and measurement can take place (Collier, Brady and Seawright, 2004b). Thus, a concept properly specified is not only imperative for intelligible theoretical discourse but also to design an inter-subjectively comprehensible and methodologically justifiable research strategy, which serves as a sound bridge between social science theory and the 'real world':

> Let it be stressed, therefore, that long before having data which can speak for themselves the fundamental articulation of language and of thinking is obtained logically – by cumulative conceptual refinement and chains of coordinated definitions – not by measurement. Measurement of what? We cannot measure unless we know first what it is that we are measuring. (Sartori, 1970, p. 1038)

> ... It should be understood, therefore, that operational definitions implement, but do not replace, definitions of meaning. Indeed there must be a conceptualization before we engage in [empirical] operationalization. As Hempel recommends, operational definitions should not be 'emphasized to the neglect of the requirement of systematic import'. This is also to say that definitions of meaning of theoretical import, hardly operational definitions, account for the dynamics of intellectual discovery and stimulation. (Sartori, 1970, p. 1045)

Of course, the presentation of this way of proceeding is ideal-typical. Each empirical researcher will and should think about the (im-)possibilities of operationalizing a concept, while working on the theoretical specification of the concept (Gerring, 2001). Otherwise she risks finding out that, after having invested considerable effort in the specification of her theoretically highly interesting concepts, the project does not fly empirically. Yet, concept specification and the operationalization of concepts must be treated separately! If, during the research process, we recognize that it is difficult to measure a concept, it is hardly conceivable to go back and change the concept's specification with a view on data availability. Concept specification is foremost guided by a particular theoretical interest. This theoretical interest is unlikely to change due to measurement problems. Thus, when facing difficulties in measuring a concept, instead of re-specifying it to make it fit the data, one should rather discuss potential problems with the validity of the measure applied (Miller, Chapter 5). The presentation in this chapter is intended to remind researchers of the often neglected but nonetheless constitutive function well-defined concepts have in our research.

The consequences of improper concept specification can be summarized in three distinct points. Concepts whose meaning is ambiguous due to insufficient specification hamper the collective and cumulative effort of (political) scientists by leading to:

1. *Theoretical infertility.* Lack of precision in the meaning of theoretical concepts renders an intelligible and critical theoretical discourse impossible and constrains improvement on purely intellectual grounds.
2. *Empirical arbitrariness.* Not clearly specified theoretical concepts have a vague empirical denotation and their operationalization and measurement is vulnerable to criticisms of arbitrariness.
3. *Invalid (empirical and theoretical) inferences.* Concepts without a clearly defined meaning risk being stretched to empirical objects with overly heterogeneous properties and/or extended to temporal and/or spatial contexts, in which the roles of the objects covered by the respective concept are far too different to subsume them meaningfully under one concept.

Practical guidelines: six rules of concept specification

In the previous paragraphs I have argued that concepts are of prime importance for doing empirical social science research. Unfortunately, however, social science concepts often leave the reader puzzled about the concept's exact meaning and its theoretical status in the author's argument. In this section I provide six practical guidelines which help to avoid conceptual problems.

1 Search the literature for specifications of the concepts you will use in your research project!

The early phase of the research process should be spent searching the relevant literature for specifications of the concepts which will eventually be used in the research project. We might recognize that we work in a field with properly specified concepts. If applying one of these well specified concepts in our own research, we have to make sure that the specification fits our theoretical and empirical purpose – and that we explicate the definition of the concepts (Rules 2 to 6). Yet, a researcher might as well discover that her field is full of dazzling concepts which do not come with specifications. She then has to come up with such definitions herself. In order to avoid contradictory terminology, the definition should be in line with the meaning normally associated with the concept.

2 Explicate clearly and exhaustively the attributes you ascribe to the concept(s) used in your theoretical framework!

Concepts are important in empirical research, because they allow for a systematic look at the objects of investigation. To exploit a concept's full potential, the attributes one ascribes to a concept must be explicated. The explication of a concept's attributes makes sure that the researcher herself as well as potential readers becomes fully aware of the concept's meaning. We thereby avoid ambiguities, which again is a prerequisite to having a meaningful scientific discourse. When a concept's intension is explicated, existing definitions in the literature must be taken into account. This saves you energy and helps to avoid terminological babble as well as concepts that increasingly lose their distinctive meaning and analytical leverage due to cross-cutting specifications.

When I state that corporatist arrangements have a positive effect on a country's macroeconomic performance, I have to state what I mean by corporatism. This is important to allow others and myself to understand the exact content of the concept and the causal hypotheses for which it is used. It also allows us to clearly demarcate an argument from other arguments which operate with the same concepts. Corporatism is defined, among other things, by interest group concentration. It will make a difference whether concentration is located at the sectoral or the national level. Knowing this will greatly help us make sense of an author's causal hypotheses. If various studies using the same concepts come to different conclusions, checking their respective concept specifications will eventually tell us why this is the case.

3   Think hard about how the attributes of the concept relate to each other – and to the concept's overall meaning!

Since the attributes ascribed to a concept define its meaning, it is important that they add up to a coherent meaning. A concept is coherent if a logical relationship between its attributes is clearly discernible. In other words: If it makes intuitive sense to group these things under one label. Thus, it makes sense to define corporatism as a 'system of interest representation in which the constituent units are organized into a limited number of singular, compulsory, noncompetitive, hierarchically ordered and functionally differentiated categories' (Schmitter, 1979, p. 13). Adding 'networked' to this list of attributes would be confusing and adding 'competitive' would be plainly contradictory. Adding attributes whose relationship with other attributes is confusing or even contradictory decreases the coherence of a concept's meaning and thus limits its analytical purchase.

4   Try to keep your concept's level of abstraction low (if it is theoretically reasonable)!

A concept's level of abstraction should correspond to the theoretical and empirical needs of a research project. It should not be formulated in an unnecessarily abstract way. An important reason for avoiding abstract concepts in empirical research is their empirical vagueness. As the level of abstraction increases, concepts loose direct reference to a concrete set of real world phenomena. As a consequence, it becomes much more difficult to choose and argue for an indicator which allows for the valid measurement of the concept. If an abstract concept is needed, the problems of operationalization and measurement are traded against the concept's theoretical generalizability. When facing such a trade-off, we should keep in mind that a concept which cannot be reasonably operationalized and measured does not allow for empirical and causal inferences.

5   Relate the concept's attributes to the units of analysis you empirically investigate!

The attributes of a concept have to be explicitly related to the units of analysis to which the respective concept refers and which are the objects of the empirical investigation. The clarification of the relationship between a concept's attributes and its empirical referents not only prevents us from inadequately stretching concepts to objects for which they are inaptly suited. The explication of the units of analysis also contributes considerably to the comprehensibility of a concept's meaning. It allows the reader to form a concrete idea about that to which the author refers with his concept. If, for example, someone hypothesizes about a public actor's supranational preferences in EU decision-making, it will help our substantive understanding to know whether the person talks about decisions in general, legislative decisions or constitutional decisions. In addition, explicating the units of analysis to which a concept refers facilitates the assessment of the validity of a concept's empirical operationalization. A researcher who argues about the European Commission's supranational preferences in EU legislative decision-making and empirically investigates the European Commission's behavior in the bargaining on the European Constitution will not be able to convince us with her empirical results.

6   Be aware that in empirical research any concept eventually needs to be operationalized and measured!

Before one can think about the operationalization of a concept, the concept needs to be properly specified. Only after the full meaning of the concept has been determined is it then possible to make an adequate choice about a concept's operationalization and measurement. Yet, when designing a research project, one should from the very beginning take into account potential problems: Data might not be easily available and it will almost certainly prove difficult to get an empirical grip on a theoretical concept. Thus, while the proper theoretical specification is the fundamental precondition to theoretical intelligibility, the practical problems in measuring a concept (Miller, Chapter 5) will finally determine whether an empirical research project is feasible.

Application: underspecified and overextended? The concept of supranationality in European Union research

When reading academic as well as journalistic accounts on European Union (EU) politics, one frequently comes across the concept of 'supranationality'. Most often in its adjective form 'supranational'. The term 'supranational' is usually used in opposition to national. Applied to EU decision-making, which will be the main subject of this section, the 'supranational scenario' (Tsebelis and Garrett, 2000) conceptualizes political conflicts in EU decision-making as struggles about more 'national' or more 'supranational' policy solutions with actors positioning themselves according to their national or supranational policy preferences respectively.

Rule 2 of this chapter's practical recommendations states that the use of a concept should always be accompanied by the clarification of the concept's meaning. 'Supranationality' as used in the literature is defined by two dimensions: An institutional and a motivational. The meaning of the institutional dimension is straightforward: The EU's institutional-legal system is supranational, since it is a system independent of the institutional-legal orders of the member states. In addition, its supranational quality results from its superiority to member state law in the sense that in cases of conflict between national and EU law, the latter dominates the former. A supranational public actor, accordingly, is one which is constituted by the EC treaty and draws its competences from it. The meaning of the institutional dimension of supranationality is thus clearly defined by the institutional-legal quality of the political system of the EU. Its defining attributes are independence and superiority *vis-à-vis* member state law.

The motivational dimension of supranationality, on the other hand, denotes actors' interests or ideas driving their actions in EU politics. The meaning of this dimension is much less clearly defined. Usually it is taken to mean that actors with supranational preferences want 'more Europe' (cf. Pollack, 2003, p. 36). Yet, how can we conceive of an actor's preferences for 'more Europe' in EU politics, that is, when the units of analysis are individual policies (Rule 5)? For constitutional politics the answer is clear: Supranational constitutional preferences are defined by the desire to further integrate policy areas, for which the member states have exclusive or predominant policy-making competences up to this point. When bargaining about further institutional integration during EU Treaty negotiations, an actor with supranational constitutional preferences wants more competences to be transferred from the member state to the EU level. In EU constitutional politics, supranational constitutional preferences thus have a clear meaning and can in principle be unambiguously identified in empirical research (Moravcsik, 1998).

At this point it becomes obvious why the two dimensions of supranationality I explicated above, should be separated analytically: The British government might have a strong preference for the (constitutional) integration of further policy areas in the EU Treaties. Yet this does not make it a supranational actor in institutional terms. At the same time, the European Commission might strongly oppose the integration of a policy area, while being a supranational actor in institutional terms. Automatically inferring from the institutional to the motivational dimension of supranationality, and vice versa, would lead to false inference. Rule 3 of the practical recommendations shall help us avoid such false inferences by clarifying the relationship between the attributes of a concept. It is of course possible to define supranationality in terms of both dimensions – in other words, to extend the concept from the institutional to motivational dimension. The analytical usefulness and validity of such a definition, however, must be empirically established.

During the last decade, EU scholars increasingly turned their attention to the everyday politics of EU legislative decision-making. Thus, the unit of analysis changed from constitutional to legislative decisions. As stated in the practical recommendations, when extending a concept to new units of analysis, the validity of such a strategy and its meaningfulness should be carefully considered (Rule 5). According to the 'supranational scenario' the pro-integrationist European Commission and European Parliament (EP) side with pro-integrationist governments to legislatively realize 'more Europe' (Hörl, Warntjen and Wonka, 2005; Tsebelis and Garrett, 2000). Thus, in the case of the European Commission and the EP the institutional and the motivational dimension are said to coincide. According to the above definition, this is clearly not the case with respect to the so called pro-integrationist member state governments.

How then can we conceive of supranational legislative preferences? If there has not been any EU legislation and a decision will establish such legislation, those actors preferring EU legislation could be conceptualized as having supranational preferences: they want to replace national with European legislation. Such a definition would then be a direct analogy to the constitutional preferences discussed above. But how can legislative decisions be conceptualized along the national-supranational continuum, which are embedded in a policy area for which extensive European legislation already exists? In these policy areas the question is not whether to replace national policies with EU policies, but rather which form and content further EU regulations shall take. The meaningfulness and accordingly the empirical usefulness of conceptualizing the EU political space along the national-supranational continuum can be seriously questioned in such a context. Thus, when the concept of supranational preferences is extended to cover legislative politics, researchers should explicate the meaning of the concept applied to the new subject matter (Rule 5). Otherwise, concepts which proved highly meaningful and useful in one context – that is, supranational preferences in EU constitutional politics – are stretched to contexts in which their meaningfulness can be questioned and should be seriously debated by the research community. The ex post imposition of old concepts to new contexts might otherwise seriously handicap rather than facilitate our understanding of decision-making processes in the EU (Hörl, Warntjen and Wonka, 2005).

Empirical results and theoretical interpretations generated by two papers affiliated to the most encompassing and systematical large-n empirical research project on EU decision-making help to point out the conceptual problems with the application of 'supranationality' in the study of EU legislative decision-making (Kaeding and Selck, 2005; Thomson, Boerefijn and Stokman, 2004). Both studies operate with the concept of supranationality and both employ similar methodological tools with which they identify comparable empirical patterns. Comparing the theoretical inferences of these two studies allows for a discussion of the importance of investigating the fit between a concept and the empirical units of analysis to which it is applied. Michael Kaeding and Thorsten Selck analyze positional data[4] of 70 EU legislative proposals which comprised 174 controversial legislative issues (Kaeding and Selck, 2005; Thomson, Boerefijn and Stokman, 2004). Their goal is to find out how the European Commission, the EP and member state governments position themselves in EU legislative decision-making. Having identified their empirical pattern, Kaeding and Selck conclude that: 'the supranational institutions seem to be largely ideological actors taking extreme positions outside the clusters. Their policy positions are significantly different from the member states ... The Commission and EP are much more pro-integrationist than any member state, a fact which our three-dimensional solution demonstrates more clearly than the existing two-dimensional studies by Selck (2003) and Thomson *et al.* (2004)' (Kaeding and Selck, 2005, pp. 282–3). From their empirical results the authors infer that the Commission and the EP are indeed institutionally and motivationally supranational actors. They thereby support the two dimensional concept of supranationality commonly used in the literature to characterize the EU's supranational institutions (Pollack, 2003, p. 36; Tsebelis and Garrett, 2000, p. 16).

Robert Thomson and his colleagues analyze exactly the same data. They employ very similar methodological tools and also rely on the concept of supranationality. With respect to the positions taken by the member state governments, the European Commission and the European Parliament in EU legislative decision-making processes, the authors conclude as follows:

> Two dimensions on which the preferences of the actors can be placed were identified. On the first dimension, the Commission and European Parliament's position are located at one end, and the reference point (the outcome if no decision is taken) at the other. The Member States are clustered at the centre of this dimension. This clustering of the Member States indicates that there are no Council members that are consistently closer to the Commission's position than others. Their support depends on the proposal at stake at any particular time. (Thomson, Boerefijn and Stokman, 2004, p. 256)

Again, the common assumption about the Commission's and the European Parliament's supranational policy preferences seems to be supported.

Yet, in scrutinizing the empirical pattern they identified and in searching for a theoretical interpretation of their empirical finding, Thomson and his colleagues did not only stretch the supranational scenario to their empirical results. Instead they checked whether the concept of supranationality can be meaningfully extended to their empirical cases. After having done this, they elaborate that '[a]lthough the ordering of actors on this dimension resembles that posited in the Integration-Independence dimension [i.e., the 'supranational' scenario, AW], we found that this ordering is neither confined to, nor even concentrated in, issues that contain choices between European harmonization versus national solutions' (Thomson, Boerefijn and Stokman, 2004, p. 256). Yet, the units of analysis of a legislative decision-making process must allow for a choice between a more 'European' and a more 'national' policy solution in order to meaningfully apply the (motivational dimension of the) concept of supranationality. If they do not, an actor's actions in the respective decision-making process cannot be driven by her preference for a more 'European' solution. Such an interpretation would amount to saying that someone who has chosen between two dishes – fruit salad and potato salad – and went for the latter was driven by her preference for meat. Specifying what the units of analysis in this case were – in other words, fruit and potato salad – excluded the 'meat preference' as a logically possible explanation for that actor's action as well as the outcome, that is, her eating potato salad. Applied to the less tasty topic of EU legislative decision-making this means that to interpret an actor's behavior in EU decision-making as supranational when 'more

Europe' is not on offer in the policy decision under investigation, one infers a wrong motive from an actor's action and erroneously proposes this motive as the cause for the political dynamic leading to the observed outcome. Such an inference is theoretically misleading.

Had Thomson and his colleagues (2004) applied the concept of the 'supranational scenario' to their empirical findings without checking the quality of their units of analysis, they would have extended the concept to referents in a theoretically misleading way. Following this strategy, they would have concluded that political dynamics in EU legislative decision-making are decisively shaped by the EP and the Commission taking 'supranationalist' positions – just as Kaeding and Selck concluded in their paper. Yet analysing the same empirical data and employing similar data analysing methods, the two studies drew quite different theoretical inferences. These differences result from Thomson and his colleagues' careful examination of their study's empirical referents. In order to interpret the pattern they identified as supranational, they checked whether the decisions in their sample involved a choice between more or less European harmonization. If it did, the expectation of the 'supranational scenario' is that the Commission – which is conceptualized to want 'more Europe' (harmonization) in the supranational scenario – positions itself on the harmonization end of the scale. Yet what they do find is that '[o]f the remaining 130 issues, we find the Commission and the reference point at opposite ends of the issue scale on 60 (46 percent) of the cases. Most importantly, these 60 issues are not concentrated in the group of 40 issues classified as harmonisation issues. Of the 60 issues on which we find the reference point and Commission at opposite extremes of the issue scales, only 16 (27 percent) referred to such harmonisation issues. Moreover, on issues involving clear choices between more or less harmonisation, the reference point and Commission were not significantly more likely to be at opposite extremes than on other issues' (Thomson, Boerefijn and Stokman, 2004, p. 253). By their close examination of their empirical data and by clear concept specification, the authors avoided the extension of the concept to units of analysis not covered by the concept. Accordingly they conclude that 'a more detailed inspection of the actor alignments does not support the supranational scenario' (Thomson, Boerefijn and Stokman, 2004, p. 252). The authors' attentive application of the concept is in line with Rule 5 of this chapter's practical applications and demonstrates how careful investigation of the units of analysis helps to avoid concept misapplication and misleading theoretical inference.

Obviously, the empirical cases analyzed by the authors of both papers show a difference in the positions taken by the Commission and those taken by the member state governments. Yet the scrutiny of the units of analysis showed that (at least in these cases) the concept of supranationality should be restricted to the institutional dimension. Extending it to the motivational dimension leads to erroneous or at least contradictory theoretical inferences. The explication of both dimensions of the concept at the beginning of this section (Rule 2, practical guidelines) allowed us to identify this restriction in the concept's applicability to EU legislative decision-making. This opens the possibility to re-specify the concept accordingly. It might as well lead to the abandonment of the concept when studying actors' behavior in EU legislative decision-making processes and lead to the application of a different concept or the formulation of a new concept – and thus to a potentially different understanding of the political dynamics governing the successive legislative integration of EU member states.

One conceptual option is to abandon the concept of 'supranationality' in order to avoid any confusion between its institutional and its behavioral dimension. Thus, one could refer to a less EU specific and more abstract concept such as 'centralization' in order to capture political dynamics leading to the harmonization of policies across EU member states. The use of this concept might invite theoretical discourse with political scientists already working with this concept, yet dealing with empirical objects other than the EU – such as for example international organizations in general (e.g., Koremenos, Lipson and Snidal, 2001). Yet the decision to abandon 'supranationality' – instead of just specifying it properly – and replacing it with 'centralization' also involves considerable costs: Instead of using the established concept – although perhaps with a slightly different specification – to relate one's argument to the rest of the literature, one first of all has to establish the new concept and relate this to the rest of the literature. Whether one takes on these costs might as well be influenced by a researcher's general interest in theoretical work. Again, these costs might be worth the effort, if the expected payoff is high enough – that is, if the chances are good that the respective scholarly community will welcome the new concept because it provides them with superior analytical leverage over their empirical field of interest.

Ideally, Kaeding and Selck had taken up the argument by Thomson and his colleagues that the concept of supranationality, defined by the institutional and the motivational dimension, cannot be meaningfully applied to the legislative cases which they analyzed to kick off a debate clarifying the concept's limits. Both studies' partly contradictory theoretical interpretations, and the careful conceptual analysis by Robert Thomson and his colleagues improve our conceptual understanding of political processes in the EU. Taking this knowledge into account when re-specifying the concept of supranationality to apply it to EU legislative research or when forming new concepts will improve our inferences from empirical analyses.

Conclusion

The aim of political science research is to add to our systematic knowledge about political facts, events and processes. To be able to achieve this we need appropriate theoretical and methodological tools. In this chapter I have argued that to profit most from the theoretical and analytical potential of concepts, their meaning has to be clearly specified. It has to be specified with respect to a concept's (unambiguous) meaning – that is, its intension – as well as its empirical referents (extension). If theoretical concepts are properly specified they serve as solid bridges between social science theory and the 'real world' social processes in which we are interested.

Ambiguous concepts not only hamper intelligible theoretical discourse, thus frustrating the improvement of social science theory. Ambiguous concepts also lend themselves to misleading theoretical ex post rationalization of empirical findings. This merely confirms perspectives on a given subject of which we grew fond, rather than revealing new insights. Thus, they are also stumbling blocks on our way to valid empirical and causal inferences. Having said all this, this chapter's final comment on ambiguous concepts is: Avoid them by all means!

Notes

1. Schmitter's (1979) article is a brilliant discussion of an overly ambiguous concept – that is, corporatism – and an outstanding illustration of how to overcome such ambiguity by concept specification.
2. However, to express the relationship between concepts – that is, to formulate causal hypotheses – formalization allows much more precise statements than does a non-formalized language.
3. Note that what I discuss here is the theoretical equivalence of a concept in different contexts. This is different from a discussion of the empirical equivalence of indicators to measure the same concept. While my discussion addresses the question whether the same concept has the same theoretical status across different contexts, the latter discusses which indicators are most

suitable to measure the same concept in different contexts (for such a discussion, see van Deth 1998 and Rathke, Chapter 6).

4. In interviews, experts positioned the EU legislative actors on a continuum from 1 to 100 on each of the 174 issues. The end points of the scale represent the extreme solutions for a respective issue. For example, no animal fat allowed in chocolate vs. 50 percent of animal fat allowed in a piece of chocolate. The actors were located on the respective issue dimension according to their preferences.

4
Typologies in Social Inquiry
Matthias Lehnert

Introduction

For a long time typologies have figured prominently among the instruments of social science. They have served as conceptual tools to simplify and order complex social phenomena such as political systems, parties and party systems or varieties of capitalism. Only recently has the usefulness of typology been questioned. Typologies, so the fundamental critique goes, do not contribute to the development of theory, because they do not contain a theoretical argument. Nor do they improve empirical knowledge since they defy empirical testing. As it seems, typologies are outdated instruments which are to be replaced by formal models and advanced empirical techniques. This critique notwithstanding, eminent scholars still invest intellectual energies in the development of typologies (see, for instance: Andeweg and Thomassen, 2005; Gunther and Diamond, 2003). Thus, there is some confusion concerning the use of typology in social inquiry: Should they be used? And if yes, for which purposes and how? It is on these questions that I concentrate here.

I will proceed as follows: First, I will present three criteria with which different 'types of typologies' can be distinguished: The dichotomy of ideal and extracted types, the level of a typology's generality, and the distinction between classificatory and continuous typologies. Next, I will discuss whether we should use typologies as instruments for describing and explaining social phenomena. I will argue in favor of typologies but will confine their use to certain purposes. In Section 3, I offer some advice on how to use typologies in political science, pointing to some important trade-offs. I will then illustrate how typologies can be used fruitfully in social inquiry by referring to a practical example, namely political institutions and their effects. Cognizant of the numerous varieties of typologies, I use a very broad definition of typology: *A typology is a theoretically or empirically derived concept which systematically orders complex phenomena according to a limited number of attributes.*

Design problem

A large number of different types and typologies can be found in the social science literature: real types, ideal types, empirical types, constructed types and extreme types, to name but a few. They differ by *construction, content* and *purpose*. Here, I focus on the aspect of construction because it provides the easiest path to understanding typologies.

One can distinguish typologies according to three criteria: the dichotomy of ideal vs. extracted types, the level of generality and the distinction between classificatory and continuous types.[1] Let me briefly dwell on these differences.

The single most important distinction to be made is between *ideal* and *extracted* types.[2] Ideal types are deductively derived constructions, or, as Weber states, 'mental images', rather than empirical observations. They are developed by isolating and combining into a coherent whole the *crucial* aspects of a phenomenon (McKinney, 1966, p. 22). Empirical cases are never commensurate to ideal types but only conform to them more or less fully. The empirical use of ideal types is thus not simply to order phenomena according to some traits but rather to confront empirical reality and theoretical construction. This gives way to a counterfactual reasoning centered on the discrepancies between empirical observations and ideal types: *What would we have observed, had the empirical phenomenon not differed from the ideal type?*

In contrast, extracted types are derived *inductively* from empirical observation. Rather than focusing on crucial features, extracted types combine features that empirical phenomena have in *common*. The difference between ideal and extracted types is fundamental: We cannot determine what should be considered crucial by merely observing empirical reality. Rather, we must ask: Crucial with regard to *what*? One can only answer this question with some theory at hand from which hypotheses can be derived. Stating which traits of a phenomenon should be considered crucial is formulating a hypothesis. In contrast, stating which traits are common to some cases is formulating a description.

The second discriminating criterion is the *level of a typology's generality*. A typology consists of at least two attributes which again can take on at least two values. Generality *increases* as the number of attributes or values *decreases*. This can best be illustrated referring to a simple matrix consisting of two dimensions or attributes. Each dimension has two values. Thus, the resulting matrix has four cells. Adding a single value on one dimension increases the number of cells to six. Adding a new dimension with two distinct values increases the number to eight cells. Now, if we assume that the number of cases under investigation remains constant, increasing a typology's generality necessarily leaves some cells less populated.[3] There is a trade-off involved: The more general a typology is – the fewer attributes and values it comprises – the more *parsimonious* the types and the broader the applicability of each type. At the same time, increasing generality makes the information a typology conveys about individual cases coarser. The typology's *discriminatory capacity* is reduced (Fuchs, 2000). One might ask why we should not generally opt for more specific typologies. Obviously, more information is better than less. However, lower generality comes at a price (see Wonka, Chapter 3): As the number of cases to which the typology applies remains constant, increasing the number of attributes and/or values might increase the number of empty or scarcely populated cells. I agree with Dogan and Pelassy (1990, p. 179) in that such 'lacunae' have often spurred both theoretical reasoning and empirical research. For a given research project, however, too fine a distinction might prove counterproductive because it limits a typology's capacity to simplify reality. Taken to its extreme, decreasing generality would imply that there are many more types than there are empirical cases. Such a typology would miss the fundamental goal of simplification.

Third one must distinguish *classificatory* from *continuous* typologies. *Classificatory* typologies refer each empirical case to exactly one type, the characteristics of which it shares. Here, structuring empirical reality is a question of 'either/or'. A classificatory typology is defective if an object in the realm to which a typology applies cannot be classified or if it can be subsumed under more than one classificatory type. Aristotle's typology of political systems is a classical example of a classificatory typology. Its first attribute is the number of rulers – one, a few or many – while its second attribute captures the rulers' intention: Do they rule for their own benefit or do they pursue the greater good. Aristotle then derives six types from his two-dimensional scheme (Table 4.1). It should now be possible to refer every case to exactly one type.[4]

Continuous types, in contrast, are not a matter of 'either/or' but rather one of 'more or less'. Empirical cases approximate a type to a greater or lesser degree. Take Lijphart's types of majoritarian and consensus democracy, for instance. There is a continuum between the two types

Table 4.1   Aristotle's typology of political systems

		Number of rulers		
		One	*A few*	*many*
Rulers strive for ...	*their own benefit*	Tyranny	Oligarchy	Democracy
	the greater good	Monarchy	Aristocracy	Polity

and each type has empirical referents which correspond to it more or less fully. It is thus possible to say that Belgium is a consensus democracy and at the same time that it is less consensual than Switzerland. Using a classificatory typology one cannot make such a statement. A lot more could be said about different types of typologies, but I think that we have now acquired a satisfactory basis for exploring the different purposes of typologies in social inquiry.

Typologies, description, and explanation

The social sciences aim at the dual goal of describing and explaining social phenomena. In this section I will discuss whether and how typologies can be used for either of the two purposes.

Describing social phenomena as part of a research project is not mere description. Rather, it involves what King, Keohane and Verba (1994, p. 55) call 'descriptive inference', a 'process of understanding an unobserved phenomenon on the basis of a set of observations'. It involves an effort of *simplification* and of *establishing order* which are exactly the purposes of typology. More specifically, with regard to descriptive inference, typologies can fulfill four tasks:

First, typologies can help to develop concepts. What King, Keohane and Verba refer to as an 'unobserved phenomenon' must be stated as a concept before it can be understood empirically. It is impossible to derive concepts from empirical analysis because they are not directly observable (also see Wonka, Chapter 3). Typologies can claim a place in the realm of concept formation and specification. It is insightful that in the methodological literature on concepts, types and typologies figure prominently (see, among others, Collier and Adcock, 1999; Coppedge, 2005; Gerring and Barresi, 2003). Dogan and Pelassy (1990, p. 183) even claim that there 'is no better generator of concepts than a good typology'.

Second, typologies can be used to focus on the systematic component of phenomena which defy quantification. Institutional settings are an important example.[5] Here, typologies come into play since they either focus on common (extracted types) or on crucial traits (ideal types). Neither strategy involves the use of quantitative instruments.

Third, since typologies combine several features into coherent concepts, they can be useful for analyzing the interactions among several variables. If we confine descriptive inference to single variables we will not be able to assess one of the major strengths of typology.

Fourth, while descriptive inference needs to be applied to both dependent and independent variables, typologies are used most successfully when dealing with the latter. The common problem of multi-causality often implies that the number and complexity of explanatory factors is much greater than that of the phenomenon to be explained. Therefore, typologies should be especially useful when it comes to managing the independent rather than the dependent variables of a causal relationship (Leuffen, Chapter 8).

This short review has pointed to some tasks in the realm of descriptive inference for which typologies might prove especially helpful: They provide us with a simplified account of complex but rather stable phenomena which defy quantitative measurement and consist of several interacting elements. For this reason, typologies are often used when comparing economic or political regimes such as types of democracy (Ganghof, 2005b; Lijphart, 1999), varieties of capitalism (Boyer, 2005; Hall and Soskice, 2001) or welfare states (Esping-Andersen, 1990).

The question whether typologies can claim a place in explaining phenomena is more difficult to answer. Typologies do not merely describe, but neither do they explain. I disagree with Brady's argument that explanation can be merely classificatory rather than causal (Brady, 2004, p. 55). To take up his example: The fact that iron appears in a certain column of the periodic table – a classificatory scheme – only tells us that it has certain properties. It does not *explain* why it has certain properties. This is what Bohr's atomic theory does. Without this theory we would not understand why iron has certain properties. The fact that Bohr's theory has not made the periodic table obsolete shows that typology and theory are complementary devices. It does not imply, however, that there are two explanations for why iron has certain properties, one causal and one classificatory. Explanation needs causal arguments which are not contained in typologies. What, then, is the role of typology in explaining phenomena? In the next section I will argue that while no typology itself explains a phenomenon, *ideal typologies* can be used as elements of explanatory approaches[6] whereas extracted typologies cannot. Extracted types can perform certain initial functions, but they are not suited for explanatory purposes. For the task of explanation we should ultimately use ideal types.[7] This is true for both factor-centric and outcome-centric designs. I will also show that the purposes a typology serves in explanatory designs partly depend on whether the research project takes a *factor-centric* or an *outcome-centric* perspective. In both factor-centric and outcome-centric research, typologies can help establish unit homogeneity. Moreover, in factor-centric research, typologies can be used to solve the problem of indeterminacy.

Typologies in factor-centric research designs

Factor-centric research aims at establishing causal links between a limited set of variables rather than at explaining phenomena as comprehensively as possible. With regard to this goal, typologies can help to address two major problems: *unit homogeneity* and *indeterminacy*.

First, typologies can help establishing unit (or causal) homogeneity. Two units of inquiry are homogeneous when we expect the dependent variables from each unit to take on the same value when our explanatory variable takes on a particular value for both units. Typologies identify cases for which the expected value of the dependent variable is equal because they share crucial characteristics. Analysis can then concentrate on cases that are subsumed to the same type while holding constant all variables that constitute the typology: 'the observations being analyzed become, for the purposes of analysis, identical in relevant aspects' (King, Keohane and Verba, 1994, p. 93). King, Keohane and Verba's statement makes clear that in order to attain unit homogeneity one cannot use extracted types. It is important that the traits which the observations have in common are *relevant*. The fact that they are shared is not enough. In order to establish unit homogeneity one must provide an argument for why we should expect the same causal mechanism at work in all the cases studied. Such an argument cannot be built on empirical observation. Thus, extracted types are not sufficient. Ideal types, in contrast, involve a hypothesis about which factors should be considered crucial. This necessarily points to some causal mechanism so that ideal types can help attain unit homogeneity.

Second, and more important, typologies can serve as a remedy for indeterminacy because they combine several variables into broader concepts, thus reducing the number of variables to be integrated into a causal model. This is especially helpful when the number of observations is small and cannot be increased. If one of the most familiar methodological suggestions – *increase the number of observations* (King, Keohane and Verba, 1994, pp. 24, 29–31, 120–1, 123) – turns out to be impractical, not everything need be lost. It is not the sheer number of observations that matters but rather the ratio of observations and variables. Thus, when increasing the number of observations is impossible, decreasing the number of variables might still be an option. Limiting the number of explanatory variables can be a viable strategy to 'maximize leverage'. However, scholars like King, Keohane and Verba favor increasing the number of observations because it comes with lesser risks of 'omitted variable bias'. By using typologies we might evade both the Scylla of indeterminate research design and the Charybdis of omitted variable bias, because typologies decrease the number of variables by *combining* rather than by *dropping* them. Ragin (1987, p. 149) states that a 'single typology can replace an entire system of variables and interrelations'. This can be especially helpful if interaction effects are in the center of interest: Using statistical methods, one might be able to attribute effects to individual variables but might find it difficult to assess interactions between variables. The number of interaction terms needed multiplies and often rapidly outgrows the number of cases or observations (Ragin, 1987, p. 15). In this case, it can be useful to focus on bundles of variables as established in types. However, there is an important trade-off involved: The price we pay for using types instead of individual variables is a lack of precision in our conclusions. We cannot attribute causal effects to particular aspects but only to types. Whether the loss of precision should be considered serious depends on the research question posed. If we expect several variables to exert an influence only in combination, the use of types would not diminish the precision of our conclusions. Instead, we might run the risk of not gaining any insight at all if we do not focus on combined effects.

With regard to indeterminacy, extracted types suffer from a lack of *interpretability*. If we try to solve the problem of indeterminacy by reducing the number of variables, we must make sure that the types can still be interpreted. Indeterminacy is not just a problem for factor-centric research designs which can be avoided by lumping together variables. Rather, it is a small-n problem: Combining variables makes sense only if the result of the effort can be interpreted. If we do not understand what the type is about, we cannot use it for explanation. Thus we must ask: Why and how do some clusters of empirically observed factors relate to the phenomenon of interest? Once we reason this way we need to switch from extracted to ideal types. The initially used extracted types have spurred concept formation and theory development, but they have not effectively solved the problem of indeterminate research designs. This could only be achieved by using ideal types because they are necessarily attached to a theory and thus can be interpreted. It seems that extracted types are of no use in factor-centric designs. This impression, however, is misleading. I have concentrated on the aspect of theory-*testing*, rather than theory-*building*. Factor-centric designs keep separate these two steps of social inquiry. It is for theory-building, rather than theory-testing, however, that extracted typologies are especially suited. Peters' understanding of typology as the 'initial stage of a theory' fits best to extracted types (Peters, 1998, p. 95).

Typologies in outcome-centric research designs

Outcome-centric approaches aim at explaining social phenomena as fully as possible. In such designs, the units studied are understood as unique wholes rather than as randomly selected examples of a larger universe. Cases are not used as a basis for inferring from samples to universes. Therefore, indeterminacy is much less of a problem in outcome-centric designs than in factor-centric designs, if it is a problem at all.

Focusing on universes rather than samples, the question of which cases constitute a universe for investigation is of prime importance.[8] Typologies 'can play a valuable role in defining the universe of cases that can productively be compared' (Munck, 2004, p. 111; see also: George and McKeown, 1985, pp. 28–9; Leuffen, Chapter 8) because they 'set boundaries on comparability' (Ragin, 1987, p. 20). At this early stage of analysis an extracted typology might be the only available instrument for case selection. Outcome-centric research can work with such blunt a tool, because it proceeds from the hypothesis that 'social phenomena in like settings ... may parallel each other sufficiently to permit comparing and contrasting them' (Ragin, 2004, p. 125). In fact, Ragin (1987, pp. 149–60) explicitly focuses on extracted typologies – or, as he calls them *empirical* typologies. They can be used to identify an initial selection of cases that is homogeneous with regard to a great number of traits. Eventually, however, ideal types are needed in order to establish the universe of cases because arguments about causal homogeneity can only be attached to ideal types. Therefore, concepts need to be reformulated during the course of inquiry. In outcome-centric designs, this is possible because, unlike in factor-centric research, theory-building and theory-testing are not sharply divided. Rather, concept formation, formulation of theories and hypotheses and empirical analysis evolve in parallel (Ragin, 2004, pp. 125–8). Scholars working from an outcome-centric perspective engage in 'ongoing refinement of concepts' (Munck, 2004,

p. 119) in which extracted types can be replaced by ideal types. This can be achieved by gradually shifting the focus from the features that cases have in common to a phenomenon's crucial features.

Practical guidelines

What can be learned from the above abstract reasoning on typologies? Beside the general point that typologies should not *per se* be discarded as instruments of inquiry, some more practical advice on *how* to use typologies can be derived.

- *Be clear about whether you use ideal or extracted types.* As I have argued above, both can be useful but not for the same tasks. Confusing ideal and extracted types can lead to misinterpreting the results of inquiry. For explanatory purposes, especially when approached from a factor-centric perspective, ideal types must be used.
- *Build typologies with regard to a precise research question.* Even if you want to construct extracted types you must focus on a somehow defined universe of phenomena. Such a limitation can be provided by a research question.
- *Avoid reification of concepts.* Keep in mind that types and typologies are conceptual tools rather than empirical phenomena to be found in the real world. Avoid any confusion about this difference between types and cases. Types cannot be observed, only their empirical referents – cases – can.
- *Be aware of trade-offs.* Most importantly, there is a trade-off between simplicity and informational content. All typologies aim at simplification. However, simplification comes with a loss of information about the individual empirical unit. Neither simplification nor informational content can be manipulated directly. The crucial variable in this respect is the number of attributes and values. The fewer attributes and/or values a typology encompasses, the more it simplifies a complex social reality. In contrast, the more attributes and values you include in a typology, the more information it conveys about the empirical referents.
- *Simplification is not so simple.* In factor-centric research, the most important alternative to combining several variables into types is the use of several variables. If there are many observations, the costs of simplification might exceed its benefits. This is especially true if interaction effects are not crucial. If, however, your theory tells you that interaction between variables matters and if the number of observations is limited,

the costs of distortion might be more easily borne than the costs of indeterminacy. With regard to outcome-centric research, 'close knowledge' of contextual settings might serve as an alternative means for achieving causal homogeneity (Munck, 2004). The trade-off remains, however: Typologies reduce complexity at the price of distortion. In contrast, 'close knowledge' avoids distortion but does not reduce the cognitive costs of dealing with complexity. Second, as already outlined above, a typology's generality involves a trade-off between parsimony and discriminatory capacity. Unfortunately, there is no rule on how to set the level of generality. Whether more general or more specific typologies should be used, depends on the research question to be answered.

- *If you use distinct categories rather than continua, construct a matrix which contains all logically possible combinations of the values you include in your typology.* It is not necessary for each possible combination to ultimately constitute a type. However, such a matrix furthers both theoretical reasoning and empirical research. It prompts the question whether there are really no empirical cases that fit into an empty cell. Moreover it can stimulate reasoning on why we would not expect to find any cases in a particular cell.

- *If all cells of your typology are densely populated consider including additional attributes and/or values.* As argued above, overcrowded cells might diminish a typology's utility. If all or most cases end up in the same box, concentrate on this one type and consider developing subtypes as a refinement strategy. This can be achieved by adding either new attributes or additional values on existing attributes or both. However, all refinements must be related to theory. *Ad hoc* refinements defy interpretation and thus diminish your typology's value.

- *If there are many empty cells consider dropping attributes and/or values.* While empty cells can serve as counterfactuals in theory-building they are useless for empirical theory-testing because there simply are no observable phenomena from which you could reliably infer; neither in large-n studies using statistical devices (King and Zeng, 2007), nor in small-n case studies.

- *Switch from categories to continua if too many combinations of values seem improbable or inadequate.* Using continua you can lump together cases that in classificatory concepts would have ended up in different cells without dropping a variable. For instance, in Lijphart's typology two cases can appear equally majoritarian although they differ with regard to some variables. Had Lijphart strictly adhered to a categorical approach these two cases would show up in different cells (on the problem of categories and continua, see the discussion in Collier and Adcock, 1999).

- *Do not overstate your case.*   The fact that you can show a robust relationship between the empirical referents of your types and some observable phenomena does not explain anything. It is a mere correlation. Always search for causal explanations.

Application

The question as to what affects different political orders has always been a major challenge in political science. Scholars have been striving to answer this question for centuries and since the very beginning of this endeavor they have used typologies.

The basic problem we are confronted with when trying to explain the effects of political institutions is twofold: Since neither political institutions nor their possible effects come in neat bundles of data which we can put into regression models, the first task is *describing* both institutions and effects (or rather: their supposed effects). However, mere accumulation of data does not suffice. Rather, we face the task of what King, Keohane and Verba (1994) call *descriptive inference*. Secondly, we must stipulate and test causal relationships between institutions and their effects. This dual task is summarized in Table 4.2.

I will concentrate on the first and fourth boxes, treating political systems as explanatory variables.

Let's start with box number one. The task of *describing* political institutions can be accomplished by using either extracted or ideal types – with probably different results.

Table 4.2   Different perspectives on institutional effects

		Object of research	
		Institutions	*Effects*
Goal of research	*description*	(1) describing institutions	(2) describing effects*
	explanation	(3) explaining institutions (institutions as *dependent* variable)	(4) explaining effects (institutions as *independent* variable)

* Note that in order to describe effects of institutions some causal argument has to be stated.

Constructing extracted types, one first pursues a 'vacuum sweeper approach' (Winch, 1947, p. 74) and collects information on as many attributes as possible. One can then use factor analysis, Boolean algebra, or simply search for clusters of values. These strategies lead to a reduced number of dimensions which span the space in which empirical cases can be located. As a final step one can identify clusters of cases in this space and establish them as types. Siaroff (2003) roughly follows this strategy in his attempt to construct a typology of parliamentary systems: He first collects data on twenty-seven different variables and then reduces the information by using factor analysis. This produces eight factors, the weakest six of which Siaroff discards. The remaining two are then combined, creating a two-dimensional space in which empirical cases can be located. Finally, Siaroff identifies three clusters of countries and turns their respective features into characteristics of three different types of parliamentarism (Siaroff, 2003, pp. 456, 460).[9] That a typology can further social inquiry almost entirely because of its descriptive value is illustrated by Arend Lijphart's typology of majoritarian and consensus democracies (Lijphart, 1984, 1999). Lijphart constructs the two types of majoritarian and consensus democracy by abstracting several institutional features from given political systems. The immediate success of his typology mostly rested on its descriptive potential rather than on its explanatory power. Rigorous critique of the typology (Ganghof, 2005a, 2005b; Kaiser, Lehnert, Miller and Sieberer, 2002; Taagepera, 2003) has spurred theoretical development and has led to theoretically more astute accounts such as Tsebelis's veto player theory (Tsebelis 2002). Just as Bohr's atomic theory and the periodic system coexist, these models have not, however, supplanted Lijphart's typology. They may provide causal explanations for some of the effects that have been found by using Lijphart's types. Ganghof (2005b) combines elements rooted in veto player theory with some features of Lijphart's approach into a new typology. His effort starts from a critique of what I call extracted types and points to the construction of ideal types. Rather than using factor analysis, Ganghof theoretically develops a notion of majoritarian democracy, which he then translates into different institutional settings. Empirical cases can exhibit one of these combinations and still must not be confused with the ideal type of majoritarian democracy. Jung (2001) follows a similar path: She first identifies two crucial principles of democracy. Both are binary in nature, so that their combination produces four logically possible combinations. Each combination is treated as a type. Jung makes clear that her types cannot be found in reality and that they are not supposed to present empirical phenomena. However, existing political systems can be ordered with regard to their accordance with the four types. In this manner, Jung's ideal typology serves as a device for empirical analysis. A final example is drawn from my own research: Together with André Kaiser, Bernhard Miller and Ulrich Sieberer, I developed a two-dimensional typology of political regimes (Kaiser, Lehnert, Miller and Sieberer, 2002). Our first dimension centers around a system's inclusiveness while our second dimension focuses on governmental responsibility and the chance of alternation in government.

Compared to Lijphart's account, our framework has at least two important advantages: Positively, it allows for a more plausible distinction between pluralitarian and majoritarian democracies. We hold that Lijphart's definition of 'majoritarian democracy' is misleading. In the proto-typical cases of what Lijphart calls 'majoritarian democracies' – the United Kingdom and New Zealand (prior to 1996) – more often than not, pluralities rather than majorities rule. Therefore, we refer such systems to the type of pluralitarian democracy while reserving the term 'majoritarian democracy' for countries which combine proportional representation on the electoral level and majority rule on the legislative level. In such systems, we contend that majorities rather than pluralities rule. Normatively, our concept leads to a more differentiated understanding of 'democratic quality' which, unlike in Lijphart's approach, is not equated with inclusiveness.

Our approach is an example of how ideal types can further our understanding of political systems, both positively and normatively. Moreover, it shows how increasing the number of attributes – and thus, types – can lead to more plausible types. We can now turn to box four and the task of explaining effects. While typologies should be constructed with regard to a precise research question, for the sake of generality I will present my example in rather abstract terms.

We cannot directly attribute observable performance to institutional settings or even particular institutions. What we observe is *national performance* which must be attributed to a country rather than a set of institutions. For instance, we can observe the growth rate of the Swedish GDP, but this is usually not what we are interested in: We are interested in Sweden's economic performance not because it is Sweden's but rather because we assume that it is somehow linked to a particular set of institutions. In other words: We are interested in *institutional capacities* which are not themselves observable. National performance must not be taken to be the empirically observable referent to the unobservable concept of institutional capacity. Performance is influenced by many factors. Outcome-centric approaches aim at developing encompassing explanations of performance which include many explanatory factors. Kaiser's book on constitutional reform in majoritarian democracies can be considered an example (Kaiser, 2002). Kaiser concentrates exclusively on majoritarian democracies – Great Britain, New Zealand, Canada and Australia – and then builds rather complex explanations for each of the four cases. One element of his theory is a typology of actors involved in the politics of constitutional reform; another is a typology of veto points. Kaiser combines the two typologies in his theory and thus accounts for both differences and similarities of processes of constitutional reform in the four countries studied. Typologies have thus served as both instruments to attain causal homogeneity and elements included in explanatory accounts.

Rather than explaining particular observable levels or patterns of performance, factor-centric designs aim at isolating the causal effect institutions have on outcomes. The methodologically appropriate test would be to constitute two (or even more) political systems in a single country at the same time and observe their effects (also see King, Keohane and Verba, p. 84). We could then alter various institutional features such as electoral systems or the number of parliamentary chambers and precisely assign each institution its partial effect on the outcome variables under investigation. Thus we would be able to assess the institutions' capacities to affect outcomes.

Unfortunately, such experiments are impossible, and we must therefore resort to second- or maybe even third-best methods. One such approach involves using a typology of political systems. The rationale is that an institutional setting has a *functional logic* which must not be confused with its *actual functioning*.[10] Many systematic and non-systematic factors influence a system's actual functioning, but only systematic factors have an impact on its functional logic. Non-systematic factors that affect a political system's actual functioning might be, for example, the health of the head of state, but could also be institutional idiosyncrasies. Using a typology we can identify cases which are sufficiently similar with regard to their supposed functional logic, notwithstanding observable differences in their actual functioning. Typologies thus lead to internally homogeneous and externally heterogeneous clusters of cases. *Ceteris paribus* we expect all cases subsumed under one type to exhibit the same observable levels of performance. In contrast, cases assigned to different types are expected to show different levels of performance.[11]

Regardless of the breadth of our research interest, the concept of functional logic can help us identify the crucial elements of political systems and combine them into an ideal typology. For instance, Bingham Powell

(2000) builds on Lijphart's typology in order to answer the question of whether and to what extent elections accomplish their task as 'instruments of democracy'. He thus infers from a sample of observations to an unobservable concept which might vaguely be called 'quality of representation'. His question is whether political institutions affect the extent to which policymakers do what citizens want them to do (Powell, 2000, p. 251). Powell is not primarily interested in the performance levels of the countries studied but rather in the record of his types or, as he puts it, visions of democracy. His typology consists of only two elements: Electoral systems and legislative committee rules (Powell, 2000, p. 39). Based on these two dimensions Powell constructs two types – a majoritarian vision and a proportional influence vision – which largely coincide with Lijphart's types of majoritarian and consensus democracy. Powell develops several criteria of performance. He then shows empirically that each vision achieves a fairly good quality of representation when judged according to its own standards. However, the proportional influence vision fares slightly better when measured against a universal standard. Powell's study exemplifies how types can be used in a factor-centric research design.

In my own research (Lehnert 2002), I have developed a modification to Powell's scheme, because I find it wanting on more descriptive ground. Powell uses distinct categories rather than continuous dimensions. Each of the two dimensions in his scheme consists of two distinct values. Logically, this gives rise to a four-cell matrix. However, Powell comes up with only two types – a majoritarian and a proportional influence vision – and a mixed category which cannot be interpreted at all and is thus lost for empirical research. Powell does not consider the two remaining logical combinations which result from his scheme. I have argued that in this manner, Powell diminishes the explanatory power of his approach, because his types are too heterogeneous and the mixed category cannot be interpreted at all, thus becoming lost for empirical research. Rather than simply taking into account the two dropped types, however, I have suggested switching from Powell's extracted types to ideal types. Underlying this is the question whether distortions in the vote-power ratio are acceptable. Taking up the distinction between majoritarian and pluralitarian democracy, I now distinguish between four types of democracy (Table 4.3).

In a second step I operationalize the types so that it is possible to sort empirical political systems. The results differ significantly from Powell's account as is illustrated in Table 4.4.

This sorting of types and empirical referents is not only a matter of different labels, however. I argue that it positively affects the results of

Table 4.3 A typology of democracies

| | | Is a distortion in favor of a *majority* acceptable? | |
		yes	no
Is a distortion in favor of a *minority* acceptable?	yes	Pluralitarian democracy	Supermajoritarian democracy
	no	Majoritarian democracy	Proportional democracy

Table 4.4 Two typologies of democracies compared

Country	Powell's typology	Lehnert's typology
Finland (prior to 1987)	Proportional influence vision	Supermajoritarian democracy
Germany	Proportional influence vision	Supermajoritarian democracy
Ireland	Mixed	Majoritarian democracy
New Zealand (prior to 1996)	Majoritarian vision	Pluralitarian democracy
Switzerland	Proportional influence vision	Supermajoritarian democracy
United Kingdom	Majoritarian vision	Pluralitarian democracy

empirical research as it leads to more homogeneous clusters of political systems, and diminishes the mixed category. While far from exhaustive, my examples show that typologies have been used successfully in attempts to describe political systems as well as in contributions explaining political outcomes.

Conclusion

Typologies have long been considered important instruments of social research. Only recently has their usefulness become a matter of debate. I have argued that typologies can contribute to social inquiry but that their use involves several trade-offs. If the goal is description of political phenomena, typologies can lead from mere description to 'descriptive inference'. If the goal is explanation, typologies can be used fruitfully in both factor-centric and outcome-centric research designs. Especially when there are few observations and many interrelated variables, typologies might help in making explanation possible. However, the simplification of complex phenomena which can be achieved by constructing typologies comes at the price of less interpretable research findings.

One last aspect deserves mentioning: Typologies link previously unrelated theories and strands of research (Kaiser, 1997, pp. 431–2). Any given typology provides descriptive knowledge that can be included in a number of causal accounts centering on different aspects of empirical reality. Each of these theories delivers insight into the part of reality it seeks to explain. By using the same typology for explaining different phenomena, we might gain some additional understanding about how seemingly unrelated aspects of reality are linked. This can prove especially important if we want to derive practical advice from a theory. Before turning from explanation to actual manipulation of reality, we are well advised to check for possible effects from as many angles as possible. In some cases, it suffices to be mindful that a variable treated in isolation within a given design is part of a more encompassing type. While the interaction effects between one's variable of interest and other factors might not be relevant for the question posed, they can be crucial when it comes to intentional action.

Both for individual research projects and the collective endeavor of social science, typologies can be useful instruments which should not be discarded. As with any tool the crucial point is to use it properly.

Notes

1. McKinney (1966) proposes additional distinctions most of which are tied to the criterion of generality.
2. I adhere to McKinney's terminology. The term and concept of 'ideal types' is, of course, most closely linked with the name of Max Weber (1988/1904). I do not discuss the methodological differences in greater detail here.
3. Note that the well-known inverse relationship between a concept's *extension* (number of empirical referents) and its *intension* (number of attributes) holds for the individual types but not necessarily for the whole typology (on the inverse relationship, see Gerring and Barresi, 2003). Adding a dimension or a value does not necessarily decrease the total number of cases to which the typology applies. The reverse is also true: As one drops a dimension or a value, a particular type might gain more empirical referents while the total number of referents remains constant.
4. Due to second attribute's fuzziness, it might be hard or even impossible to refer any given case to one and only one criterion. Try it with contemporary democracies and you will understand what I mean.
5. To be sure, quantitative measures and indices have been developed *on the basis of typologies* (see, for instance, Crepaz, 1996; Lijphart, 1999, pp. 247, 312–14). Note, however, that such instruments presuppose the existence of a typology.

6. I will concentrate on the distinction between ideal and extracted types, because I think that both the level of generality and the use of categories or continua must be decided upon with concrete research questions at hand rather than in an abstract discussion.

7. Interestingly, Ragin (1987, pp. 149–60) demonstrates that his approach of truth tables can be used as a means for building extracted types. He fails to link this entirely descriptive endeavor with the rest of his book which is focused on explanation. I maintain that ultimately the types constructed with the help of truth tables are not 'up to the task' because they lack an argument about relevance of factors. This is not to say that Boolean algebra must not be used for typology construction. Neither do I warn against the use of extracted types.

8. This is especially true if one follows a deterministic view of reality in which a single observation can refute an explanation (see Ragin, 1987, pp. 51–2).

9. Here is not the place to discuss the intricacies of Siaroff's approach, some of which are highly questionable. I have chosen this example because it neatly illustrates how extracted types are constructed.

10. It is not necessary to subscribe to a functionalist view of political systems implying that systems act through themselves. The term 'functional logic' simply marks a difference between the actual observable functioning of a given system on the one hand and the way this system would function if we could abstract from all nonsystematic effects. If there was no functional logic but only actual functioning, the whole purpose of institutional design and institutional learning would be pointless.

11. Types can significantly reduce the number of explanatory variables, but they do not make the use of control variables obsolete (see Sieberer, Chapter 9).

Part III
Measurement

5
Making Measures Capture Concepts: Tools for Securing Correspondence between Theoretical Ideas and Observations

Bernhard Miller

Introduction

'Perhaps the most fundamental barriers to good comparative research are measurement and the problems of comparability of measures.' (Peters, 1998, p. 80) A quick glance at the contents of this book reveals that this is a bold statement. Given the sheer number of challenges we face designing our research projects, it might even be an overstatement. But whether or not we share Peters' view, measurement as the link between theory and empirical reality is the backbone of empirical research and therefore at the core of research design, irrespective of whether research is quantitative or qualitative (based on large-n or small-n), or, for that matter, whether it is comparative or not. The central role of measurement in research design goes some way to explain the skepticism of one distinguished commentator on the subject who is 'doubtful, that any amount of study ... can teach you how to measure social phenomena, though it can conceivably be helpful in understanding exactly what is achieved by a proposed method of measurement or measuring instrument' (Duncan, 1984, p. 154). This is what this chapter sets out to do.

I proceed by addressing two sets of issues: First: What are the challenges we face devising measures? And: Which tools can we employ to help us solve them? Particularly for the readership of this volume it will be helpful to look at research design problems from the vantage point of what is to be achieved. Accordingly, measurement should be understood in functional terms as the process of arriving at persuasive empirical tests of research hypotheses (Geddes, 2003, p. 157). More narrowly, and as a part of this process, measurement is 'the assignment of numbers to objects or events according to rules' (Stevens, 1951, p. 22).[1] While this definition is coined for quantitative researchers, it can be generalized to qualitative research. Measurement attributes (relative) *values* to observations according to pre-defined rules. In the following, I stress the design of measures – and only discuss in passing issues of measurement error (Brady and Collier, 2004; King, Keohane and Verba, 1994).

This chapter is written for the researcher engaged in political science research outside of survey research[2] and combines insights from both a more abstract as well as from an application oriented perspective on measurement. It is structured as follows: In the first section I discuss measurement as the process of operationalization, validity- and reliability-testing. In the second part I discuss how careful index-construction can help alleviate problems of measurement and provide a compact list of practical advices for researchers. The application part ties these recommendations to my own research and illustrates their usefulness. The conclusion summarizes the main points.

Design problem

Measurement problems are manifold and affect both large-n and small-n studies. For large-n studies, measurement is often said to be reductionist, based on inadequate indicators and thus resulting in poor data quality (Geddes, 2003, p. 216; Collier, Brady and Seawright, 2004b, p. 206). Measurement in small-n studies on the other hand has drawn criticism because of potential subjective biases (King, Keohane and Verba, 1994; Geddes, 2003). There is little in these contributions, however, which translates directly into practical tips for the research process (Thomas, 2005).

As Wonka (Chapter 3) stresses, the necessary preconditions for measurement are clear and unambiguous concepts. Measurement needs to proceed from there. To discuss just how, we need to delineate what we mean by measurement. Everyone has an intuitive idea of what measurement is. This intuition probably involves commonplace measures such as temperature. The process of establishing temperature is quite simple: You pick a thermometer and know the temperature. Changes in the object of interest are easily observed, readily quantified, reliably reproduced, and can easily be documented. Most readers would sigh in relief if measurement in our discipline was as straightforward.[3] In order to discuss differences, difficulties and remedies, I shall use the temperature example to take a closer look at the elements of which measurement consists (Figure 5.1). The concept we are interested in is temperature – different degrees of warm and cold in our environment. In and by itself the concept is unobservable and of little help. Research into the characteristics of mercury has enabled inventors to link the volume of this metal to changes in temperature. This step is called operationalization and results in an indicator (change in volume). Operationalization is often conflated with measurement (Brady, 2004). I suggest to maintain the distinction, however, as there is a specific set of problems associated with operationalization justifying the term. Once we measure temperature it is important to establish whether the value is in fact related to how warm or cold it is. That is, the validity needs to be established (it could be possible for example that our measure only works for certain ranges of temperature). Finally, in order to be able to produce a reliable measure we need to make sure that its results are reproducible, that is, any researcher must be able to arrive at the same result using the same measurement under the same circumstances.

The scheme in Figure 5.1 shows that measurement can usefully be described as a process (Carmines and Zeller, 1994, p. 2). With concepts specified we know what we theoretically want to observe. Latent variables are our theoretical constructs while observed variables are empirical manifestations thereof.[4] The latent variable is what a researcher

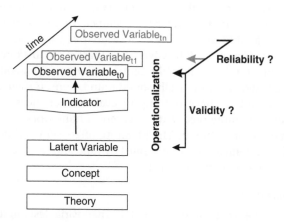

Figure 5.1 The measurement process

would ideally like to observe (politicians' true policy preferences for example). Usually, direct observations are not possible, however, and indicators need to be identified through which the researcher arrives at her observable variable. This part of the measurement process is called operationalization. After the data are collected, the researcher needs to make sure that they are valid (how closely does the observed correspond to the latent variable?) and reliable (are the values for the observed variable identical if measurement is repeated?). What is worth emphasizing is that the measurement process is identical whether the research is large-n or small-n, quantitative or qualitative (King, Keohane and Verba, 1994, p. 152). As Brady stresses, '*qualitative* comparisons are the basic building blocks of any approach to measurement' (2004: 63, italics original; see also the discussion on typologies in Lehnert, Chapter 4). The notion that measurement is more of a quantitative playground thus lacks a basis. What differs is the operationalization (Brady, 2004, p. 65, fn 14) and the means to assess validity and reliability. As questions of measurement apply to all dependent and independent variables it is also insubstantial whether the design is outcome- or factor-centric. To discuss the research design problem let us begin with a list of criteria for good measures and then proceed by discussing the difficulties involved in achieving them.

How to design a good measure

In the ensuing part, I outline criteria for the design process. The design aspect is particularly central in political science as there are many extensive theoretical concepts which are not directly observable (the size of a constituency is observable, corporatism and democracy are not). Virtually all measures in the social sciences are derived measures, i.e. they are based on another indicator (Hempel, 1952). Corporatism for example is – among other things – measured as the degree of union concentration (Siaroff, 1999). Given the mostly complex relation of concepts and empirical reality, the central criterion for a good measure is that it be based on theoretically sound foundations. If there is no theoretical blueprint we have nothing to evaluate our measure against. Furthermore: the more precise the theoretical framework, the easier to develop means for testing it. The literature offers standard demands – data need to be comparable, results must be valid and reliable – but more concrete criteria are hard to come by.

Operationalization

A central challenge to measurement is that variables might not be observable (King, Keohane and Verba, 1994). King and colleagues recommend restricting research to observable concepts. This, however, is not helpful – amongst other things because our research should be determined primarily by theoretical concerns. The task then is to find sensible observable variables for our concepts.

'Observable' as a term evidently entails some ambiguities. I therefore resort to the distinction between latent and observed variables (Bollen, 1989). For example, an actor's preferences are a latent variable – what is observable on the other hand, are revealed preferences only. Parties do not write their preferences into a manifesto without trying to anticipate voter reactions. Thus, what is revealed might not correspond to what we want to measure. The deviations which might exist need to be explored and taken into account. I present a simple measurement model to illustrate the assumptions operationalization entails. A measurement model is a formal representation of the relation between latent and observed variables to elucidate I provide an example below:

$$x_j = \lambda_{ji}\, \xi + \delta_i$$

x_j is the observed variable which is composed of the latent variable ξ, scaled by λ_{ji} to assure for comparability over all j. δ_i is the error term. As a modification, one could introduce another systematic error term to account – in the above example – for deviations of revealed and true preferences which might vary between different objects of observation.

Take, for example, 'terrorism prevention' (adapted from Rohwer and Pötter, 2002). We might be interested in how much effort states put into protecting their citizens from terrorist activity and consider as terrorism prevention all assets spent on military and police projects above the average level of spending before terrorism was on the agenda. Our observed variable then is the amount of money spent. However, it makes little sense to treat every additional € spent on the prevention of terrorism as equally important in every country. In small countries, citizens profit more from increased spending than in larger states (because longer borders and more people are harder to protect). Therefore our measure is scaled by the population or area for λ_{ji}. The error term δ_i serves to remind the researcher that each measurement might to some degree be erroneous.[5] In small-n research, it is relatively easy to explicate the substantial effect of potential measurement errors by describing the myriad of influences to which an indicator is subjected; both qualitative and quantitative researchers should make more use of this. In large-n research, there are methods to correct for measurement error (Bollen,

1989). The advantage of measurement models is that they explicate assumed causal relations and encourage thinking about alternative explanations or different causal relations between latent and observed variables.

Finding indicators is often the driving force behind measurement. Tensions between the theoretically desirable and the empirically available are therefore often barely disguised. Unless correspondence between concept and measure can be taken for granted, however, a measure is not worth much. Therefore criteria for operationalization should be documented. In cases where different indicators can be used – and there is no compelling theoretical reason for or against one – the differences between the operationalizations need to be documented. These alternative operationalizations should be presented and interpreted. This strengthens the robustness of the results and enhances the confidence we can have in them rather than weakening them.

Operationalization is often discussed in close connection with scale types. Which is the appropriate scale to use for a variable? The literature distinguishes between nominal, ordinal, interval and ratio scales (Stevens, 1946).[6] The higher the scale, the more information it contains. Yet higher scales are not inherently better – there is no *inherent* reason for assigning ordinal values to different interest groups or religions for that matter. Obviously, there will be research questions suggesting other scales. However, the issue must not be stressed too much, because ultimately it is not about the substantive meaning of a measure but only a technical characteristic. Geddes (2003, pp. 70–1), for example, uses a dichotomous measure of regime type as she is interested in the beginning and end of regimes only. Scales are important when it comes to the difference between small- and large-n research. While King and colleagues rightly assert that the scales apply to both approaches (1994, p. 151), qualitative analysis of interval scales would seem difficult if not impossible. Language does not lend itself to precise differentiation.[7] Measures in small-n studies can often be justified more thoroughly and therefore offer the potential for more accurate measurement. It is misleading to say that measures need to be more tightly specified in large-n research (Peters, 1998, p. 81). Thus, the differences between these two types of operationalization are worth exploring a bit further. Geddes (2003, p. 144) seems to suggest that quantitative operationalization is mainly restricted to picking 'off-the-shelf' measures, whereas qualitative operationalization forces the researcher to specify clear criteria. This differentiation clearly is not helpful. In both research approaches, any ambiguity in the design of a measure must frustrate our efforts to provide an intersubjectively relevant argument which lends itself to testing and developing hypotheses.

What must be stressed, however, is that any operationalization will be more plausible when it corresponds closely to a given concept. A nominal concept (war – yes or no) should be operationalized nominally – even though one could certainly find interval indicators (e.g., number of civilian casualties). Intermediate values would have no theoretical basis and would thus render the indicator devoid of sensible interpretation – or even lead to wrong conclusions.

To sum up, operationalization, in order to assure close correspondence between a concept and the measure needs to specify how latent and observed variables are related and whether or not there might be alternative ways to operationalize a concept. The researcher should also explicate all potential deviations between latent and observed variables.

Validity

The next three sections discuss how to scrutinize data once it has been generated. Once suitable indicators have been identified the question is: How can we make sure we have a measure which actually measures the concept we are interested in. King and colleagues recommend that researchers adhere to data and not 'allow to let unobserved or unmeasurable concepts get in the way' of achieving validity (1994, p. 25). It is not clear what implications one can draw from this recommendation. However, it seems to suggest that there are concepts which are easily observable, and thus are preferable to use in measurement. Yet, as we have seen, there are not many directly observable concepts. The best way to avoid this problem, then, is to use theoretically well-grounded and explicit operationalization as sketched in the last section. The validity tests which the literature suggests to test a measure are usually (Bollen, 1989; Duncan, 1984; Rohwer and Pötter, 2002)[8]: (1) Content validity; (2) criterion validity; and (3) construct validity. As I will demonstrate, there are significant problems with two of these validity tests – particularly for small-n studies but also medium large-n studies below the level of surveys.[9]

1. To test for *content validity* the analyst judges whether – or to what degree – a measure reflects its underlying concept. In technical terms, the researcher looks at a sample of measured values and then draws inferences as to how closely they correspond to the concept. The ensuing critique (Carmines and Zeller, 1994, p. 14), then, is that without random sampling the representativeness of the sample cannot be assumed. Furthermore, there is no criterion for when content validity is achieved, particularly given more abstract or extensive constructs (Carmines and Zeller, 1994, p. 14). A qualitative approach allows for a more straightforward interpretation which is also tied closely to the subject matter. Logically, there is no way to ever test for or find exact correspondence between observed and latent variables – simply because the latent variable can never be observed. Suggesting anything different is misleading. The central idea underlying content validity is to test to which degree an indicator reflects its domain. This invites qualitative testing by experts on a given subject. This intersubjective 'test' will thus probably fail to yield clear results, but it is ideally suited to test the correspondence of indicators and concepts – in a given context. Only experts can weigh in other factors which might potentially distort the results. However, there are trade-offs: Published expert opinion might not speak directly to the research question and thus needs to be interpreted with great care. This is the case if interviewed experts are potentially subject to time constraints or unable to answer in terms of the analytical categories provided to them. These are substantial problems and need to be approached carefully. In contrast, 'objective' validity tests, as discussed below, define such criteria but cannot provide insight into the substantial value of an indicator. The more complex a measure, the harder to match its correspondence to qualitative data – while measures such as disproportionality indices can be validated relatively easily, it is harder to assess measures of democracy, which take into account a number of different dimensions.[10] This approach is thus compatible with both large-n and small-n research.

2. *Criterion validity* is a large-n test. Its logic, however, can also be applied to small-n research as it assesses the degree to which a measure is related to another relevant measure. In other words, the test is based on correlation with another *existing* indicator (Taagepera and Grofman, 2003). A correlation in and by itself is useless to determine if the indicator actually measures the intended concept. Unless we know that the reference indicator is valid, the validity problem comes full-circle. In order to apply criterion validity, the researcher should either use the existing literature or qualitative information to assess correspondence to the concept. Alternatively, one can, of course, correlate a measure to another one if either of the two is highly contextual. Epstein and O'Halloran (1999), for example, measure the amount of discretion the US Congress delegates to the executive branch by manually coding the pertinent legislation. Another measure for the same concept is based on

the length of statutes (Huber and Shipan, 2002).[11] Finding a high (negative) correlation between the two indicators would therefore validate the Huber and Shipan measure as we can be sure that there is a content validity to the Epstein and O'Halloran indicator. Criterion validity is therefore a useful test but one which needs to be applied carefully and with explicit reference to the concept under investigation.

3. The final test is the so-called *construct validity*. These are tests based on *hypotheses*. To elucidate: If we hypothesize a positive relation between the frequency of back-ache and visits to the doctor, finding such a relation would lead us to conclude that the indicator produces valid results. The logic of construct validity thus is identical to theory testing. It compares a finding to theoretical expectations (however derived) and a match is considered to corroborate the measure. The measure, however, is not in any way more or less valid than before! Since this test lacks an *independent* confirmation of validity, this method has a serious logical flaw – it tests for plausibility of an indicator, not for its validity and thus does not serve the purpose of a test (for similar critiques, see Bollen, 1989; Rohwer and Pötter, 2002).[12] The deficits of this test lead me to recommend avoiding it.

While not explicitly discussed as a validity test in the literature, an analyst can also use outlier analysis as a qualitative technique to gauge validity. Usually outliers are seen as a good way to test hypotheses or explore alternative explanations (Collier, Brady and Seawright, 2004b). A similar logic holds for validity tests. In any distribution, extreme values should reveal clearly identifiable differences particularly in case-by-case comparisons. While it is hard to validate exact differences between cases, the outlying nature facilitates finding evidence for or against the validity of these cases. This technique lends itself to quantitative research in particular. Extreme values on a quantitative measure should correspond to rather distinguishable characteristics in qualitative sources. A single case in a typology cell in small-n research would be another example for application of this test. Brady (2004, p. 63) in any case argues that, ultimately, all measures are based on qualitative comparisons.

To conclude: The best, if most demanding, test of validity is based on qualitative information which allows the researcher to assess in detail the correspondence of a measure to a concept. This content validity, however, needs to be at the basis of other tests based on correlations as well. Tests which do not allow for empirically tying a measure back to a concept are logically unsuited to assess validity.

Comparability

To note that observations need always be valid *given* a specific context is crucial. Any comparative study – both over time and across contexts – needs to address the problem of comparability as we already saw in the Peters quote at the beginning of this chapter. In different settings the relation between observed and latent variables might vary or, put differently – a perfectly valid measure in one context might measure another thing entirely somewhere else. Federalism, for example, might mean completely different things to people in France – without any pertinent experience – and Germany where it is a subject of permanent discussion. The literature has come to speak of the 'problem of equivalence' (van Deth, 1998). There are two broad strategies to assure equivalence (Rathke, Chapter 6; van Deth, 1998): One is to assure that indicators are exactly identical, that is to make sure no problem of equivalence exists. As pointed out, this strategy is hardly a promising remedy. The second strategy is to either choose concepts at a (higher) level of abstraction at which equivalence exists between contexts or to rely on inference. Increasing the level of abstraction (Wonka, Chapter 3) will in most instances not be adequate to the research question (why, otherwise, choose a more specific concept in the first place?). Relying on inference in this context means to use a different set of indicators which, based on qualitative background knowledge, can be assumed to actually measure the same concept. This strategy, needless to say, is demanding (Spector, 1981, p. 26). The shifting of focus from direct observation to inference is consequential, and it requires that attempts to assure validity are increased. Beyond this very general discussion, there is little which can be recommended irrespective of a concrete research design to deal with the problem of comparability (Przeworski and Teune, 1970, pp. 11–12). When drawing up a research design, we need to nevertheless keep comparability in mind.

Reliability

Validity and comparability, however, do not suffice to test a measure; Reliability is crucial. It indicates that the *same method* is supposed to arrive at the *same results* for the *same phenomenon*. Therefore reliability cannot be tested if the conditions for data gathering have changed (King, Keohane and Verba, 1994, p. 26). As every social researcher knows, there are plenty of research areas for which conditions are not the same (Rohwer and Pötter, 2002). It is here that research on institutions is privileged as changes are both rare and well documented. Therefore, data based on secondary sources is more amenable to reliability testing, as coding procedures can relatively easily be reproduced. The trade-off involved is, of course, that it is more difficult to assess the validity of the sources the analysis is based on. It is crucial, therefore, that researchers document the instrument used in obtaining data – and ideally base their information on more than one source. Returning to the point of expert information I mentioned in the last section: Comparing expert estimates (in analogy to standard deviation) will yield an estimate of how reliable a measure is.

For small-n research there is the concern that 'thick description' might sacrifice reliability for validity (King, Keohane and Verba, 1994, p. 152). King and colleagues' recommendation is not to rely on subjective data which could be influenced by the researcher's own hypotheses. Yet external sources are often not a viable solution. Other means to assure reliability therefore deserve attention. Most importantly, all coding needs to proceed along precise and unambiguous criteria – documented in a codebook (Geddes, 2003, p. 147). In more qualitative work – but also when using quantitative indicators based on qualitative data – the sources a decision is based on are necessary to make the data construction transparent. Döring (1995) or Franchino (2007) illustrate, however, that it is often feasible to base one's coding on qualitative expert data which are not in danger of being influenced on behalf of the researcher. Finally, when using secondary sources, the researcher should alert the reader to the fact that the sources diverge, and justify why one was chosen over another. This, however, points to a reliability problem of the secondary sources and cannot be controlled on the part of the researcher herself.

Summary

Theory, all authors agree, is central to measurement. This at the same time is probably one of the most significant problems with most of the more technical literature on measurement, but also with much of the literature on research design in general. Unless theory is put first and measurement second, it is hard to see how correspondence between concepts and measures is to be achieved. Operationalization needs to be tied closely to theory and should follow clear guidelines. In due course, the measure needs to be validated with recourse to qualitative evidence – even if there are additional quantitative tests of validity. Reliability, as I argued, requires first and foremost a well documented data gathering process.

Practical guidelines

Whole books have been dedicated to measurement and the discussion here necessarily needs to be limited in scope. Moreover, it is hard to offer generalized, practical advice on issues like operationalization. I therefore focus on a topic which can be helpful for many applications. Measurement entails the problem that with increasing complexity a measure is more difficult to validate. Indices are an attractive, yet often neglected, way to put this recommendation to use. They provide, as I shall argue in the third part, a means to tackle several problems or uncertainties researchers will often be confronted with. A second part briefly outlines trade-offs in practical research and recommends solutions. A final part summarizes all suggestions discussed in this chapter.

Indices

As I have argued in the last section, validity tests should be based on qualitative evidence or expert judgments. While experts might be able to validate more complex measures, we have seen that there might be a trade-off with reliability. The data generated might be unduly influenced by the expert. Asking multiple experts can alleviate the problem – but this will often not be feasible. More complex measures also render data collection more demanding. It is therefore attractive to resort to simple and parsimonious indicators (Geddes, 2003, p. 157). On the other hand, the simpler the indicator, the easier to validate. This leaves us with a seemingly contradictory recommendation – find simple indicators for complex concepts.

Application

The solution I suggest may seem somewhat old-fashioned, but indices have some substantial arguments in their favor. Indices are composite measures which combine two or more indicators on the basis of pre-defined rules. There are three particularly important areas in which indices are useful. First, many theoretical concepts require a look at more than one variable – indices reduce multiple indicators to one.[13] Second, researchers might have a number of different operationalizations for the index at their disposal, but little theoretical reason to favor one over the other. Indices can combine such different options, and different combinations can be compared. The reader might object that this is the kind of a-theoretical testing against which contributors to this volume strongly argue. Indeed *only* if a concise concept specification is still insufficient to yield an unambiguous operationalization – that is, in cases where we cannot make conclusive assumptions about the relation between latent and observed variables – should a more empirical solution be employed. The third reason is related: In some cases it might be possible to directly measure a concept, but the causal connection between latent and observed variable might be hard to trace. In order to avoid arbitrarily opting for one measure, an index comprised of different indicators of the same concept might be used as a basis to test validity.

Construction of indices

In this section I discuss the difficulties of constructing indices both in theory and in practical applications. As the term 'constructed variable' indicates, these variables are based on existing measures which are combined to be theoretically useful. It is therefore imperative that measurement problems be solved before an index is computed (Duncan, 1984, p. 231) and that the measures upon which an index is based are reliable and valid. The researcher's task is then in justifying the aggregation and testing the validity of the construct itself. If the researcher suspects specific index elements might involve problems, she should assess the robustness of the index by testing the impact of removing (or exchanging) the critical elements (for an example see Kaiser's [2004] alternation indices discussed below).

To construct an index, the researcher has to specify aggregation rules and justify why individual components are to be combined in a specific fashion. Many indices are additive and attach equal weight to their elements. To add up elements furthermore requires the assumption that all components affect the index in the same direction (that latent and observed variables correlate with the same sign). This unidirectional relation is important as indicators otherwise cancel each other out. In variation, weighted indices attribute more impact to some elements. Weights can be endogenous – party positions can, for example, be weighted by the seat percentage – or exogenous. An index of influence might, for instance, consider money to be twice as important as other lobbying efforts. Additive and weighted indices are particularly useful for combining several conceptually related (but distinct) elements into one measure as I will demonstrate in the next section. An index may also be based on any other mathematical transformation. Whenever an index is constructed, the analyst needs to make sure that its elements are indeed related to the latent variable and might not reflect some other construct. The logic corresponds to controlling for alternative explanations. It has to be certain that it is not some other concept, 'hidden' in the index that enters the analysis.

There are some theoretical and some more operational criteria to be observed when constructing an index:

- *Indices based on ideal types.* Indices can be built around ideal types (Lehnert, Chapter 4). Shugart and Carey (1992), for example, construct their presidentialism-index on the basis of an ideal-typical concept of presidentialism. The ideal type is defined by theoretically derived states of all variables in the index. Deviations from the defined extreme then constitute changes in index values. Indeed, a typology can form the basis of an index – the theoretical challenge is to align the types identified on one dimension.

- *Theoretically justified index values.*   Taagepera and Grofman (2003) review 19 indices of disproportionality. They demand that for each index the minimal and the maximal values of the index should be defined and that there needs to be a theoretical rule to decide which units of observation should enter the index.
- *Weighting.*   Weighting is crucial, as minimal changes to weights might alter the nature of the whole index. At this point indices probably are most prone to manipulation. Therefore weighting criteria need to be justified, and, if appropriate, different weights need to be discussed with explicit reference to the theory.
- *Discussion of empirical effects.*   The researcher should contemplate counterfactually how extreme values (e.g., in the case of Taagepera and Grofman [2003] a large number of very small parties) would affect the index results and whether such effects are theoretically desirable.
- *Multiple possible operationalizations.*   A more practical recommendation is that indices can be used to incorporate more than one way to operationalize a concept. Kaiser and colleagues (2002) argue that alternation is an element of democratic quality. In developing a measure to test the argument, Kaiser (2004) suggests three indices each using slightly different interpretations of alternation. This allows him to document the implications and trace them back to shades in the theoretical argument.
- *Test of index robustness.*   Kaiser (2004) also demonstrates how the robustness of an index can be tested by removing data generated in a potentially problematic way.[14] Robustness can be tested for two scenarios. One, a whole variable for which measurement is problematic might be removed. Alternatively single cases (outliers) can be removed. If the change barely affects the index values, the measure can be considered robust with regard to the potential measurement problem.

Trade-offs

At the end of this section on practical guidelines let me briefly consider some trade-offs which so often occur in everyday research practice.

Some trade-offs might seem less important than others, but all deserve consideration:

- First and most importantly, there is *no* inherent trade-off between theoretically desirable measures and empirically available indicators. Despite limited time and money, effort should be invested in identifying the most suitable indicator. Picking off-the-shelf indicators is a legitimate alternative but might lead to a trade-off of quality for availability. Therefore, extra efforts need to be made for testing the validity of such indicators.
- In many cases available empirical information will capture theoretical concepts reasonably well. If not, there is a likely trade-off between the resources required for gathering new data and the quality of the measures. There is little to be said about this trade-off except for noting that researchers should try to find creative ways of digging up useful data.
- A trade-off exists between the complexity of measures and their reliability. The more discretionary decisions involved, the harder to test the reliability. Indices, as I have argued, might be a way of solving the problem as they consist of several elements which can each be of reduced complexity.

A summary of practical recommendations

The following list translates points from the discussion above into hands-on advice:

1. The scale of a measure should not deviate from the scale suggested by the concept.
2. In your operationalization, always explicate relations of the indicator to the concept, and clearly delineate different categories or subunits.
3. Be careful not to assume validity all too easily. Make sure that there is qualitative evidence which supports correspondence to your concept.
4. If there are multiple ways to operationalize, discuss the implications of the different choices.
5. Break down complex constructs into simple and parsimonious elements and aggregate into a composite index (explicating the construction logic). This simplifies validity and reliability tests.
6. When building indices, pay attention to justifying the aggregation rules.
7. If multiple measures exist, attempt to select based on theory. Whenever this is not possible, compare and discuss potential differences.

8. As a minimum, use (or refer to) qualitative validity tests – not only for outliers, but systematically. Other methods can be used in a complementary fashion.
9. Use outliers to support quantitative measures with qualitative evidence. They are potential sources for uncovering errors in measurement.
10. To ensure reliability, follow a codebook and document all coding decisions with the respective sources.

Application

This section illustrates the practical application of some of the recommendations above. I discuss the steps from concept to measure on the basis of my own work on informal institutions, and illustrate index construction based on research on the ombudsman.

Coalition Committees (CoC) are informal institutions in the sense that they have no basis in either legal statutes or constitutional law. Thus their existence, procedural rules, and decisions are beyond enforcement by state institutions. CoCs are most often seen as conflict-management mechanisms (see contributions to Müller and Strøm, 2000; Andeweg and Timmermans, 2007).[15] Given the prevalence of coalition governments in Europe, the question of how coalition partners maintain their cooperation through CoCs is both theoretically and empirically interesting: Theoretically, because the literature essentially assumes that coalitions, once established, are stable unless terminated by (rare) exogenous events; empirically, because there is no information on how these informal institutions operate. I address this topic for the German case.[16] Conceptually, I focus on 'reliance on informal institutions' defined as the recourse of political actors to informal venues while at the same time a functioning set of formal institutions exists. Some problems emerge: Given the informality, it is difficult to observe reliance. First, it is a data problem. Second, it is a problem of correspondence between latent and observed variable. The former problem is ameliorated by two factors. Many coalitions fix up the frequency of CoC meetings in their coalition agreements (the 2005 coalition agreement of the CDU/CSU, SPD coalition in Germany, for instance, mandates one meeting of the CoC per month). In addition, the German media report on some CoC meetings – at least in instances where important issues are on the agenda. Tackling the second question: How closely do the observed variables – frequency as agreed in the coalition agreement and reports in the media – represent the latent variable? The first indicator (frequency in coalition agreement) is unsuitable to uncover the flexibility in the use of informal institutions the literature leads us to expect. The second (frequency according to media reports) compensates for the limitations of the first, but might be biased (see Thiem, Chapter 7) since in some instances the media will be preoccupied with other issues and decide not to cover a CoC meeting. Still, given the limitations, 'reliance' can be operationalized as the frequency of publicly visible meetings, and achieve close correspondence based on the assumption (which needs qualitative backup) that in publicly visible cases the reasons to resort to informal structures are particularly important. A precise indicator is still required, and the research design needs to make up for this deficit through qualitative evidence. Given this operationalization the measurement model assumes a true score *and* an unknown but systematic error (the media bias) as well as the standard error term. Securing reliability for these indicators is not a problem: I ran a full text search with a set of terms the substantial meaning of which is stable over time. Validity is harder to assure. For one thing, there are few sources for comparing my results. However, tests were confirmatory for the cases where it was possible. More important is a qualitative analysis on the basis of interviews a) of meetings not covered in the press (were they to some degree different?) but b) also of the meetings in the measure (were they really more important so as to support the assumption above?). Such tests obviously can only be conducted for some meetings, and the test itself is potentially biased as the participating actors might not remember all details from the CoC after some time. In this case, there is no quantitative test that could even potentially be used to assess validity.

In Miller (2006), I analyze reasons for the institutional design of national ombudspersons responsible for overseeing the administration in 25 democracies.[17] The theory leads me to expect variance with respect to both the competencies the institution enjoys during investigations, and also with respect to the degree to which it is free from the influence of other institutional actors. The two concepts I specify are (1) 'investigative competencies' and (2) 'independence'. While competencies directly imply measurement along a catalogue of statutory competencies, independence could be defined either behaviorally or institutionally. Since my theory models the establishment of the ombudsman as a principal-agent relation, however, I need to look at the formal basis of the institution and not at potential deviations from it in actual practice. As both concepts are highly abstract, it is not possible to find one indicator which would capture them to any satisfying degree.[18] The literature, however, helps to identify a set of indicators, most of which are nominal. Since all indicators have a unidirectional relation to the latent variables and there is no compelling reason why some indicators should be more important than others, I have developed an unweighted additive index for each concept. The scaling of the indices (between 0 and 1) in order to achieve theoretically sensible extreme values was not as straightforward, though. For the independence dimension there are ten indicators which, if they all apply, can indeed be taken to indicate a maximum of independence.[19] For 'investigative competencies', it does not make sense to define abstract, extreme values: First, some competencies always exist (limiting variation) and, second because there is no theoretical reason to demand that all indicators be positive in order to speak of an institution with 'complete' competencies. I therefore scaled the second dimension empirically, using the countries with the highest and lowest number of existing competencies as extreme values. The example shows how two rather abstract concepts can be measured in a useful manner with the help of indices. Both can be interpreted as a continuous variable ranging from a totally independent / resourceful ombudsman to an institution which is tied to its political principals and / or has limited means to conduct investigations.

The remainder of the discussion only looks at the independence index. To assess its validity, the index was tested based on qualitative evidence in the literature. I identified outliers and extreme values and compared these values to the literature which usually comments on independence and the competencies of ombudspersons. Paired comparisons (is *a* really x units more independent than *b*?), however, was not a feasible option because there is no naturally observable equivalent to what the index as a whole measures. Since the index elements had been qualitatively established to be important for independence, however, this is not disadvantageous but rather shows the strength of indices. The reliability was fostered through the use of a rigorous coding scheme and an objectively identifiable basis for the data (statutes and constitutional provisions).[20]

These examples demonstrate that measurement design is to be clearly and explicitly connected to theoretical constructs. While in many cases this is probably done already, spelling it out allows for more transparency and renders this aspect of research design easier.

Conclusion

This paper has provided an overview of measurement – and the design of measures in particular – in research design. I have stressed the role of theory and concepts as crucial parts of any measurement process. Linking measures to theory is central both for design and for testing the correspondence of a measure with the underlying latent variables. I have argued that empirical tests of measures such as correlation analysis cannot and should not substitute more qualitative approaches for assessing validity. Researchers applying these techniques should bear their limitations in mind. The contrast between the qualitative small-n and quantitative large-n approach, portrayed by some as profound (Thomas, 2005), has not played much of a role in the discussion. This is due to the similar requirements each of the two approaches suggest for treating measurement. The overall challenge is – to reiterate Geddes's (2003) call – to provide theoretically convincing empirical tests for our hypotheses. If this purpose is served, then measurement contributes to research in a meaningful way.

Notes

1. There are, of course, other definitions of measurement – all of which, however, are covered by a definition of measurement as a process (Brady, 2004; Duncan, 1984; Schmidt, 1994, p. 257).
2. While the steps described here are, of course, applicable to any kind of social science research, methods available in survey research (especially when data are directly collected) exceed those available to others.
3. Those of us who thought that measurement in the natural sciences was straightforward would be surprised by just how substantial difficulties are (De Bièvre, 2006).
4. The term 'latent variable' is often used synonymously with 'concept'. I maintain the distinction to indicate that they are used in different literatures but also to accentuate the difference between the theoretical task of specifying a concept and the empirical aspect of testing it. Moreover, some concepts such as policy space can only be operationalized with two (or more) latent variables.
5. While the error term here is assumed to have a mean of zero, the very fact of the existence of error is important to take into account.
6. Nominal measures consist of different and distinct categories (e.g., gender), ordinal scales allow for an ordering of different states (degree of citizen participation in dictatorships, feudal states, and democracies), interval measures allow for a comparison of distances (GDP) and, finally, ratio scales have a defined zero-value (temperature).
7. This should not be seen as a weakness. Measurement error – read imprecise classification – will often render quantitative measures inaccurate – a fate qualitative measures do not share (Brady, 2004).
8. There are further types of validity tests. The ones presented here, however, are broadly representative.
9. Surveys allow for controlled and different operationalizations of concepts which then facilitate tests unavailable to most other research designs.

10. These indices assess the correspondence between voteshare and seatshare of a party in a given system (Taagepera and Grofman, 2003).

11. They argue that length is a valid proxy for the amount of detail in legislation and is thus inversely proportional to the amount of discretion.

12. Bollen (1989) suggests convergent and discriminate validity as one further set of tests. The term refers to a multi-method design where indicators of two or more concepts are measured by two or more methods each. Correlations are employed to estimate the validity. Correlations of different measures of the same concept need to be higher than correlations between concepts. Also, correlations between the same measure of different concepts need to be higher than correlations between different measures of different concepts. If applicable, this method would indeed provide a quantifiable measure of validity of the respective measures. While the objection that correlations cannot prove correspondence to the latent variable is still valid, this test makes it much more plausible that the measures actually measure the same thing. However, in research designs which cannot rely on surveys, it will not be possible to even devise such a validity test.

13. Multidimensional concepts cannot, however, be combined in an index.

14. Kaiser (2004), for example, argues that to measure the end of a cabinet on the basis of the exchange of a prime minister might be misleading as the basis for his alternation variable – as policy might depend more on parties than on its personnel.

15. Helmke and Levitsky (2004) provide an outstanding overview on the conceptualization and measurement of informal institutions.

16. For a collection of essays on the German CoC, see Rudzio (2005). Kropp (2004) provides some of the same arguments in an English contribution.

17. The data are based on bills or articles of the counties' constitutions; that is, they are prescriptive. Therefore the indicators need not be adjusted to the specific context.

18. The institution's annual budget might serve as a proxy for independence. It could, however, also measure all sorts of organizational peculiarities and would misinform our judgment in countries where the ombudsman-institution need not cover all expenditures from its own budget.

19. Since all indicators are for the most part explicitly related to specified aspects of ombudsman independence, interference of another – unspecified – latent variable is unlikely.

20. Inter-coder reliability was not an issue as all data were coded by one person only – on the basis of coding instructions.

6
Achieving Comparability of Secondary Data

Julia Rathke

Introduction: why comparing?

'Comparison is the methodological core of the scientific study of politics' (Almond, Powell, Strom and Dalton, 2001, p. 399). Political scientists compare to find either particularities or generalities. In the first case, different contexts are used as 'objects of analyses' and are themselves the centre of attention (Kohn, 1987, p. 714). For instance, a researcher comparing Norway with Finland and Sweden is not primarily interested in testing general hypotheses about Scandinavia but wants to learn something about Norway. The second, more prominent field of research makes comparisons to test general assumptions in different contexts, which are then the 'units of analyses': 'The more evidence we can find in varied contexts, the more powerful our explanation becomes, and the more confidence we and others should have in our conclusions' (King, Keohane and Verba, 1994, p. 30; cf. pp. 208–9). The logic behind this argument is clear: The more often a theory test is repeated, the more telling the results. Investigators can expand their number of observations by looking at diverse geographical or cultural contexts (for example, nations, regions, cities), by comparing across time, by relying on different levels of aggregation or different datasets. Irrespective of the decision which way investigators follow, they first have to check 'whether the new units are appropriate for the replication of [their] hypothesis' (King, Keohane and Verba,1994, p. 229). Second, researchers must be aware that the examination of *new units* often causes or rather requires *new measures* (Alwin, Braun, Harkness and Scott, 1994, p. 30). Thus, they also have to check whether these *measures* are 'appropriate for the replication of [their] hypotheses'. Are the chosen measures really measuring the same, are they comparable? For instance, Voltmer and Schmitt-Beck (2006) test different hypotheses on the effects of mass media on the development of democratic orientations in new democracies. In order to compare two different contexts of democratization they consider four new democracies: the former communist countries Bulgaria and Hungary as well as Chile and Uruguay, both with a history of military dictatorship. All four chosen units share the attribute 'new democracy' and two couples have different backgrounds in common. Since general indicators of media usage are not appropriate they gathered information about significant newspapers and television programs in the particular countries. Such problems of comparability (as well as the answers to them) are relevant for all kinds of research looking at more than one existing dataset. For this reason, the crucial question is not whether a research design is cross-cultural but whether it relies on primary or on various secondary data.

In order to direct the attention of researchers to this fact, this chapter explicitly uses a mono-cultural example. Two primary questions are addressed here: (1) How can the number of observations be increased by relying on secondary analysis? (2) How can comparability be achieved in secondary analysis? The chapter is structured as follows: The next section deals with problems of comparability in comparative research and shows how shifting notions of identity to approaches of equivalence expands possibilities for making comparisons. Section 3 provides some practical guidelines for finding appropriate datasets and indicators as well as making them comparable. Section 4 presents an example from my own research on effects of social capital on political orientations in Germany to demonstrate the use of the given advice. The chapter then finishes with a short conclusion.

Design problem: comparability of various secondary data

As stressed above, any use of various secondary data is a comparative approach and hence has to deal with problems of comparability. The most obvious way to avoid any comparability problems would be to completely avoid secondary data. The data would then be collected for the purpose of the researcher's hypothesis, which may heighten the validity of the measurement. Some investigators therefore argue that only fresh data assures the appropriateness of the measures and consider that 'collecting new and better data is almost always an improvement on trying to use existing' (King, Keohane and Verba, 1994, p. 27). But primary research is expensive and therefore not always an alternative, especially for young researchers. Moreover, given the high costs of data collection and the rich information content of the collected data, it would be quite inefficient to use data only once. That data is collected for the purpose of primary research does not mean that it may not be suitable for analyzing other research questions. Second, resuming and challenging previous findings is a crucial part of scientific knowledge processing, and secondary data allow for new tests of hypotheses. Third, previous results have to be examined, and in the social sciences, re-analysis of existing data is the functional equivalent of repeated experiments in natural sciences. Secondary data is therefore fundamental for a sceptical verification of scientific assumptions (van Deth, 2003). Fourth, large-scale cross-national surveys have become very important in social science, and provide manifold – partly unique – possibilities for analyzing research questions with secondary data.[1] Finally, only secondary data provides the possibility to make comparisons over time. As surveys cannot discover the past, data gathered over many years are an indispensable source of information. To sum up, secondary data analysis is cost-effective and reasonable both from a conceptual (for example, best or sole data for comparative research) as well as a methodological (such as replication, re-analysis, longitudinal analysis) point of view (Frankfort-Nachmias and Nachmias, 1992).

There are nevertheless limitations to secondary data analyses. For instance, not all data are available for secondary analysis. Moreover, the process of data collection and construction may be documented only fragmentarily or inadequately, which leads to inaccuracy in analysis and interpretation (van Deth, 2003, pp. 292–4). In addition to these practical problems, there is at least one conceptual problem, namely that the use of different secondary datasets breeds usage of different measures, and researchers must check whether these measures are comparable. Incomparability of measurement instruments seems to be no problem for measures which are identically formulated. This is, however, not necessarily the case. For instance, the usage of identical or, rather, verbatim translated standard research questions about aspects of political efficacy in China and Mexico show people in Mexico being *less* convinced that they can influence political affairs than people in China, although Mexicans have in fact *more* chances to influence politics than Chinese (King, Murray, Salomon and Tandon, 2004, p. 203). This example depicts a well-known problem in comparative research: 'The "generalized" contexts constituted by the objective social structure of the countries ... pose a problem for ... the comparability of information gathered in different nations' (Alwin, Braun, Harkness and Scott, 1994, p. 30). Although the measurement instruments are identically formulated or rather verbatim translated, they produce incomparable results. Thus, since the literal replication (or translation) of an indicator obviously does not assure that it measures the same concept in different contexts, primary investigators sometimes have good reason to use different measurement instruments. For instance, the effectiveness of items dealing with gender-related attitudes diminished since their first adoption in the 1960s, because the role of women in western societies changed as well. Hence, only later surveys about gender-role attitudes included 'male-items' to counterbalance the superior number of 'female-items' (Braun, 1998, p. 116). To take social change into account, the investigators had to integrate new instruments to measure the same concepts. Such comparability problems are not restricted to cross-cultural or longitudinal research. Since surveys differ in conceptualization without any 'good reason' – ranging from the mode of data collection, the population, the sample method and size or the number and character of variables – any investigator relying on existing datasets from various sources, faces problems of comparability.

Irrespective of whether the indicators are *literally equivalent* (identically formulated or verbatim translated), indicators must measure the same concept in different contexts. This so-called *conceptual equivalence* is a necessary condition for *any* comparison (van de Vijver, 2003, p. 148; Westle, 1998) and means that 'the observations being analyzed become, for the purposes of analysis, identical in relevant aspects' (King, Keohane and Verba, 1994, p. 93). For these reasons, secondary researchers can neither rely on the sameness of similar variables in different contexts, nor do they have to restrict their analyses to identical measurements. Instead they have to check whether *literally equivalent indicators are conceptually equivalent* and whether they can *establish conceptual equivalence of literally different indicators*.

The diverse strategies to ascertain conceptual equivalence can be broadly summarized in two categories: Increasing the level of abstraction and establishing functional equivalence by relying on inference (see Figure 6.1). *Increasing the level of abstraction (1)* means to disregard context specific, irrelevant properties of indicators and 'accept two indicators to be equivalent exactly because these properties are deleted' (van Deth, 1998, p. 10). For instance, in order to compare apples with oranges, it is necessary to move to the more abstract conceptual level of fruits (van de Vijver, 2003, p. 148).

Whereas concept abstraction (Wonka, Chapter 3) seeks to broaden a given concept as long as context specific (but irrelevant) differences are deleted, attempts to establish *functional equivalence* ((2)–(5) in Figure 6.1)

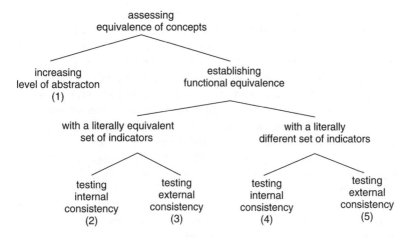

Figure 6.1   Main strategies for assessing conceptual equivalence in comparative research

Source: Following van Deth, 1998, p. 10.

maintain the original concept and seek to find indicators that are related to the concept in the same way *despite* (irrelevant) context specificity. 'The aim is to find items which show an identical structure over all units of analysis' (Przeworski and Teune, 1966, pp. 555–7; Westle, 1998, p. 26), so that it can be concluded that they have an 'identical relationship to the intended theoretical dimensions' (Alwin, Braun, Harkness and Scott, 1994, p. 39). To find indicators of the concept 'significant newspaper' in different settings, for example, one can either abstract the concept to 'any newspaper' (and use this concept further on) or find functional equivalent indicators that fit into the already specified concept 'significant newspaper' (Wonka, Chapter 3). Thus, the difference between the two ways to establish conceptual equivalence lies in the measurement process (Miller, Chapter 5): increasing the level of abstraction takes place *before* operationalization, and establishing functional equivalence becomes a crucial part of the operationalization process itself.

How functional equivalence can be established then depends on the commonalities of the indicators. If there is a *literally equivalent set of indicators* ((2) and (3) in Figure 6.1) in different contexts, investigators have to assess their conceptual equivalence. However using this strategy may restrict the analyses and may cause unnecessary, context-specific information loss. For instance, solely concentrating on national newspapers would ignore local newspapers. Thus, an alternative strategy enables the researcher not only to rely on common measures but to use *literally different* ones as well ((4) and (5) in Figure 6.1). In the case at hand, national newspapers constitute the common set of indicators and several local newspapers would be added. Then the common and non-common 'indicators combined provide a scale for reliable and valid measurement of the same phenomenon' in various contexts (Przeworski and Teune, 1966, p. 568). But what if there are no common measures, for example no national newspapers (for example in Switzerland) available? For this problem, Przeworski and Teune present a way of creating equivalence by analyzing relationships within the units and comparing them across units (Przeworski and Teune, 1966, p. 565). Whether the selected indicators of the concept are functionally equivalent must be assessed through empirical verification of their consistency. A further differentiation regards the kind of consistency test investigators rely on: 'Internal consistency means that the stimuli or items used should show more or less the same structure in different environments; external consistency means that indicators are related in the same way to an element not belonging to the initial set of indicators' (van Deth, 2003, p. 303). For instance, whether the chosen newspapers are functionally equivalent can be assessed via internal criteria ((2) and (4) in Figure 6.1) like the print run, the number of subscribers or advertising customers and/or via external criteria ((3) and (5) in Figure 6.1) such as the evaluation of experts.

Practical guidelines: increasing the number of observations and achieving comparability in secondary data research

The problem discussed so far can be summarized as follows: Identically formulated or *verbatim* translated (that is, literally equivalent) measurement instruments used in different settings may have different meanings and produce incomparable results. Thus, primary investigators often use different *conceptually equivalent* measurement instruments. As a consequence, *secondary investigators* can neither rely on the sameness of literally equivalent indicators, nor should they necessarily restrict their analyses to them. Instead, any secondary researcher using more than one dataset has to think about the conceptual equivalence of the chosen indicators, acting thereby either on a conceptual level via concept abstraction and/or on an empirical level via the establishment of functional equivalence. In the following sections, several guidelines for secondary investigators are provided which show ways to increase the number of observations, as well as to make efficient use of information inherent in divergent datasets.

Guideline 1   Select those datasets that include indicators which seem to be appropriate to measure the central theoretical concepts.

After having specified the theoretical concepts (Wonka, Chapter 3) and deciding to use more than one dataset, investigators must look at existing data and check which of them might be appropriate for answering the research question at hand. This includes aspects like the conformity of the population definition to the research design, or the availability of documentation like codebooks and questionnaires (van Deth, 2003). What is more important with regard to the problems of comparability discussed above is that appropriate measurements of the central theoretical concepts should be included. The aim is to select a manageable number of datasets out of the multitude of existing data without unnecessarily decreasing their number. Following King and colleagues' advice 'to find as many observable implications of your theory as possible' (1994, p. 208), one practical guideline is to go ahead multi-faceted. Thus, even though one ought to have an idea what the most adequate measure would be, this should not narrow the search too much (van Deth, 2003, p. 296). It is not necessary to exclude datasets at that early stage if measurements are not identical to the perfect ones, or to measurements included in other datasets. Moreover datasets need not contain perfect measures for all of the main theoretical concepts. Instead at least *one* perfect indicator for *one* of your main concepts should be included in each dataset.

Guideline 2   Look at the datasets carefully and check each of them separately to determine whether they include at least one adequate indicator for each of the main concepts.

Until now one has just got a selection of datasets which *might* be appropriate for answering the research question. Whether this is *really* the case should be decided only after a careful consideration of the available datasets. Thus, after the first phase of data screening investigators should become more familiar with the data. Whereas the main concern so far was with the appropriateness of the *datasets*, now the capability of the included *indicators* to measure the theoretical concepts is at the centre of interest. Therefore one should examine each selected dataset *separately* and check which of the available indicators might be consistent with the research objective. The minimum criterion for selecting the datasets (at least one adequate indicator for one of the main concepts) now no longer holds. Instead, within each dataset there must be at least one adequate indicator for each of the main concepts. Although more indicators do not automatically result in more reliable measures, the main goal in this working step is to find as many indicators for as many of the considered theoretical concepts as possible (Alwin, Braun, Harkness and Scott, 1994, p. 35). Following this strategy has several advantages: First of all, while a well-selected list of indicators is usually the most powerful tool, in this early working stage it is hard to decide whether a list of indicators is well-selected. Second, measuring difficult concepts (for example attitudes) is much easier with multiple indicators mapping different aspects, problems, and perspectives. Third, whether a multiple set of indicators might be reduced or simplified should be an empirical question. Finally, the more indicators are collected within each dataset the more detailed information is offered and the greater the likelihood of finding a set of indicators comparable in *all* datasets (Johnson, 1998, p. 23; Spicker, 2004, p. 438). Though acting upon this advice makes it possible to maximize the use of information inherent in the datasets, there is a *trade-off.* The amount of data which has to be processed is probably immense. In order to avoid getting overwhelmed by the quantity of datasets and indicators, it is useful to make a systematic overview of all appropriate indicators in tabular form. Such a table should show the variable name, the *exact* wording of the questions, as well as the number and labels of the answer categories for each dataset and for each appropriate indicator. Surveys that – despite this broad search for adequate measures – still miss any indicator for one of the central theoretical concepts should now be excluded. So the result of this step is a table displaying how potentially appropriate variables are measured in the selected datasets. The next steps then deal with the different possibilities for making measurement instruments comparable.

Guideline 3   Literally equivalent indicators can be used directly or harmonized if investigators are certain of their conceptual equivalence.

After careful consideration of the several datasets, the *differences between the datasets* (or more exactly, the measurement instruments) are important. Thus, investigators should shift from looking at the datasets separately to a comparative view, and divide the indicators into literally equivalent and literally different ones. Literally and conceptually equivalent indicators from different datasets can be used directly or harmonized. Since any value of a variable for a given observation indicates an answer to an interview question, there are two possible sources of variation: The interview question and the answer categories. Indicators are literally equivalent only if there is similar question wording as well as labeling of the answer categories. Hence literal equivalence is normally given only for a very limited number of simple measurement instruments, for instance year of birth. If conceptually equivalent indicators vary in the number or pooling of answer categories, the variables have to be harmonized. 'Harmonization means that for different studies a common scheme is used to code interview questions and answer categories and/or for analyzing variables derived from those inputs' (van Deth, 2003, pp. 297–8). For instance, for the harmonization of occupational status in cross-national studies, several classification systems (for example ISCO-88) exist which can be meaningfully compared across various contexts, are stable, and account for the variety of work.

In contrast to the direct use of measurement instruments, there is a *trade-off* between a loss of information inherent in the single piece of data and the use of more observable implications of the theory which occurs when harmonization is necessary. As the direct usage of similar indicators is seldom possible, harmonization results on the one hand in information *gain*. On the other hand, harmonized data will always be 'at the level of the lowest common denominator, providing less rather than more detail; distilling information, rather than amplifying it' (Glover, 1996, p. 35). However, there are two more problems with this guideline. First of all, the differentiation between literally equivalent and different indicators is sometimes not easy to carry out. Thus it is recommended that the researcher record the *exact* question wording (quoted from the questionnaire) and not only the variable label. Second, and more important, investigators must be sure that the literally equivalent indicators are conceptually equivalent as well. When in doubt, investigators should act on the assumption of disparity. They then have to empirically assess the conceptual equivalence of indicators by establishing functional equivalence.

Guideline 4   The only way to make conceptually different indicators comparable lies in concept abstraction.

As was stressed above, conceptual equivalence is a precondition for any comparison. Consequently there are different strategies to assess the comparability of literally different indicators, whereas there is strictly speaking no way to make conceptually different indicators comparable. Instead it is necessary to raise the level of abstraction of the concept until the indicators are no longer conceptually different. As was mentioned above, it is then possible to compare apples and oranges. Once again, a *trade-off* occurs by doing so; although the abstraction of concepts makes it possible to compare non-common indicators, the strategy is not without pitfalls such as the typical 'fallacies of "concept stretching", "pseudo equivalence", or simply shifting problems' (van Deth, 1998, p. 11; Sartori, 1970). In order to avoid these pitfalls investigators always have to keep the rules for concept specification in mind (Wonka, Chapter 3). Furthermore, after having abstracted concepts and having selected indicators, their functional equivalence should be established as well.

Guideline 5   For conceptually equivalent indicators, different strategies to establish functional equivalence are possible.

To assess the conceptual equivalence of literally equivalent as well as literally different measurement instruments, functional equivalence must be established. 'Functional equivalence refers to the requirement that concepts should be related to other concepts in other settings in more or less the same way' (van Deth, 1998, p. 6). Since functional equivalence is a relational notion, it is a result of inference not of data collection. There are two alternative procedures for assessing the functional equivalence of indicators in different settings. On the one hand, investigators can rely on tests of internal consistency, asking for each setting whether the indicators are related to *one another* in a similar way. On the other hand, they can use tests of external consistency, asking for each setting whether indicators are related to *another concept* in a similar way. Whereas internal consistency requires at minimum two indicators of a concept, external consistency can be examined with just one indicator per concept.

To sum up: In any comparatively designed secondary data analysis, one must consider that 'increasing the N has a downside – specifically, it may take the analysis outside the domain where given concepts are appropriate and measurements remain valid' (Collier, Brady and Seawright, 2004a, p. 204; Thomas, 2005, p. 858). In order to increase the number of observations and leverage the information inherent in several datasets, a stepwise approach is recommended. First, investigators should start a broad search for potentially appropriate datasets. Secondly, the appropriateness of the available indicators should be carefully examined. Therefore, the comparability of the selected indicators must be assessed. Depending on whether the indicators are literally and/or conceptually equivalent, possibilities range from direct use to concept abstraction or the establishment of functional equivalence. The following section provides a practical application of the five guidelines using my own dissertation project as an example.

Application: social capital and the political orientation of young people in Germany

Since Putnam's (1993) seminal work about 'civic traditions in modern Italy,' several authors sought to prove or disprove his conclusion that 'social capital is the key to making democracy work' (Putnam, 1993, p. 183; Farr, 2004; Fischer, 2005). In my research, I sought to analyze whether social capital theory applies to adolescents as well, and concentrated on the consequences for political orientations in Germany (Schäfer, 2006).

Guideline 1   Select those datasets that include indicators which seem to be appropriate to measure the central theoretical concepts.

A first global search in the database of the *Zentralarchiv für Empirische Sozialforschung (ZA)*,[2] a major source for German social science data, with the term 'youth' over all fields yielded 256 results. Since appropriate data had to be representative for young people in Germany (no local studies, no particular GDR- or FRG-data), the number decreased to 32. Furthermore, 12 datasets included at least one perfect measure for at least one of my central theoretical concepts. As three of those datasets were not publicly available I ended up with looking more closely at a manageable number of nine instead of the original 256 youth studies.

Guideline 2   Look at the datasets carefully and check each of them separately to determine whether they include at least one adequate indicator for each of the main concepts.

For each of the nine datasets I had to find *as many observable implications of the theory as possible* and therefore made a systematic compilation of the interesting variables in the different datasets. As the complete table contains more than 100 indicators, Table 6.1 displays just some examples: To analyze the consequences of social capital for political orientations, indicators of both concepts – 'social capital' (Putnam, 1993, p. 167; 2000, p. 19) and 'political orientations' – are needed. The minimum criterion for selecting the datasets in this second phase of data screening requires at least one adequate indicator for each of the main concepts within each dataset. For this reason DJI 2000 and Spiegel 1994 – where at least one indicator for one of the main concepts is missing – is sorted out for the subsequent analyses.

Table 6.1 Table for a compilation of the interesting variables in the different datasets

Variable name	Exact question wording	ZA-number categories 19xx	2323 Shell 1992	3434 KJE 1996	2564 Spiegel 1994[1]	2930 Shell 1997	x* Shell 2000	3694 Shell 2002	2527 DJI 1992	3298 DJI 1997	3609 DJI 2000[1]
Y_birth	Note respondents year of birth	19xx	x	x	x	x	x	x	x	x	x
Indicators of the concept 'social capital'											
memb_d	Are you a member of any organization? I will now show you a list of different organizations. For each of them please answer yes if you are a member of the organization.	0 no, 1 yes (d)	x	x	x	x	–	–	–	–	–
memb01	professional organization	0 no, 1 yes (d)	–	–	–	–	x	–	x	x	–
memb02	religious or church organization	0 no, 1 yes (d)	–	–	–	–	x	–	x	x	–
memb03	charity or social-welfare organization	0 no, 1 yes (d)	–	–	–	–	–	–	x	x	–
memb04	local home associations	0 no, 1 yes (d)	–	–	–	–	x	–	x	x	–
memb05	youth association	0 no, 1 yes (d)	–	–	–	–	x	–	x	x	–
memb06	sports club or outdoor activities club	0 no, 1 yes (d)	–	–	–	–	x	–	x	x	–
memb07	other club or association	0 no, 1 yes (d)	–	–	–	–	–	–	x	x	–
memb08	other voluntary organization	0 no, 1 yes (d)	–	–	–	–	x	–	–	–	–

		1	2	3	4	5	6	7	8	9
memb09	environmental organization	0 no, 1 yes (d)	–	–	–	–	x	–	–	–	–
memb10	cultural, musical, dancing or theatre society	0 no, 1 yes (d)	–	–	–	–	x	–	–	–	–
memb11	fan club	0 no, 1 yes (d)	–	–	–	–	x	–	–	–	–
memb12	trade union	0 no, 1 yes (d)	–	–	–	–	x	–	x	x	–
memb13	political party	0 no, 1 yes (d)	–	–	–	–	x	–	x	x	–
trust	Generally speaking, would you say that most people can be trusted, or that you can't be too careful in dealing with people?	0 careful, 1 can be trusted (d)	–	–	–	–	–	x	–	–	–

Indicators of the concept 'political orientations'

		1	2	3	4	5	6	7	8	9
P_trust5	I will now read out names of different institutions. Please tell me how strongly you trust each of these institutions	0 no trust at all, 5 very strong trust	–	x	–	–	–	x	x	x	x
P_trust7	I will now read out names of different institutions. Please tell me how strongly you trust each of these institutions	0 little trust, 7 very strong trust	x	x	–	x	x	–	–	–	–

Notes: (d) dichotomous; x integrated; – not integrated; ¹ not used. * The 13th Shell Youth survey 'Youth 2000' (=Shell 2000) is not available via the ZA but has to be bought from *psydata*.

*Guideline 3   Literally equivalent indicators can be
used directly or harmonized if investigators are certain of
their conceptual equivalence.*

In general, indicators should only be used directly if literal as well as conceptual equivalence is given. In the case at hand, this holds for no more than one indicator, the year of birth. In contrast, for instance the indicators for political trust are literally different: Even though they do not vary in question wording, the number and labeling of the answer categories is different. Thus, only the variable 'y_birth' can be used directly.[3]

*Guideline 4   The only way to make conceptually different indicators
comparable lies in concept abstraction.*

Following Putnam (1993, p. 167) '[s]ocial capital here refers to features of social organization, such as trust, norms, and networks'. The structural aspect of social capital – the concept 'networks of civic engagement' (Putnam, 1993, p. 173) – is used as an example for assessing conceptual equivalence of indicators. Organizational membership is one of the most often used indicators for the concept 'civic engagement' (Gabriel, Kunz, Roßteutscher and van Deth, 2002). But as Table 6.1 reveals, there are two different problems. First of all, there are completely different measurement instruments in the various youth studies asking whether the respondent is a member of *any* organization (variable *memb_d)* on the one hand and whether one is a member of *several, specific* organizations on the other hand (variables *memb01 – memb13)*. As one cannot 'add' information to an already collected variable, the only way of creating comparable indicators is to reduce the information inherent in the more complex version. One must therefore summarize the information in one variable and dichotomize the resulting index by contrasting respondents who declare membership in at least one of the organizations with respondents who do not. Second, the studies including the more detailed measurement instrument vary in respect of the types of organizations for which membership is asked. For instance, membership is asked for 'cultural society' in Shell 2000 but not in the remaining ones. DJI 1992 and DJI 1997 include the categories 'other hobby club/society' and 'other club or organization', but this is not true for the other datasets.

Since the selected datasets contain both common and non-common organizations it is possible to apply all five main strategies for establishing equivalence recommended by van Deth (1998), increasing the level of abstraction by employing the broader concept of 'membership in *any*

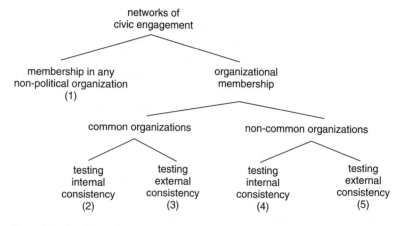

Figure 6.2   Applying the main strategies for establishing conceptual equivalence

non-political organization' instead of 'club membership' (1) and relying thereby on inference, using only the organizations *common* in all datasets and the criterion of internal (2) and/or external consistency (3). Finally, one may employ those variables that satisfy the criteria of internal (4) and/or external consistency (5) even though they are *non-common* in the several datasets. The application of the main strategies can be summarized as illustrated in Figure 6.2 and will be shown in detail for each case.

1   Increasing level of abstraction

'Organizational membership' is one of the most often used indicators for civic engagement (Gabriel, Kunz, Roßteutscher and van Deth, 2002), but Putnam first defines the term *civic engagement* very vaguely as 'active participation in public affairs' (Putnam, 1993, p. 87). In his latter publication about the trends of civic disengagement in the United States, he specifies the concept of *civic engagement* in order to distinguish 'official membership in organizations' (Putnam, 2000, p. 49) from several other forms of civic engagement, like political participation, religious participation, participation at the workplace or informal connections. Often, however, the operationalization of this concept is not possible as it requires information about the kind of organization for which respondents report membership. As Table 6.1 shows, this is the case for only three out of the seven datasets. One possibility for making the different measurement instruments comparable is to increase the level of abstraction. As *membership in any organization* (variable *memb_d*) is the abstract measurement instrument to which the more specified ones should be comparable, the most obvious way to establish equivalence is to increase the level of abstraction and simply consider membership in *any* organization. The trouble with this conceptualization is that it mixes up political and social participation. This not only makes the concept vague but is problematic for the research question. In order to investigate the influences of social capital on political orientations, a clear classification of 'political' and 'social' is required. It is therefore more appropriate to specify the concept and only include *membership in non-political organizations* (ignoring 'political parties', *memb13*).

Guideline 5   For conceptually equivalent indicators, different strategies to establish functional equivalence are possible.

As long as the rules for concept specification are adhered to, the solution to use all indicators about membership in any non-political organization (*memb01–memb12*) could be maintainable from a theoretical point of view. Yet whether the several non-political organizations are really functionally equivalent measures of the theoretical concept 'civic engagement' is an empirical question.

2   Establishing functional equivalence: Common indicators – internal consistency

One possible threat to comparability may result from the fact that the so constructed additive indices include non-common (literally different) indicators in the different datasets. For instance, 'charity or social-welfare organizations' are included in DJI 1992 and DJI 1997 but not in the other index. One alternative is to ignore those six organizations not included in all datasets and concentrate on the common organization types, but the question whether the common indicators are really measuring equivalent constructs is still unanswered. One strategy to assess the functional equivalence of the common indicators is to rely on the criterion of internal consistency: Do the common indicators have the same structure in different contexts? A rather uncomplicated means of getting a first impression of the internal consistency of indicators is a matrix of tetrachoric correlations. In the case at hand, a 6 x 6-table is already quite complex. Therefore, the correlation matrix was factor-analyzed to detect a single structure. The results are reported in Table 6.2. Instead of recording the exact numbers, fields are in bold text if the factor loadings indicate that variables can be assigned to a common concept.

Such factor analyses done with the common six indicators in Shell 2000, DJI 1992 and DJI 1997 separately show different structures every

Table 6.2 Common indicators: internal consistency

	Shell 2000	DJI 1992	DJI 1997
professional organization	x	x	X
religious or church organization	x	x	X
local home associations	x	x	X
youth association	x	x	X
sports club or outdoor activities club	x	x	X
trade union	x	x	X

Notes: factor analyses of tetrachoric correlation matrices; one factor extracted; fat: factor loading greater .400.

time.[4] Three types of organizational membership, however, can be assigned to one latent concept in all three datasets: Membership in 'religious or church organization', in 'youth associations', and in 'sport clubs or outdoor activities club'. Thus, following the strategy of concentrating on literally equivalent indicators and using the criterion of internal consistency results in a highly comparable variable. Yet the *trade off* is obvious; only three out of the six common and 12 totally available indicators would be used.

3 Establishing functional equivalence: Common indicators – external consistency

To assess the equivalence of common indicators in different settings, the criterion of external consistency can be used as well. The question then is whether the common indicators are related to another concept in a similar way. For instance, it is often assumed that civic engagement is positively related to education. Equivalent indicators of civic engagement should therefore show a positive association to education in all datasets. Whether this is really the case, can be analyzed with linear regressions of the several (common) indicators of organizational membership on education.

Table 6.3 reveals that three out of the six commonly available organizations show a positive association with the concept education. The results mirror those of the test of the internal consistency of the literally equivalent variables done before. Memberships in 'religious or church organization', 'youth organization' and 'sport club or outdoor activities club' seem to be functional equivalences of the concept 'civic engagement' in all three datasets. Irrespective of the criterion of consistency

Table 6.3   Common indicators: external consistency – membership in organizations and education

	Shell 2002	DJI 1992	DJI 1997
	education		
professional organization	n.s.	n.s.	n.s.
religious or church organization	+	+	+
local home associations	n.s.	–	–
youth association	+	+	+
sports club or outdoor activities club	+	+	+
trade union	–	–	–

Notes: linear regression, +: significantly positive (p <.005), –: significantly negative (p<.005); n.s.: not significant; highlighted fat: significantly positive in all datasets.

used, the strategy of concentrating on common organizations results in an indicator which, while highly comparable, ignores a substantial number of indicators.

4 Establishing functional equivalence: non-common indicators – internal consistency

If investigators consider not only the common but also the non-common (or literally different) indicators, they can avoid this information loss. Again, they can use the criterion of internal consistency as well as of external consistency. Table 6.4 provides a summary of factor analyses of the tetrachoric correlation matrices of all available organizations.

In contrast to Table 6.2, in which only common organizations were examined and results therefore had to be interpreted line-by-line, table 6.4 should be read column-by-column. Whereas the concentration on common forms of organizational membership would result in an indicator containing three aspects of civic engagement, the strategy to not ignore literally different indicators produces indices consisting of up to seven forms of membership. For instance in Shell 2000, membership in 'other voluntary organization', 'environmental organization', 'cultural/musical/dancing/theatre society' as well as 'trade union' would be added to the three common memberships 'religious or church organization', 'youth organization' and 'sport club or outdoor activities club'.

Table 6.4 Non-common indicators: internal consistency

	Shell 2000	DJI 1992	DJI 1997
professional organization	x	x	x
religious or church organization	x	x	x
local home associations	x	x	x
youth association	x	x	x
sports club or outdoor activities club	x	x	x
trade union	x	x	x
other club or association	–	x	x
charity or social-welfare organization	–	x	x
other voluntary organization	x	–	–
environmental organization	x	–	–
cultural/musical/dancing/theatre society	x	–	–
fan club	x	–	–

Notes: factor analyses of tetrachoric correlation matrices; one factor extracted; –: indicators not included, fat: factor loading greater .400.

5 Establishing functional equivalence: non-common indicators – external consistency

The fifth strategy to establish conceptual equivalence is to use a non-common set of indicators and rely on external consistency. In contrast to the criterion of internal consistency, external consistency is not restricted to concepts for which at minimum two indicators are available. Moreover, as it is now possible to establish functional equivalence of non-common indicators, a comparison of the dichotomous general organization-membership-indicator and the more differentiated kind-of-organization-membership-indicator is possible. Hence for the current example the strategy of using non-common indicators and the criterion of external consistency pose the only possibility for establishing functional equivalence in all six data sets for all 13 indicators. Once again, we start from the assumption of a positive association between organizational membership and education and use regressions to assess the functional equivalence. From the fact that the different organizations in different datasets are associated positively with education, it could be concluded that there is a common structure.

The results summarized in Table 6.5 show that the general membership-indicators ('membership in any organization', *memb_d*) are significantly

Table 6.5 Non-common indicators: external consistency – membership in organizations and education

	Shell 1992	KJE 1996	Shell 1997	Shell 2000	DJI 1992	DJI 1997
			education			
membership in any organization	+	+	+	-	-	-
professional organization	-	-	-	n.s.	n.s.	n.s.
religious or church organization	-	-	-	+	+	+
local home associations	-	-	-	n.s.	–	–
youth association	-	-	-	+	+	+
sports club or outdoor activities club	-	-	-	+	+	+
trade union	-	-	-	–	–	–
other club or association	-	-	-	-	+	+
charity or social-welfare organization	-	-	-	-	n.s.	n.s.
other voluntary organization	-	-	-	–	-	-
environmental organization	-	-	-	+	-	-
cultural/musical/dancing/ theatre society	-	-	-	+	-	-
fan club	-	-	-	–	-	-

Notes: linear regression, +: significantly positive (p <.005), –: significantly negative (p <.005); n.s.: not significant; -: indicators not included.

positively associated with education. It can therefore be concluded that they are functionally equivalent. In contrast, the coefficients for membership in several kinds of organizations indicate that not all of them are functionally equivalent. For instance, membership in 'other clubs or associations' is significantly positively associated with education in DJI 1992 and DJI 1997; this is not the case for membership in 'other voluntary organization' in Shell 2000. Within this dataset, membership in 'environmental organization' as well as 'cultural/musical/dancing/ theatre society' seems to be functionally equivalent to the membership-variables used in the other datasets as well as to other organizations such as 'youth organizations' within Shell 2000.

In sum, the different strategies for establishing functional equivalence produce different results, and there are at least two ways to cope with this variation. First, investigators could choose the one strategy that is most appropriate for answering their research question. For instance, relying on a non-common set of organizations in each dataset would mean having four different indicators: the general-organizational-membership indicators in four datasets and three indicators based on different indices in the remaining studies. This complicates the interpretation of the subsequent analyses. For this reason, the most appropriate strategy to assess functional equivalence seems to use common indicators and the criterion of internal consistency. A comparable indicator then definitely includes membership in 'religious or church organization', 'youth organization' and 'sport club or outdoor activities club'. The second way to deal with the different results would be to decide on the least common denominator and consider only those organizations for which all four strategies indicate functional equivalence. Although in the example at hand the result would be the same ('religious or church organization', 'youth organization' and 'sport club or outdoor activities club'), this must not necessarily be the case.

Conclusion

Even though the strategies described focus on researchers working comparatively and relying on existing data, most social science research is sooner or later confronted with the question as to how the collected information can be best used. This chapter tried to provide practical advice and examples to illustrate ways to increase the number of observations as well as to maximize the information inherent in divergent datasets. It has been shown how King and colleagues' (1994) guidelines to *collect data on as many of its observable implications as possible* can be combined with an *efficient use of the relevant information* inherent in different existing datasets. With these guidelines in mind, secondary researchers working comparatively no longer have to restrict their research to already pooled datasets. Instead they can use datasets from various sources with literally equivalent as well as literally different indicators and make them comparable through the establishment of functional equivalence. On the other hand, the problems discussed in this paper should direct secondary researchers' attention to the fact that even already pooled datasets should be handled with care. One should carefully examine whether the pooled measures are really conceptually equivalent. For this reason, secondary researchers must be familiar with their questionnaires, datasets, contexts, and so on and communicate any uncertainty to the reader. As one source of uncertainty is the reasoning about the incomparability of their different measures, 'the qualitative aspects involved in any judgment on functional equivalence must ... be documented, open to criticism and systematized' (King, Keohane and Verba, 1994, pp. 32, 76; Niessen, 1982, p. 88; van de Vijver, 2003, p. 144). Therefore investigators should give a detailed description of the different indicators, variables, questions, and the like used in their statistical analysis. To cite Gerring, however, the conclusion of the discussion presented here can be formulated as follows: 'The existence of multiple cases brings other problems in its train – for example cases that are of questionable comparability – but it is still, *ceteribus paribus*, a desirable quality in a research design' (Gerring, 2005, p. 184).

Notes

1. See van Deth (2003, p. 305) for a table displaying 'Important Cross-National Survey Programs and Data Bases'.
2. See homepage: http://www.gesis.org/ZA/; there are several corresponding institutions for other countries; see, for example, van Deth (2003) for more information.
3. For a detailed description of harmonization strategies see van Deth (2003) or Braun and Mohler (2003).
4. This result mirrors common challenges in cross-cultural research about organizational membership, where normally '*none* of the structures found can be reproduced in all countries' (Roßteutscher and van Deth, 2002, p. 5; van Deth and Kreuter, 1998).

Part IV
Case Selection

7
Dealing Effectively with Selection Bias in Large-n Research

Janina Thiem

Introduction

The potential for selection bias exists whenever one draws inferences from a non-random sample to the population of interest. As a variety of empirical social research relies on research designs and/or on data sets that are vulnerable to selection effects, it is one of the central methodological problems in social science. Selection is problematic as it leads to biased results of regression estimates if observations are selected in a way by which they are not independent of the outcome of the study or if the dependent variable is truncated (that is, observations on the dependent variable do not reflect the full variance) (Winship and Mare, 1992, p. 327). However, to rely exclusively on research designs that are free from selection bias is to 'rule out a vast portion of fruitful social research' (Winship and Mare, 1992, p. 327). Therefore, it is crucial to identify selection bias when present in order to be able to estimate and evaluate the selection effects. King and colleagues (1994) as well as others (Collier, Brady and Seawright, 2004) recommend that scholars should always take into account the possibility of selection bias: What kinds of events are likely to have been recorded? What kinds of events are likely to have been ignored? This especially concerns the dependent variable. If selection bias cannot be avoided, 'we should analyze the problem and ascertain the direction and, if possible, the magnitude of the bias, then use this information to adjust our original estimates in the right direction' (King, Keohane and Verba, 1994, p. 133). This is, however, easier said than done.

The goal of this chapter is to fill the gap between such rather abstract recommendations which can be found in research design textbooks on the one hand and, on the other hand, econometric articles which are usually highly technical and address statisticians. Therefore, this chapter exemplifies and discusses decisions with which researchers are usually confronted when selection bias is present. Although it is possible to estimate the selection effects statistically, dealing with selection bias should first and foremost be theory-driven. This is neglected in most textbooks on selection bias. As an appropriate evaluation of selection effects can only be ensured in the light of theoretical considerations, the importance of a theoretical approach to selection bias is pointed out in this chapter, which is structured as follows. First, I illustrate the design problem of selection bias: When can it arise and why is it problematic? Developing practical guidelines of how to deal with selection bias, I focus on research decisions and trade-offs that especially concern the question of whether estimating selection effects statistically is helpful. Thereby practical advice will be given to scholars who abstain from statistical estimation when dealing with selection bias. I then turn to an application which refers to my own work on selection effects in roll call votes (RCVs) in the European Parliament (EP). Since several studies on voting behavior rely on this data which proved to be vulnerable to selection problems, I expose how the selection process may influence the results of these studies. The application presents ways of dealing with the selection problem and discusses the advantages and shortcomings of statistical and non-statistical proceedings.

Design problem

Selection bias arises if observations are chosen (the so-called selection rule) in a way that the inferences drawn from such a sample about the population of interest lead to an over- or an underestimation of the true causal effects. In this chapter, 'sample' refers to the selected observations, while 'population of interest' refers to the population about which inferences will be drawn. Therefore, it is indispensable that the population of interest is at least theoretically identified. If a researcher limits her conclusions to the selected observations, the problem of selection bias can be neglected. In most cases, however, the researcher is interested in inferences about the population so that selection effects have to be considered.

Exemplarily, this can be illustrated with regard to roll call votes. Roll call votes, in which the individual voting behavior of Members of Parliament is identifiable, are usually a sample of all votes taken in a parliament. The criteria as to which votes are taken as roll calls vary among parliaments. In the European Parliament, a group leader can initiate such a vote and may do that for strategic reasons. This has to be taken into consideration if one wants to draw valid conclusions about the population of votes and not just about the roll call sample. This selection problem can be neglected if the researcher limits her conclusions to the roll call sample.

Selection bias is particularly problematic with regard to the dependent variable: '[I]f the explanatory variables do not take into account the selection rule, *any selection rule correlated with the dependent variable attenuates estimates of causal effects on average*' (King, Keohane and Verba, 1994, p. 130; emphasis in original). The reduced slope of the regression line for the selected sample results from a correlation between the error term and the independent variables, which is caused by the truncation of the dependent variable.[1] This violates the standard assumption of linear regressions that the independent variables and the error term must not be correlated. Whereas this type of selection bias leads to underestimated causal effects, an overestimation of causal effects can occur as well. This is the case if causal effects vary over the units. A selection rule correlated with the size of the causal effect leads to a bias of average causal effects. Selecting observations with large (or small) causal effects and averaging these effects during estimation, for example, induces an overestimation (or underestimation) of the average causal effect (King, Keohane and Verba, 1994, p. 139).

In contrast to a selection rule correlated with the dependent variable, the truncation of explanatory variables does not represent an inference problem. This selection rule does not predetermine the outcome of the study since the variation in the dependent variable is not restricted (King, Keohane and Verba, 1994, p. 137; Winship and Mare, 1992, p. 322). Nevertheless, researchers should bear in mind that this procedure may limit the generality of their study. If the *selection rule* is correlated with at least one of the independent variables *and* with the dependent variable, however, omitted variable bias arises. This can be the case in sample selected data where the observation of the dependent variable depends on another variable (see below).

In a truly random sample, selection bias cannot occur because the random rule is, by definition, uncorrelated with all possible explanatory and dependent variables. Every potential observation has an equal probability of being selected into the sample.[2]

To illustrate the logic of selection problems, several types of samples that may lead to biased inferences can be differentiated. Breen (1996, p. 4) distinguishes three: censored, sample selected and truncated samples. In censored samples (or data), the values of the dependent variable

(y) are known exactly if some criterion defined in terms of the value of y is met, such as $y < t_1$. In other words, the values of the dependent variable below the threshold t_1 are known exactly while the values of the dependent variable above this threshold are unknown. For instance, this is the case if a researcher wants to analyze factors associated with time in office of Members of Parliament and only gets the exact time for those MPs who already left Parliament at t_1. While the exact duration time of those MPs who are still in office at t_1 remains unknown, their characteristics (such as sex, age, party membership, former occupational status) which may serve as independent variables are known. In this case, y is a truncated random variable and the whole sample is called censored. The explanatory variables are observed for the entire sample, regardless of whether y is known exactly.

In sample selected data, y, a truncated random variable, is observed only if some criterion defined in terms of another random variable, z, is met, such as if $z_i = 1$.[3] This is, for example, the case if one analyzes factors that affect Supreme Court decisions (y) (King, 2004). As some cases get decided in lower courts, y cannot be observed for this subset of the data. In this case, $z_i = 1$ if the i th decision is granted certiorari, $z_i = 0$ otherwise. In sample selected data, the explanatory variables are observed for the entire sample, regardless of whether y is observed.

A truncated sample is similar to the censoring problem as y is observed if some criterion defined in terms of the value of y is met, such as $y > c$. Again, y is a truncated random variable. The central difference to a censored sample is that the explanatory variables in a truncated sample are observed *only* if y is observed (Breen, 1996, p. 4).[4] When analyzing factors that influence the amount of campaign contributions, a researcher is, for example, confronted with a truncated sample if the contributions are published only if they exceed EUR 20.000. So the researcher does not receive any information on contributions below this value – neither about the exact amount of money nor about potential independent variables like the organization or person that contributed it. Table 7.1 summarizes types of selection problems and ways to model selection effects in large-*n* data.

As truly random samples are rare in political science, researchers should always be aware of selection bias. While in some cases the random character of a sample can be tested empirically, theoretical considerations about the potential selection process are essential in order to assess the selection effects appropriately. Although it is possible to correct for selection bias in large-n data, it remains a matter of judgment whether selection influences the results substantively. This depends on

Table 7.1 Types of selection problems

Sample	Dependent variable	Independent variables	Estimating selection effects in large-n studies
Censored	y is known exactly only if some criterion defined in terms of the value of y is met, such as $y < t_1$. y is a truncated random variable	x variable values are observed for all of the sample, regardless of whether y is known exactly.	Estimating selection effects is possible → Tobit model (Stata commands '-cnreg-' or '- tobit-').
Sample selected	y is observed only if some criterion defined in terms of another random variable, z, is met, such as if $z_i=1$. y is a truncated random variable.	The explanatory variables for both, the selection and the outcome stage (w and x) are observed, regardless of whether y is observed.	The estimation of the selection and the outcome stage is possible → Heckman model (Stata command '-heckman-').
Truncated	y is observed only if some criterion defined in terms of the value of y is met such as $y > c$. y is a truncated random variable.	The explanatory variables are observed only if y is observed.	Only the outcome stage can be modeled (Stata command '-truncreg-').

Note: See Breen, 1996, p. 4

the theoretical considerations about the selection process. If a substantive influence can be excluded, a process of sample selection may even be ignored (Breen, 1996). This is the case if the selection rule is neither correlated with the dependent variable nor with any of the independent variables. However, if it is conceivable that the selection process affects inferences to a significant degree, the researcher has to decide in a second step how to deal with the selection bias. Whether this can be done formally depends on the research question and on the sample at hand. The researcher should in any case give attention to the potential mechanisms of the selection process. This is not only indispensable when estimating selection effects, but it also facilitates the interpretation of the result if one does not consult statistical procedures.

For large-n studies, the econometric literature offers several procedures to estimate and evaluate selection effects. Usually, these procedures consist of two stages of analysis. In the first stage (selection stage), the probability that the i th observation is included in the sample is estimated. In the second stage (outcome stage), the expected value of y_i conditional on having been included in the selected sample can be modeled.[5] With regard to the different types of selection bias, different procedures are available for estimating the selection effects. For censored and sample selected data, both the selection stage and the outcome stage can be modeled so that in these cases the selection effects can be estimated (Heckman, 1976, 1979; Tobin, 1958). The central goal of theses procedures is to yield unbiased estimates of the effect of the independent variables on the dependent variable. However, an important precondition in applying these procedures is that data is available for both the selection and the outcome stage. For truncated data, only the outcome stage can be modeled because of the lack of information about the selection stage. This leads to a truncated error distribution of the dependent variable. Thus by assuming a truncated rather than a normal error distribution, this problem can be tackled and estimated, for instance, by using the command '-truncreg-' of the general purpose statistical program *Stata*.

However, one should bear in mind that relying solely and uncritically on estimating selection effects is not recommended, as the respective statistical procedures are vulnerable to violations of their distributional assumptions. Even if the assumptions are violated, however, the estimation of selection effects may be useful if one considers the reasons that have led to violating the assumptions. One can then compare the results with the theoretical considerations about the selection process. When abstaining from estimating the selection effects, one may lose relevant information about the selection process.

Practical guidelines

According to the methodological discussion, what practical advice can be given with regard to the question of how to deal with selection bias? The following guidelines focus on research decisions that have to be taken when selection bias is likely. They are illustrated in Figure 7.1.

- *How to identify selection bias?* Generally, one should always take the possibility of selection bias into account by considering the potential selection process: what kinds of events are likely to have been (systematically) recorded? What kinds of events are likely to have been (systematically) ignored? Does selection occur with regard to the dependent or the independent variables? The researcher should evaluate possible implications of the selection process for the research question in the light of these theoretical considerations. If they indicate that selection occurs according to the dependent variable or that the selection rule is correlated (with at least one of the independent variables

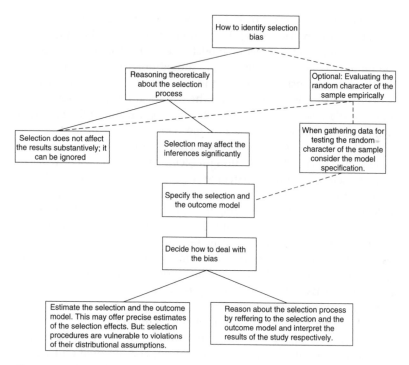

Figure 7.1 Illustration of practical guidelines

and) with the dependent variable, it can be assumed that the selection process substantively influences (that is, biases) the results of the study. In this case, both the selection and the outcome model should be specified in order to facilitate dealing with the bias. If, however, the theoretical considerations suggest that the selection process does not affect the outcome of the study, it can be ignored. This is the case if the selection rule is neither correlated with the dependent variable nor with any of the independent variables. In theory, there is no selection bias present if the sample at hand does represent a truly random sample which can be tested empirically against known quantities of the population of interest. Therefore, information on the characteristics of the population are needed (for an example, see section 4) and must often be gathered by the researcher herself. One should bear in mind that this can be very time-consuming. If the researcher decides to evaluate the random character of the sample empirically, and if she gathers the data herself, this should occur in the light of theoretical considerations about the selection process (maybe even after the process of model specification) (see, for instance, Gschwend, 2005). In this way, she ensures that she can use the data not only for testing the random character of the sample, but also for estimating the selection model if necessary. However, evaluating the random character of the sample should only be supplementary to the theoretical considerations about the selection process and must not be seen as a substitute for it. Since the empirical findings do not allow one to explain why selection occurs, the researcher should be aware of *ad hoc* explanations of the selection mechanisms.

• *Model specification.* If the researcher has found that the sample at hand is characterized by selection problems, she has to properly specify both the selection and the outcome stage. Here, it is helpful to identify the selection type at first. Once again, the model specification should be deduced theoretically by referring to the considerations about the selection process. The specification of the selection stage is useful even if one has not planned to estimate the selection effects, as it forces the researcher to clarify the mechanisms underlying the selection process. This should facilitate the interpretation of the outcome model as it allows one to assess the selection effects more properly.

• *How to deal with selection bias.* Dealing with selection bias can either be done formally or non-formally. While in the first case, the selection effects can be estimated statistically, the second case usually leads to limiting the scope of interpretation. For censored and sample selected data, different estimation procedures are available. A precondition to apply these procedures is that data is available for both the selection and the outcome stage. If the researcher decides to estimate the selection effects and if data is not already available for the selection stage, she should collect the data according to the model specification. In this way, she ensures that all variables of her model are incorporated in the data set. One should take into consideration that the process of data gathering can be very time-consuming.[6] Moreover, it is useful to compare the estimation results with a theoretical evaluation of the selection process, since the combination of statistical and non-statistical proceedings may shed more light on the selection process than concentrating on only one of these options.

• *Estimating selection effects.* Estimating selection effects is only possible if the data is, in the terms of Breen (1996), censored or sample selected. For these types, several statistical procedures (like the Heckman or the Tobit model) are available for estimating selection effects.[7] The advantage of applying these procedures is that they offer good estimates of the effects of the independent variables on the dependent variable. However, the Tobit and Heckman models are both parametric procedures which rely on strong distributional assumptions. As they are sensitive to violations of their distributional assumptions, their application can be problematic. The researcher should therefore assess which reasons may have led to violating the assumptions and which consequences this has for the interpretation of the results. However, in recent years, semi- and non-parametric approaches for estimating selection problems have been developed. These approaches relax the strong assumptions of (full) parametric procedures, but 'at the cost of weakening the conclusions that can be drawn from the data' (Greene, 2003, p. 435) as they provide only ranges of probability but offer robust conclusions.[8]

- *What should be done if the selection effects cannot be estimated?* If estimating the selection effects is not possible (either because of non-available data or due to limitations of the model), the researcher must nevertheless cope with the selection bias. In this case, one can try to ascertain the direction of the bias and, if possible, its magnitude and then use this information to adjust the original estimates in the right direction (King, Keohane and Verba, 1994, p. 133). What does this mean, however, in concrete terms? The researcher can build on prior scholarly work when assessing selection effects. For instance, other researchers may have already investigated the selection problem with which one is confronted. If it is too specific, referring to studies about selection processes in similar areas may also be helpful. Furthermore, additional data gathering may be useful to further yield information about the sample at hand. Moreover, the researcher should use the specified selection and outcome model to evaluate the character of selection by reasoning about how the respective dependent and independent variables of the two stages are related. Thus model specification is absolutely recommended even if selection effects are not statistically estimated.

Application

Having laid down practical guidelines of how to deal with selection bias, I turn now to an application by referring to my own work on selection problems in European Parliament (EP) roll call data. For the outcome model, I refer to a study by Hix (2004).

Selection bias in European Parliament roll call data

Several studies about voting behavior, party cohesion, or conflict dimensions in the European Parliament are based on roll call votes (RCV) (Faas, 2003; Hix, 2001, 2002; Kreppel and Hix, 2003; Whitaker, 2005). In the present EP (2004–09), one Political Group (in other words, party group) or at least 37 MEPs are able to initiate a roll call vote. Usually, RCVs are requested by party group leaders. Since only one-fourth of all votes are taken as roll call in the European Parliament, these studies (implicitly) assume that a) either the roll call sample represents a *random selection* of all votes or that b) predominantly *legislative* votes are taken by roll call. While in the first case, a generalization of the results to the universe of all votes would be unproblematic, in the second case general statements about *legislative* votes could still be possible. However, if one wants to analyze voting behavior in legislative votes and if legislative roll call votes are still a subsample of all legislative votes, one has to guarantee that the selection rule is not correlated with the dependent variable (nor with any of the independent variables) in the respective outcome model. This could be the case if the legislative roll call sample systematically reveals higher levels of voting cohesion than the population of all legislative votes would do. Therefore, selection bias can also arise if one wants to draw inferences from a subsample of the RCVs (all legislative RCVs) to a population of interest (all legislative votes). If, however, the researcher makes explicitly clear that she has limited her conclusions to all *roll call votes* – or to all *legislative roll call votes* – the problem of selection bias is not present. In light of the respective research question, however, this limitation might not be satisfactory.

The considerations about possible correlations between the selection rule and voting behavior also hold for the entire sample. Roll call votes may be requested for strategic reasons such as in an effort to exert party discipline or to signal policy positions to voters or interest groups (Thiem, 2006). This might influence the voting behavior of MEPs and could lead to systematically high levels of party group cohesion in the roll call sample. A generalization based on the roll call sample to all votes without correcting or controlling for the selection rule would therefore overestimate party group cohesion.

(a) How to identify selection bias

In this section, a theoretical examination of the selection process of RCVs will be presented. Based on these considerations, it must be decided if selection is substantively important. First of all, I present the outcome stage to which the theoretical examination on the selection process will refer. Second, I discuss if the roll call occurrence could be correlated with the dependent variable of the outcome stage. While this general theoretical discussion on the selection stage will be illustrated, the following model specification will not be presented in detail since it strongly depends on the specific research question.

For the dependent variable of the outcome stage, I will refer to Hix' study on 'electoral institutions and legislative behavior' (Hix, 2004). Hix finds a positive and statistically significant correlation between the electoral institutions under which an MEP is nominated and the probability of voting defection from the party group line. His argument is as follows: MEPs can be considered as agents of two principals, the leader of their national party delegation[9] and the political group leader, who both are able to exert voting discipline over MEPs (Hix, 2004). While the former principals control nomination lists for the re-election of MEPs, the latter are formally more influential over the likelihood of MEPs obtaining attractive positions in the EP. Since electoral institutions differ among the member states, national parties are unequally likely to be able to punish the voting defection of MEPs. Therefore, 'when there is a conflict between an MEP and her national party, she is unlikely to vote against her European party group – unless she is elected under institutions that enable her national party to punish her to a politically appreciable extent' (Hix, 2004, p. 206). Despite the two principals, Hix generally expects a high level of party group cohesion since the majority decision of the European party group is endogenous to the level of conflict among the national delegations within the group (Hix, 2004, p. 204). The underlying assumption of this study is that similar voting behavior of party group members is not just preference-driven (Krehbiel, 1993), but can be enforced by party leaders through 'threats and promises' (Cox and McCubbins, 1993).

In contrast to Hix, I argue that the central causal factor explaining party discipline (either towards the transnational party group or the national party delegation) is the occurrence of both a roll call vote and the factors leading to a roll call vote. Only in this case is voting behavior recorded, and party leaders are able to control it. Therefore, MEPs should have an incentive to behave loyally towards their party leaders in order to avoid their sanctions. As the majority decision of a Political Group is endogenous to the level of conflict within that group, MEPs of one Political Group should vote uniformly in RCVs. If the interests of their national delegation diverge from those of their Political Group, MEPs are supposed to vote in line with that principal who possesses stronger instruments of party discipline. Therefore, vote defection from the party group line can also be considered as party discipline if MEPs vote according to their national delegation. Usually, MEPs vote by the show of hands or electronically; in these cases their individual voting behavior is unregistered. As party leaders are neither able to punish nor reward voting behavior they do not know, MEPs should not have strong incentives to behave loyally toward their party group leader or the leader of their national delegation when the vote is not recorded. In terms of Hix' model, this means that the detected correlations between electoral institutions and voting defection from the party group line should attenuate if the selection process is taken into account. In addition, the relatively high levels of voting cohesion of Political Groups should disappear for the same reasons. The underlying assumption again is that the individual preferences of party group members are not totally similar and that cohesive voting behavior is usually enforced by party discipline.

Based on these considerations, I assume the dependent variable of the outcome stage (probability of vote defection from the party group line) to be correlated with the selection process. Due to the public character of RCVs, party leaders are able to enforce party discipline in such a way that the whole variance of vote defection is not revealed in the RCV sample. While the sample should rather reveal votes characterized by high levels of group/delegation cohesion due to the enforcement of party discipline, it should hide low levels of cohesion expected to show up in non-recorded votes.[10]

In addition to these theoretical considerations, data is actually available to test the random character of the RCV sample at least for the first year of the fifth EP election period (Carrubba, Gabel, Murrah, Clough, Montgomery and Schambach, 2006).[11] The dataset includes information on: (1) the method of vote; (2) the type of motion; (3) the responsible committee for each legislative motion; and (4) the requesting group for each RCV.[12] On the basis of this dataset, Carrubba and colleagues (2006) demonstrate by chi-squared tests that the RCVs do not represent a random sample of all votes in the EP. The roll call sample is biased with respect to at least three dimensions: Issue area, requesting group and legislative importance. With regard to issue area, some committees are overrepresented in the roll call sample, while other issue areas are totally excluded from the sample. Further disproportionality is shown for party groups requesting a roll call vote. The most interesting finding by far is that the evidence suggests that legislatively binding votes are specifically not decided by roll call. Thus, these findings show that both assumptions having legitimated the use of roll call data in EP research are not correct.[13] However, such empirical findings can only serve as a supplement to theoretical considerations about the selection process as they do not allow for explaining why selection occurs.

(b) Model specification

With regard to the specification of the selection stage, one has to reason about the conditions under which party group leaders are likely to request a RCV *and* about their motivations not to initiate a RCV. However, I abstain from presenting the model specification stage in this chapter since a model specification for the selection stage can be found in my own work (Thiem, 2006); for the outcome stage it is presented in Hix (2004). I rather concentrate on discussing the advantages and disadvantages of formal and non-formal proceedings for the example at hand.

(c) How to deal with the bias

Due to the data gathered by Carrubba and colleagues (2006), information about the character of the population of votes should generally be available. However, in order to estimate the selection stage the dataset has to include all relevant variables that are defined in the model specification. If not, one has to gather the respective missing variables or to rely on interpreting selection effects in a non-formal way. When explaining roll call request in the EP (Thiem, 2006), I was confronted with this problem. In order to test my theoretical model I needed information on all votes including single amendments. As the dataset by Carrubba and colleagues (2006) does not contain single amendments, I had to gather the data myself.

Since an introduction to the Heckman model can be found in Breen (1996) and since applications of the model are also available in political science (Plümper, Schneider and Troeger, 2006), I discuss the advantages and shortcomings of this procedure but abstain from applying it to the example at hand.

(d) Estimating selection effects

Since the observation of MEPs' voting behavior (y) depends on the occurrence of a roll call vote ($z = 1$), the RCV sample can be considered as sample selected data. Thus, it is possible to estimate the selection effects. The Heckman procedure (Heckman, 1976, 1979) offers the possibility of acquiring good estimates of the effects of the independent variables on the dependent variable in the outcome model if sample selection is present. The estimation can be illustrated in two steps.[14] In the first step (selection stage), the probability that a roll call vote occurs would be estimated. It is assumed that the selection bias results from correlation ρ (= Rho) between the error terms of both stages. Therefore, in general terms, the correlation coefficient of the error term and the inverse Mill's ratio, which is usually symbolized by λ_i, would be used as independent variable in the outcome stage. The inverse Mill's ratio can be interpreted as the probability that z_i *had not been observed* (i.e. $z_i = 0$). According the theoretical considerations about the selection process for the example at hand, I would expect the selection effects to significantly influence the results of the outcome stage. If the Heckman procedure was actually applied, this should lead to a reduction in the correlation between electoral institutions and voting behavior detected by Hix (2004). If the correlation coefficient of the error terms had not been included as an independent variable in the outcome model, selection bias would have the same consequences as omitted variable bias (King, Keohane and Verba, 1994, p. 169).

The Heckman model also allows for testing whether the estimates of the effects of the independent variables in the outcome stage are unbiased:

- 'In samples in which the selectivity problem is unimportant (i.e., the sample selection rule ensures that all potential examples are sampled), λ_i becomes negligibly small so that [the selection effects need not be corrected and] least squares estimates of the coefficients [...] have optimal properties' (Heckman, 1976, p. 479). Similarly, if the correlation of the error terms of both stages (ρ) is equal to 0, selection and outcome can be seen as independent (Breen, 1996, p. 37).

- If the correlation between the estimate of λ and any independent variable (say x_k) in the outcome model is zero, then the OLS estimate of this variable's coefficient, β_k, will be unbiased (Breen, 1996, p. 37). This corresponds to the omission of an independent variable which is not correlated with any other independent variable in the model. Hence, the omission of that variable is unproblematic and does not produce omitted variable bias (King, Keohane and Verba, 1994, p. 169). This holds at least for factor-centric approaches (see Chapter 1). However, when omitting an explanatory variable that is uncorrelated with the other independent variables but affects the dependent variable, one loses some accuracy in explaining the dependent variable. This is relevant for outcome-centric approaches when mapping all of the systematic variation in the dependent variable which is prevented by the omission of one relevant independent variable (King, Keohane and Verba, 1994, p. 169).

Nevertheless, the Heckman model remains a parametric procedure characterized by the assumptions of these approaches. Primarily, these are the assumptions about the linear relationship between the error terms of both stages and the normal distribution of the error term in the first stage. Hence, the results of the Heckman estimator 'may be sensitive to violations of its assumptions about the way that selection occurs' (Winship and Mare, 1992, p. 327). The precision of the estimates depends on how effectively the probit model at the first stage predicts which observations are selected into the sample. The better the prediction, the more precise the estimates will be (Winship and Mare, 1992, p. 341). However, applying the Heckman procedure *can* yield precise estimates of the selection effects. When interpreting the estimation results one should thus consider a possible violation of the distributional assumptions and a potential ineffectiveness of the probit model in the selection stage.

(e) What to do if the selection effects cannot be estimated?

If the researcher decides not to estimate the selection effects, she has to reveal the mechanisms underlying the selection process on the basis of the model specification and to interpret the results in the light of these considerations. With regard to the example at hand, the theoretical considerations suggest that the findings of the outcome model are not entirely effects of the independent variables like electoral institutions, but may also result from selection effects. That means that the correlation Hix detected should be limited to the RCV sample and should not be found to that extent if the population is considered. According to the theoretical considerations about the selection process, one should thus abstain from inferring these results to the population of all votes taken but instead consider the selection effects in the interpretation of the results. Since the RCV sample represents a disproportionately low degree of legislative votes (Carrubba, Gabel, Murrah, Clough, Montgomery and Schambach, 2006; Thiem, 2006), in which researchers are usually interested, one should also discuss why particularly these votes remain hidden from the public.

Even though formal approaches to estimate selection effects may discourage statistically inexperienced readers, non-statistical ways of dealing with selection bias are not less challenging. This is often ignored by researchers. The most crucial task in non-statistical approaches is to deal with the bias in an open and sincere way. In terms of the outcome model at hand, this means that one has to discuss the detected correlation between electoral institutions and voting behavior which can be the result of voting discipline in roll call votes, and may attenuate or even vanish in the entire sample. In addition, one can refer to prior empirical and theoretical work, for example by Carrubba and colleagues (2006) or Thiem (2006), to assess the selection effects more properly.

Conclusion

Generally, researchers should always be aware of selection bias as it is one of the central methodological problems in social sciences. The consequences of not detecting it are potentially very serious since inferences from a sample suffering from selection problems to a population of interest can lead to an over- or underestimation of the true causal effects. As truly random samples are rare in political science, this chapter served as an introduction to how to deal with selection bias. The first crucial task is to identify selection bias. This should be done by considering the potential selection process and can be supplemented by empirically examining the sample at hand. Having found that selection is existent, the researcher has to assess whether it substantively affects the results of the study. Thereby, it is essential to examine the selection process theoretically and to specify the selection and the outcome model, even if the selection effects are not estimated statistically. In this way, selection can be evaluated (more) appropriately. On the basis of the model specifications, the researcher has to decide how to deal with the bias which can either be done with statistical procedures or theoretically. However, selection problems can be ignored if the selection stage and outcome stage are independent of each other. In this case, selection is inconsequential for the research question.[15]

In order to illustrate how to deal with selection bias, I discussed selection problems with recourse to my own work on roll call votes in the European Parliament. I thereby concentrated on a theory-driven evaluation of selection effects since this is missing in most research design textbooks. While the Heckman and Tobit models can offer precise estimates of the selection effects, the researcher should take into account that these procedures are vulnerable to violations of their (restrictive) distributional assumptions. When applying Heckman or Tobit, one should thus assess such a potential violation and consider it in the interpretation if necessary. It is therefore generally recommendable to combine both theory-driven and statistical approaches when dealing with selection bias.

However, the most important task when dealing with selection bias is that reasoning about the selection process is theory-driven. This means that developing a concrete theoretical idea about the selection process before evaluating potential selection effects is indispensable. Therefore it is absolutely recommendable to specify both the selection and the outcome model conceptually even if one has not planned to estimate the selection effects statistically.

Notes

1. Truncation of the dependent variable means that observations on y do not reflect the full variance of that variable.
2. In political science truly random samples are rare, some would even say they are an ideal type. So, in survey research randomly drawn samples are treated as 'quasi-random samples' if their response rate exceeds an acceptable threshold, say 40 percent.
3. Sample selection is a form of censoring, but one in which the truncation of the dependent variable is a function of a second variable (Breen, 1996, p. 3).
4. Long (1997) uses the terminology 'censoring' and 'truncation' differently from Breen (1996). Please note that in this chapter I refer to the terminology used by Breen (1996).
5. In technical terms, Ordinary Least Squares (OLS) models are biased and inconsistent if the error term of the second stage is either correlated with the error term of the first stage or with at least one explanatory variable of the first stage (Winship and Mare, 1992).
6. To reduce the number of observations for which data has to be collected, it might be helpful to draw a random sample of the population of interest for estimating the selection stage. The proceedings to estimate selection effects remain the same. Please note that using a random sample for the selection stage does not diminish the selection effects as the distribution of the dependent variable of the outcome model is not affected by the random sample.
7. For an introduction, see Breen (1996).
8. Discussing these procedures would go beyond the scope of this chapter. For an introduction to semi- and non-parametric approaches, see Greene (2003, chs 16 and 18).
9. The transnational Political Groups are composed of MEPs from different national delegations belonging to the same ideological party family.
10 A similar interpretation of RCV request can be found in Carrubba and Gabel (1999).
11. This is the period to which Hix (2004) also refers.
12. The method of vote measures whether the vote is taken by roll call. The type of motion indicates whether the vote is a non-binding resolution or occurred in the context of a legislative procedure. In the case of the latter, the respective legislative procedure is recorded, as well. The responsible committee serves as a proxy for the issue area. The requesting group measures which party group, if any, initiated the RCV.
13. The problem of selection bias in roll call data is not restricted to the European Parliament, and it is discussed for other chambers as well (Hug, 2005; Koford, 1989; Rosenthal, 1992; Snyder, 1992; Vandoren, 1990). However, the considerations in this chapter concentrate on the European Parliament. One must

thereby bear in mind that the selection effects in roll call data can be different in other Parliaments.

14. Most statistical programs combine these two steps in the estimation procedure, for example by using Maximum Likelihood Estimation.

15. In statistical terms, this means that the error terms of both stages are uncorrelated. This can be found either by applying an estimation procedure or, again, by reasoning theoretically about the selection process.

8
Case Selection and Selection Bias in Small-n Research*

Dirk Leuffen

Introduction

Designing social research is often a blood, toil, sweat and tears experience, with the road to publication usually long and winding. Constantly, the researcher has to weigh different options, and case selection is often considered a particularly delicate and demanding step. For King and colleagues (1994, p. 115), 'poor case selection can vitiate even the most ingenious attempts, at a later stage, to make valid causal inferences.' In small-n as well as in large-n approaches 'the cases you choose affect the answers you get' (Geddes, 1990). However, case selection usually differs between those two approaches – and for good reasons. Whilst large-n studies generally seek representativeness, for example by random sampling, case selection in small-n research usually follows an intentional logic. Intentional does not, however, mean arbitrary. In the end, the types of cases you select determine which inferences you can draw.

In an idealized research cycle, case selection usually takes place after the formulation of the research question, elaboration or compilation of theories and concept specification. Case selection thus links theory development and the empirical testing of these theories. As they usually select their cases non-randomly, small-n researchers are particularly in jeopardy of introducing selection bias. A selection bias results from a faulty inference that wrongly attributes the properties of the scrutinized cases to the larger universe of cases. In this chapter, I will first identify different types of selection bias. I will then introduce some strategies for case selection that are commonly applied in small-n research. I will argue that case selection in small-n research should be considered a theory-guided iterative process. Theory defines the variables that are to be included in the research design. On the basis of these variables we can construct multi-dimensional classification schemes that structure the possible universe of cases on theoretical grounds. Such typologies help in selecting cases as well as discussing the generalizability of one's findings. In this chapter, I will illustrate some methods of case selection by referring to my own research on the consequences of French divided government. Referring to my own research allows me to point out some problems and trade-offs around the issue of case selection that can arise during the research process. Methodological treatises often tend to merge the steps of case selection, data collection and data analysis. This, however, is not the practitioner's view. In practice, for example, the universe of cases is often not known right from the start, and case selection must take place behind a veil of ignorance. But how should one proceed when the universe of cases is 'clouded in mist'?

In general, when it comes to case-selection there is not one road to salvation, rather 'earthly sinners' must find their own paths. Some paths, however, seem more appropriate than others. Researchers should first of all be conscious about the pitfalls of case selection and be as transparent as possible when describing their case selection strategies. Verbalizing the problems around case selection and discussing the principal trade-offs is already a step that helps the reader gauge the impact of possible bias.

Design problem

This chapter analyzes case selection and selection bias in the social sciences. A case here is considered a unit or an object of comparison. It takes a particular value on each dimension that is submitted to the comparison (Eckstein, 1992, p. 125). As stated above, a selection bias is a systematic error that results from improper inferences drawn from a sample (Collier and Mahoney, 1996, p. 59). Accordingly, in 'configurative-ideographic studies' (Eckstein, 1992, p. 136), 'atheoretical' or 'interpretative case studies' (Lijphart, 1971, p. 691) selection bias is not a big problem since those kinds of research focus on cases *per se*. However, to therefore conclude that we should all refrain from drawing generalizations and inferences altogether is certainly not a satisfying response. In fact, such a strategy would correspond to suicide from fear of death.

In theory, we can distinguish between different types of bias. In a real world or contingency bias, the universe of available cases is biased by historical contingencies. For instance, in comparative country studies the number of available cases is clearly determined by the historical development of nation-states (Ebbinghaus, 2005, p. 138f.). If, however, nation-building is linked to what we wish to explain, such a contingency bias may raise some delicate problems of endogeneity (Hug, 2003, p. 257). In this chapter we will, however, mostly focus on researcher-induced bias. Such bias results from improper measurement or non-random case selection strategies. Measurement bias can be attributed to unreliable indicators or biased sources. Hug (2003, p. 258), for instance, shows that an analysis of social movements that primarily relies on media reports is likely to suffer from a bias. The media pre-select cases according to their own logic. For example, newspapers might over-report violent forms of participation. Similarly, legislative datasets can be biased. Mayhew's (1991) study on divided government, for example, is criticized by Fiorina (1996, p. 90) for only analyzing the production of legislation and neglecting its demand. Edwards and colleagues (1997) and Binder (1999) in response use data-sets that include unsuccessful proposals as well. This, indeed, brings forth more nuanced findings about the consequences of divided government.

Self-selection, volunteer or participation bias is closely related to the measurement process. Pre-selection mechanisms such as response or non-response non-randomly determine who participates in a survey or experimental sample. In the case of such bias the sample does not mirror the target population properly. Whereas real world and measurement bias equally applies to large-n and small-n research the bias resulting from an intentional or non-random selection of cases is more of a problem for small-n research (Achen and Snidal, 1989, pp. 160–1; King, Keohane and Verba, 1994, p. 140). In small-n research, cases are generally selected intentionally. An intentional selection of cases, however, leaves room for manipulation. A rather obvious selection bias occurs if a researcher only selects cases that confirm the initial theory. Conspiracy theories most clearly display such confirmation bias. Conspiracy designers only collect information that support their theory and do not report any opposing evidence. Almost anything can be claimed by such a method; however, such practice does not at all meet the standards of social scientific research. A more common type of confirmation bias, however, consists in selecting cases that share the same value on the dependent variable (Achen and Snidal, 1989; Geddes, 2003; King, Keohane and Verba, 1994, p. 129). When interested in revolutions, researchers study revolutions (Skocpol, 1979), when interested in prosperity they analyze economically successful countries. Not including 'negative' cases, however, can lead to the false conclusion that any characteristic that these cases share should be considered a cause. Finally, selection bias does not only occur in cross sectional analysis.

Also in longitudinal designs there is a risk of leaving out important information. For example, when complaining about the present without comparing the past there is a selection bias. If the previous values of our variables remain unknown, how can we judge a causal effect?

Understanding what to avoid is one thing. Knowing how to proceed is a different matter altogether. How shall cases be selected in small-n research? Before introducing different techniques for case selection in small-n research, I will shortly address the question of why small-n in the first place. Given the enormous challenges of small-*n*, why do researchers still engage in such dangerous research strategies?

Why small-n?

If case selection is such a crucial research step that bears such enormous risks in small-n research, why then choose a small-n design in the first place? It is generally accepted that the formulation of research questions and interests should precede the elaboration of the research design. If you are interested in a particular topic you should work with the best methods available to solve your research puzzle. Subject to the research question there are basically two reasons for choosing a small-n design. First, data properties might restrict the number of available cases. Second, methodological objectives such as getting a better grip of causal processes or mechanisms can incite a researcher to choose a small-n approach. As a matter of fact, for numerous research questions, just a few cases exist out there. Think, for example, of revolutions, international monetary systems or interim Presidents in the Fifth Republic. This is not to say that such topics can never be related to broader concepts; for example, when interested in revolutions one could also include mutinies in the analysis. This, however, often comes at the price of *concept stretching* (on concept specification and its pitfalls see Wonka, Chapter 3). When interested in the extinction of dinosaurs it might not be advisable to study today's endangered species since the particular conditions and potential causes such as pollution might differ a lot.

There are other research questions that relate to larger populations of cases in the real world. However, systematic data-sets do not exist. Can the researcher afford to collect new data? Data collection always comes at a high price in an imperfect world with limited resources. In addition, external restrictions such as data secrecy, for example, often hinder the analysis of political decision-making. Political processes often lack transparency, and decision-makers try to hide their strategies and preferences from the public. This applies equally to international relations as well as to domestic and comparative politics. For example, in my own research on French European policy-making in the context of divided government, both sides of the split-executive generally emphasize their influence in the executive decision-making process. When there is reason to doubt available information – for example, when you are confronted with severe inconsistencies – the researcher has to collect additional data. The application of different data sources to one issue – methodologists speak of triangulation – is, however, time-consuming. In such a situation opting for a small-n design might therefore be the only viable solution.

On the other hand, the choice for small-n can be methodologically motivated. For example, small-n research is often employed to uncover causal mechanisms. Techniques such as process-tracing (George and Bennett, 2005) enable us to at least theoretically include a great number of variables in a within-case analysis. By testing necessary causes we can narrow down the scope of potentially relevant variables and thereby foster theory development. This particularly holds for research programs that are still in their infancy. For Goldthorpe (2000, p. 59) detailed case studies can play a *heuristic* role in the 'context of discovery', prior to the testing of any resulting theory against further, independent cases in the 'context of validation'. More specific theories can then be submitted to more rigorous tests in a following step.

In the remaining sections of this chapter, I will concentrate on data property motivated small-n designs. That means that the universe of cases is actually quite large, yet accurate information is not available to the researcher. If the universe of cases is clouded in mist, how should one proceed?

Practical guidelines

In 1843 John Stuart Mill introduced the methods of difference and agreement. Originally designed for experimental research – that means research in which all relevant variables can be manipulated while everything else is held constant – these methods of inference have frequently been referred to in non-experimental case selection as well (Meckstroth, 1975). The methods of agreement and difference are useful tools to test necessary conditions (Ebbinghaus, 2005, p. 143). In the method of difference you select two or more cases that differ on the key independent variable while otherwise being as similar as possible. This is why Przeworski and Teune (1982, p. 32) speak of a 'most similar systems' design. If the dependent variable – *ceteris paribus* – varies in correspondence with the key independent variable, we detect a causal effect. King and colleagues (1994) basically recommend this method for case selection. These authors suggest selecting observations 'according to the categories of the key causal explanatory variable' (King, Keohane and Verba, 1994, p. 137).[1] They find that this reduces the risk of introducing a bias since the selection procedure does not predetermine the study's outcome. Once the categories of the independent variable are defined, the cases should carefully be matched across the different categories. For example, when comparing decision-making in a coalition or single party government we should select similar types of decisions for both categories of this independent variable.

Fine examples of an application of the method of difference are Dreze and Sen (1995) as well as Haverland (2000). In order to test the 'goodness of fit' hypotheses for implementation records in the European Union, Haverland studies the implementation of the European Packaging and Packaging Waste Directive in Germany, the Netherlands and the United Kingdom. These cases are carefully selected along the categories of the independent variable. The 'goodness of fit' theory predicts that conformity between European provisions and national rules and practices can best explain the degree of national adjustments to European law. In this particular case Germany shows the best fit, the United Kingdom the least best, and the Netherlands scores in between. Haverland's in-depth case studies, however, cannot confirm the causal relationship that was hypothesized by the 'goodness of fit' hypothesis. In fact, the adaptation of the directives follows a different logic altogether. Whereas the UK did well in implementing the directives, Germany showed great difficulties. Haverland therefore comes up with an alternative explanation. He claims that institutional veto points can better explain national adjustments to European provisions.

In the method of agreement, the cases should agree on the dependent variable as well as on the key independent variable. The other variables should, ideally, differ between the cases. In the method of agreement, 'the investigator employs the logic of elimination to exclude as a candidate cause (independent variable) for the common outcome (dependent variable) in two or more cases those conditions that are not present in both cases' (George and Bennett, 2005, p. 155). The method of agreement is often linked to Przeworski and Teune's (1982, p. 34) 'most different systems' design. However, the selection of cases that agree on the dependent variable has lately been criticized by many methodologists (Achen and Snidal, 1989; Geddes, 2003; King, Keohane and Verba, 1994, p. 129). In fact, the serious shortcomings of Mill's methods in non-experimental social research have extensively been addressed in the literature (George and Bennett, 2005, pp. 153–60; Goldthorpe, 2000, pp. 49–50; Lieberson, 1992). First of all, these methods rely on the rather weak assumption that all candidate causes can first be identified and then included in a small-n research design. In social reality, cases are rarely as neatly ordered as demanded by this theory. They score more or less similarly on the different variables of interest. In addition, neither the method of agreement nor the method of difference can account for equifinality or multiple causation (King, Keohane and Verba, 1994, p. 87).[2] If a variable exerts its causal power only under specific conditions or in combination with other variables it will nevertheless be eliminated by Mill's methods. Methodologists therefore speak of 'false negatives' (George and Bennett, 2005, p. 156).

Mill's most important contribution, on the other hand, probably consists of drawing our attention to the importance of introducing variance in our designs. The cases we compare should somehow differ. In general terms, causal analysis needs variance.

How to make use of theory-guided typologies

Constructing multidimensional classification schemes or typologies (George and Bennett, 2005, p. 235; Lehnert, Chapter 4) can be a useful starting point for case selection. In order to do so the researcher should first identify the independent variables. This is a theoretical task. Of course, a review of the existing literature is generally the first step. Once the independent variables are identified, they constitute the different dimensions of our typology. This gives us a clearer picture of the potential universe of cases. We can now classify the different cases and derive theoretical predictions about the values of the dependent variable. Our classification scheme also helps us relate our cases to other cases as well as to the universe of cases. This helps in judging the direction and magnitude of possible biases. Although typologies are primarily descriptive in character, they are a valuable starting point for causal analyses. In the end, when it comes to generalizing findings, qualifying one's cases and relating them to the larger universe of cases is also facilitated by typologies.

Pliny's strategy: not many things but much!

In addition, theory-guided typologies allow researchers to control for alternative explanations (Diesing, 1972, p. 189; George and Bennett, 2005, p. 237; George and McKeown, 1985, p. 45). Control is a central element of case selection. Whereas George and McKeown (1985, p. 28) suggest filling as many cells of a typology as possible, I take here a different stance. Following Pliny the Younger's dictum '*multum non multa*' – not many things (*multa*) but much (*multum*) – I propose to start off by consciously narrowing down the domain and focusing on a set of theoretically interesting cells. Only after some certainty is established in these clearly delineated domains, for example, by analyzing more than just a single case per cell, we should move on to other cells and/or dimensions. When theories are weak – and that is often precisely the *raison d'être* of small-n social science – it is often unclear which variables should be taken into account in the first place. This can be a particular challenge for small-n research in which we can only test a very limited number of variables due to a lack of degrees of freedom (Goldthorpe, 2000, p. 49; Lijphart, 1971, p. 686; King, Keohane and Verba, 1994, pp. 118–124).[3] The *multum non multa* approach, however, averts the degree of freedom problem by limiting the number of variables being tested. Of course, if a theory is very sophisticated – for example, if we can derive precise expectations for each and every cell – and data on the entire range of cases can possibly be collected, there is no reason not to follow George and McKeown's suggestions. However, when confronted with the trade-off between scope and certainty it often makes sense to opt for certainty given the restrictions of small-n research. More robust findings about particular types of cases clearly contribute in a building block fashion to the cumulative development of the social sciences (Geddes, 2003).

Sinatra's strategy: select 'hard' cases!

Once a theory-guided typology is constructed we can select cases that promise the best possible answer to our research question – always given the restrictions of a non-ideal world. In general, it is always good to submit our theories to hard tests. Accordingly, a useful small-n strategy can consist in selecting particularly 'hard' cases. Hard cases are cases that represent a tough test for a theory. A typology is a useful tool for identifying such cases on theoretical grounds and relating them to the larger universe of cases. If a theory holds in a particularly hard case it is more generally supported. The underlying logic could be called the 'New York inference' following Sinatra's song line 'if I can make it there, I'll make it anywhere.' Such 'hard' cases are also called '*a fortiori*' cases: if a theory beats alternative theories in a particularly difficult context it should all the more hold under more favorable conditions. For example, I relied on a New York inference when generalizing from my findings on 'high politics' in my analysis of French European policy-making during divided government. I argue that if the Prime minister can increase his influence on European Council decision-making it is very likely that he, equally, should play an important role in 'low politics.' An equivalent logic respectively applies to the selection of most likely or easy cases. A theory can best be called into question when it fails to explain cases that should be an easy game on theoretical grounds. Turning Sinatra upside down we could respond: 'if the theory can't make it there, it won't make it anywhere!'[4] Designs that rely on New York inferences can thus test theories on the basis of just a few cases. However, the researcher must assure that she is not focusing on outliers.

Case selection as a theory-guided, iterative process

How many cases should be included in a small-n research project? The number of cases generally depends on the number of variables that you want to investigate. However, the Sinatra inference underlines that there are exceptions to this general rule. In general, even in small-n studies there usually is a diminishing marginal utility in terms of depth of analysis. At some point the additional utility gained by deeper investigation into a single case can become very small. In very general terms, case analysis should therefore be as deep as necessary – the most important characteristics of a case, of course, need to be grasped – and as wide as possible as to the number of cases. If cases are easily accessible or data is available why should we not include such information in our research?

Small-n case selection should be considered a theory-guided iterative process. Knowing about the trade-offs in the process of selecting one's cases is important. The researcher should be aware of the advantages of the different approaches when designing social inquiry. In the following I will illustrate some techniques and trade-offs around the issue of case selection by referring to my own research on the consequences of French divided government.

An application: gauging the effects of French divided government

In my PhD-thesis I analyzed the consequences of divided government in France. The so-called cohabitation is a split-executive government in which the French president stands in opposition to the parliamentary majority and to the Prime minister (PM). So far, the Fifth Republic has seen three cohabitations: in the first cohabitation President Mitterrand had to govern with PM Jacques Chirac (1986–88), in the second cohabitation President Mitterrand had to govern with PM Balladur (1993–95) and in the third cohabitation President Chirac had to cope with a government of the *gauche plurielle* under PM Lionel Jospin (1997–2002).

The literature was divided about the effects of cohabitation. When compared to the sophisticated literature on the consequences of the US-divided government, the French case clearly seemed understudied.

In a first step, the research question had to be narrowed down. Since the effects of cohabitation should vary considerably across different policy areas, I decided to restrict my analysis to one field, European policy-making. This was a theory-based decision. The effects of divided government depend on the decision-making procedures and on the policy-preferences of the actors (Milner, 1998, p. 774). In a rational institutionalist perspective, if the actors share the same preferences, divided government does not matter since the outputs of the political game do not change. In addition, decision-making should be shared between the divided actors. Only if there is some cooperation between the branches of government can divided government have a systematic effect on 'system production' (Mayhew, 1991, p. 35). These conditions clearly apply to the field of European policy-making. In France, the President has only limited formal power in the legislative process. On the other hand, the French Constitution is ambiguous as to who – the President or the PM – should be responsible for foreign policy-making. This ambiguity also covers European policy-making since this domain can be situated between the domestic and international realms. I also assumed that this proximity to domestic politics makes Europe a more controversial and partisan subject as compared to more traditional foreign policy issues. Thus, in European policy-making the two conditions for an effect of cohabitation were met.

After narrowing down the research question how did I proceed? The theory that cohabitation matters, expects that the vote-maximizing PM during cohabitation strives for utmost influence on formulating the positions that France holds in the European arena. In contrast, during unified government the President dominates French European policy-making. The PM thus challenges this supremacy during cohabitation. The literature is divided about how the split-executive formulates France's European policies. Some authors find that the PM, indeed, dominates the process; others, however, maintain that the President is still the most important actor. A third branch argues that European policy-making should be considered a *domaine partagé*. Based on an account of the actors' resources and the institutional setting, I follow this third read and propose to test a veto-player theory of French European policy-making during cohabitation (Tsebelis, 2002). Veto-player theory generates a precise hypothesis on the effects of cohabitation. This theory claims that the number of veto-players rises during divided government since the PM should be added as an additional veto-player. On average, the size of the French acceptance sets thus shrink. Following Schelling (1960, p. 28) this should also affect decision-making at the European level (Putnam, 1988). In such a view, cohabitation should thus systematically slow down European integration.

In order to test this theory I introduced some simple models on core executive decision-making (Dunleavy and Rhodes, 1990; Laver and Shepsle, 1994). The models generate different predictions about the positions France should hold in the European arena. Which cases did I select in order to analyze the effects of French divided government? Most studies on the consequences of US divided government rely on statistical techniques (Cameron, 2000; Mayhew, 1991). In the US, the relations between the President and Congress are extremely well documented. This, however, does not apply to the intra-executive French decision-making processes. The government archives are closed for 25 years and since both sides had a strategic interest in exaggerating their respective influence during cohabitation, the available data on the formulation of French positions and the initial preferences of the actors must be handled with great care. The available sources are thus weak, which is why I opted for a triangulation of the data. However, triangulation, as data collection in general, is time-consuming. Therefore the number of cases I was able to study in-depth was clearly restricted. Of course, an in-depth study of only a few cases promised to provide a clearer picture of the decision-making mechanisms.[5] Unveiling the mechanisms is a general advantage of comparative case-study approaches.

Which cases did I select for in-depth analysis? The research question on the effects of cohabitation is factor centric. The logic underlying this question relates to Mill's method of difference. I argue that – all other factors being equal – the switch from unified to divided government changes executive decision-making. This, in turn, affects the positions France holds in the European game. If there are systematic differences between unified and divided government, cohabitation matters. If we do not find any systematic differences there is no causal connection between unified or divided government and the European positions that France holds. King and colleagues (1994) have argued that cases should be chosen according to the categories of the key causal variable. In my research the key causal variable comprised the two categories of divided and unified government. Therefore decision-making processes during divided as well as during unified government should be analyzed. To every rule, however, there is an exception. Such an exception is also acknowledged by King and colleagues:

> However, most research is part of a literature or research tradition … , and so some useful prior information is likely to be known. For example, the usual range of the dependent variable might be very well known when the explanatory variable takes on, for instance, one particular value. The researcher who conducts a study to find out the range of the dependent variable for one other different value of the explanatory variable can be the first to estimate the causal effect. (1994, p. 146)

This precisely fits the case of cohabitation. Unified government decision-making has been analyzed extensively in the past and, in fact, there is little doubt about the dominance of the French President. In contrast, our knowledge about decision-making during divided government is very limited. I therefore decided to focus my in-depth case studies on decisions that were taken under the conditions of cohabitation. My analysis of unified government, on the other hand, is based on the literature.[6] Since in the end I finally compare European policy-making during divided and unified government, there is no selection bias (Gerring, 2004, p. 347; King, Keohane and Verba, 1994, p. 137). Because I concentrate my in-depth analysis on decisions taken under divided government, I am able to better understand the decision-making processes during cohabitation. Had I decided to carefully match cases – for example, by adding the Maastricht negotiations or another budgetary round as, for example, the Delors-II-package – I would have only been able to study three or four cases from each of the two categories of the independent variable. This is thus where a trade-off comes into play. I opted for increasing the variance of cases during divided government since this category of the independent variable had been understudied in the past.

But which of the numerous possible cases should be selected from divided government? This is now where I rely on a theory-guided typology. Whereas George and McKeown (1985) suggest filling as many cells as possible, I decided to concentrate on a few important cells and leave it to future research to fill the rest. For example, I decided to restrict my analysis to 'high politics', that means policies negotiated at the level of the European Council. The analysis thus controls for 'range of decision'. As I did not include 'low politics' in my in-depth analysis, I can only make preliminary statements as to how cohabitation matters in such decision types. However, there are theoretical reasons that allow for formulating such expectations. If I am able to show that the President lost power in 'high politics' this should all the more apply to 'low politics'. Given the President's limited administrative resources, his influence in such decisions should clearly be restricted. In an ideal world, I certainly should have tested this expectation. This, however, would have exhausted my resources which is why I kept this question for future research.

While I restricted my analysis to 'high politics' European policy-making, I decided to maximize the variance between the remaining cases by including other control variables. These control variables were 'issue area', 'decisional scope' and 'personalities'. Accordingly, the cases that were finally chosen covered different issues; they contained intergovernmental conferences as well as 'normal' European council decisions and were selected from all three cohabitations.

A final criterion for my case selection was a bit idiosyncratic. In order to test my models I needed to analyze some kind of conflict amongst the actors (Stokman und Thomson, 2004, p. 10; Thomson, Stokman, Achen and König, 2006). Without any initial differences between the actors we can hardly measure the impact the actors have on the decision-making processes. From a large-n view such a restriction should bias my findings. However, this research does not establish frequency distributions. I do not make precise claims on how often there is conflict amongst the actors of cohabitation, but rather I analyze how decisions are made during unified and divided government. In my research on cohabitation I finally analyzed seven cases in depth and added four mini-case-studies.[7] The mini-cases are less detailed but support the results of the other cases. They thus increase the robustness of my findings.

Typological theorizing can finally be useful when it comes to general-izing one's findings (George and Bennett, 2005, pp. 233–62). The reader has to know which cells have been filled by your research and what remains to be done. The typology helps to discuss the conditions under which your theories seem to hold. You have to be clear about whether there are potentially relevant conditions that you were unable to test. Another useful technique for assessing the generalizability of one's find-ings consists in establishing links to other similar data-sets or causal process observations. How does my data, for example, correspond to other data sets on governance in the Fifth Republic and beyond? How do the findings relate to the case of US divided government and the con-flict between the President and Congress?[8] When generalizing findings, one should always come to nuanced assessments and inform the reader about the remaining uncertainties. Careful formulations, such as '[those] preliminary observations indicate' (Haverland, 2000, p. 100), help to better assess the scope of your findings. A modest stance on one's findings is a virtue not just in terms of professional ethics but also in terms of efficiency. It contributes to the cumulative development of the social sciences.

Conclusion

In the beginning social scientific research often resembles a roller coaster ride. The researcher moves up and down the ladders of abstraction, the various levels of analysis, between data and theory fascinated by a theoretical or empirical puzzle. When streamlining one's research there are, however, many trade-offs the researcher must face. This also applies to case selection. Since the empirical findings of a study depend enormously on the cases studied, the importance of case selection can hardly be overrated. This is why case selection is considered a major step in designing social research.

In this chapter, I analyzed case selection and selection biases in small-n research. After introducing standard procedures of case selection, some applications of these methods were highlighted by my own research on divided government in France. In general, case selection in small-n research can be considered a theory-guided iterative process. There is no uniform rule as to how to proceed in case selection. Of course, the cases you select first of all depend on the questions that you ask. There are, however, some strategies that might help to avoid the most pertinent pitfalls of case selection. After carefully narrowing down the research question and formulating theories, one should select cases that guarantee sufficient variance in terms of our research question. However, given the restrictions of small-n research it is sometimes difficult to maximize the variance between the cases of our analysis. Here typologies can help to select theoretically interesting cases. Sometimes it can be an asset to restrict one's analysis to just a few interesting cells and relate one's findings to the literature. In general, the smaller the domain, the more certain one's findings are likely to be. However, we lose out in terms of scope.

In general, our case selection mechanisms should be made as transparent as possible so that the reader can estimate the magnitude and directions of possible bias (Geddes, 2003, p. 25). While designing social inquiry, you are constantly confronted with possible trade-offs. Such trade-offs should explicitly be addressed when publishing one's findings: which options did I face? Why did I finally choose this particular strategy? Discussing the pros and cons of your case selection is a sign of maturity and methodological awareness. If you enable the reader to gauge possible bias and restrictions of your own analysis, you take an important step towards improving the quality of social scientific research.

Notes

* The author thanks the participants of the MZES working group on research design for many vivid and thought-provoking discussions. Many thanks also go to the editors of this volume as well as to Markus Haverland, Guido Schwellnus, Stefan Seidendorf and Stefanie Walter for helpful comments and suggestions.

1. Their suggestion also relates to Mill's method of 'concomitant variation'. This method relies on at least ordinally scaled key independent and dependent variables and assumes that there is a proportional causal relation. Luebbert's (1987) study on the development of interwar regimes in Europe is a good example of an application of the method of concomitant variation (cf. Mahoney, 2000, pp. 403–4).
2. We speak of equifinality if different causes or combinations of causes bring about the same effect.
3. However, the careful collection and analysis of causal process observations can counterbalance some of these effects.
4. A good example for such logic is Lijphart (1968). Studies that rely on such reasoning additionally employ qualitative techniques in order to investigate the mechanisms that bring about the observed results (King, Keohane and Verba, 1994, p. 477; McKeown, 1999, p. 173; Rogowski, 1995). Within-case analyses can thus support a theory in terms of causal mechanisms (George and Bennett, 2005, p. 206; McKeown, 1999, pp. 173–4).
5. Static comparisons of preferences and negotiation outcomes often neglect how certain results come about. For example, in the case of my research on cohabitation I was able to show by careful process-tracing that President Mitterrand during the first cohabitation had less influence on the internal French decision-making processes than commonly believed. Since the results of the European bargains were closer to Mitterrand's than to Chirac's initial positions many commentators had falsely inferred that Mitterrand was able to impose his will on Chirac. The process-tracing, however, revealed that Chirac – for example in the budgetary negotiations of the Delors-I-package – finally accepted the European agreement in order to gain utmost financial support for French farmers. Thus, Mitterrand's influence was not decisive.
6. In addition, I analyzed two cases that started during unified government and ended during divided government. One case is on the GATT-negotiations. These negotiations started under the socialist government but were only concluded in 1993 and 1994 under the Balladur government. The second case is on the Amsterdam treaty. In this case the Juppé government was replaced by the government of the *gauche plurielle* shortly before the final negotiations at Amsterdam. Such case-studies include two sub-cases and have a quasi-experimental structure (George and Bennett, 2005, p. 81). Most other factors do not vary but there is a change from unified to divided government.

7. The case studies cover, for example, the budgetary Delors-I-package and the Amsterdam intergovernmental conference. Such decisions usually combine various issues. Therefore the number of observations on which my results are based is actually higher than the number of case studies (cf. Gerring, 2004).
8. A similar technique is applied by Gschwend and Leuffen (2005) when these authors back their quota-sample data by comparing it to other sources (cf. Gschwend, 2005).

Part V
Control

9
Selecting Independent Variables: Competing Recommendations for Factor-Centric and Outcome-Centric Research Designs

Ulrich Sieberer

Introduction

The decision as to which variables should be included in a quest for explanation is both a fundamental and a tricky decision in any research design. On the one hand, it is practically impossible to include all variables that could possibly have any explanatory value. On the other hand, it is equally problematic to focus completely on one variable considered important and thereby ignore all others. This chapter discusses some basic methodological choices which must be confronted when selecting independent variables for a research project and the trade-offs associated with these choices.

What would happen if we just stuck to the two extreme positions outlined above? If we included all potentially relevant variables, we would create a model as complex as the world itself and thus miss one main goal of scientific explanation – sorting out important and marginal causes. Even worse, our model may be overdetermined, that is, it may include more explanatory variables than observations so that we would not be able to estimate the causal impact of any of the explanatory variables. If instead we focused completely on one independent variable, we would be unable to claim that an effect we found based on observational data is indeed causal as it may also just be the result of other variables not included in the analysis.[1] These two basic problems of research design emerging from either extreme position are often discussed under the labels 'indeterminate research design' and 'omitted variable bias' (King, Keohane and Verba, 1994).

The decision on which independent variables to include has both a theoretical and a more directly methodological dimension. First, researchers have to explain in theoretical terms why and how potential independent variables should be expected to affect the phenomenon under investigation. In this step, the state of theoretical knowledge in the field may offer important guidance and, if well advanced, may in fact predetermine many of the independent variables to be addressed. In less developed fields and exploratory studies, however, the researcher must also justify the inclusion of variables theoretically.

With regard to the more narrow methodological research design problem, I will argue that the status of independent variables, especially control variables, differs greatly depending on whether a researcher is interested in testing one particular causal mechanism involving one or few key causal variables in a factor-centric research design, or instead seeks to account for specific outcomes as completely as possible in an outcome-centric research design. In the first case, much of the advice given by King and colleagues (1994) on selecting control variables is applicable. In the second case, the very term "control variable" is misleading. (This is the reason I constantly use double quotation marks with the term when referring equally to factor-centric and outcome-centric research designs.) Instead, we are dealing with explanatory variables of equal logical importance, in other words alternative explanations for the observed outcomes.

Most of the research I use to illustrate my points employs large-n methods. From a methodological point of view, though, there is no reason why the lessons drawn should not be applicable to small-n work as well (Dür, Chapter 10). The logical status of control variables depends less on the use of large-n or small-n tools than on the factor-centric versus outcome-centric focus of a research design (see Chapter 1).

The chapter proceeds as follows: In the next section, I discuss the research design problems relevant to my question. I first emphasize the role of theory in guiding the decision on which variables to include and point out the importance of consistency for any theoretical model. Second, I contrast the answers that factor-centric and outcome-centric scholars give to the question of which "control variables" to include in a research design and point out the inherently different logical status of "control variables" under the two approaches. In subsequent sections, I extract practical guidelines for research from the methodological discussion and illustrate these points using work on explaining party unity in legislative voting. I refer to a factor-centric research question about the effect of party size on majority party unity in the US House of Representatives and an outcome-centric attempt to explain levels of party unity in Western parliamentary democracies.

Design problems

The role of theory in guiding the selection of independent variables

The state of theory development provides initial guidance on the selection of independent variables. In well-studied fields, a scholarly consensus has often emerged on the array of relevant variables. Thus the selection of independent variables may be pretty obvious, and the task often is to test rivaling established theories on new data, to apply existing theories to new empirical phenomena, or to derive conditions under which a theory or competing theories hold empirically.

If you add a new independent variable in your particular research project (something often done in PhD work), you cannot simply ignore variables that have been proven to matter in previous research. Instead, these variables have to be dealt with on a theoretical level. You have to argue why your new variables makes an important contribution to our understanding of the studied phenomenon. This may be the case if the new variable is causally prior to the one that is currently used for explaining the phenomenon. In such a case, it is your new variable that explains both the outcome and an intervening variable that is currently considered the cause of the outcome. Therefore a causal explanation has to focus on your variable. Depending on the factor-centric or outcome-centric nature of your research design, these variables may also have to be included in an empirical test of the theoretical model (see below).

Sometimes little prior research may exist with regard to a question so that there is little theoretical guidance on relevant independent variables. In this case, the scholar has to develop his or her own theoretical framework. This does not mean that s/he is completely free in choosing variables. Instead, every decision to study a particular variable has to be defended theoretically with arguments about why and how this variable should affect the dependent variable.[2] Especially scholars in a small-n tradition insist on the importance of spelling out causal mechanisms (George and Bennett, 2005; McKeown, 2004), but more large-n-oriented scholars emphasizing 'causal effects' instead of 'causal mechanisms' also agree that theoretical guidance is essential for valid inferences (King, Keohane and Verba, 1994, ch. 3).

In order to arrive at valid causal inferences, spelling out the causal mechanisms behind your variable(s) of interest is not sufficient. Instead, you have to come up with (ideally) all variables that could affect and possibly bias the effects you are interested in – you have to think about which control variables are relevant to your question. Thus theory remains essential to guide empirical research in less-developed fields as well.

Nevertheless, it may not be recommendable to include all variables that could distort the causal effect under investigation into one theoretical and/or empirical model. The importance of theoretical consistency urges us to use theories cautiously and not to combine them at will. All theories are built on certain fundamental ontological assumptions from which they cannot be detached. For example, a rational choice theory in which actors are allowed to act irrationally is no longer a rational choice theory.[3]

The need for theoretical consistency forces us to be careful when testing rivaling theories in a single empirical model. If these theories are built on fundamentally different assumptions, such tests would not allow us to draw any valid inferences about causal effects and thus would not help us to adjudicate on the relative success of rivaling theories. If, to glance forward to the example in Section 4, a theory explains the voting behavior of parliamentarians as motivated by rational self-interest in the light of different structural incentives, we should not include an independent variable like cultural norms that suggests a different rationale for action (that is, norm-abiding behavior). Such a model could be estimated empirically, but its results could not be interpreted consistently.

What we can do, of course, is to estimate different models for the same dependent variable built on different theories (in the example above one model each built on the assumptions of rational and norm-abiding behavior) and then judge the relative success of the respective theories. Sometimes one researcher will run these competing models herself, but more often these comparative tests are performed by the discipline as a collective enterprise (Laitin, 2002; Lichbach, 1997). Different researchers coming from different theoretical backgrounds study the same phenomenon based on their assumptions, ideally using the same (or at least easily comparable) data. It is then up to each scholar and the discipline as a whole to judge the relative success of these attempts and to recognize certain theories as corroborated and others as falsified or at least severely damaged (De Bièvre, Chapter 11).

The role of theory in guiding variable selection is closely tied to the aim of a specific research project. As two main goals of scientific inquiry we can distinguish between gathering descriptive information and explaining outcomes in the past. I do not deal with description and the problems of descriptive inference here (see the discussion in King, Keohane and Verba, 1994, ch. 2), because this chapter focuses on dependent and independent variables which presupposes the goals of explanation.[4]

A quest for explanation can be either 'factor-centric' or 'outcome-centric'. The distinction and its broader relevance for research design are discussed at length in the introduction to this volume. In this chapter, I show that this distinction is also vital for the decision of which 'control variables' to include.

Indeterminate research designs, omitted variable bias, inefficiency, and the theoretical status of 'control variables' in factor-centric and outcome-centric research designs

The newer literature on research design offers different and at times contradictory advice on which 'control variables' to include. I begin with the factor-centric approach as advocated by King and colleagues (1994) and contrast it with an outcome-centric approach in the causal modeling tradition.

The main rules for selecting independent variables in factor-centric designs are stated clearly in King, Keohane, and Verba's *Designing Social Inquiry* under three headings: The necessity of a determinate research design, the problem of bias introduced by omitting relevant control variables, and the loss of efficiency associated with the inclusion of irrelevant explanatory variables. Before discussing those, it should be pointed out that the factor-centric approach starts from a clearly articulated theory asserting causal effects of one or a few key explanatory variables. *Designing Social Inquiry* is mainly concerned with how to test such theories and does not focus on theory development.[5]

Their first advice is simple: Do not include more independent variables than you have observations (or degrees of freedom, to use the statistical term) and do not use two explanatory variables that are perfectly correlated. In the first case, we cannot make inferences about causal effects, because the observed outcomes are compatible with several different combinations of the independent variables. In the second case, there is no way to determine to which of the two perfectly correlated variables an observed effect should be causally attributed (King, Keohane and Verba, 1994, pp.118–24). This advice is crucial for both factor-centric and outcome-centric research designs.

The main goal of a factor-centric research design is estimating the effect of one or a few independent variables tied to a theoretical model. Accordingly, other independent variables are only included if their omission would result in a bias when estimating the causal effect of the key causal variable(s).[6] These variables are literally *control* variables – in other words, we are not substantively interested in their effects on the dependent variable. Starting from this premise, there are two rules when including a variable as control variable. First, include a control variable if it is correlated with both the dependent variable and the key explanatory variable to avoid 'omitted variable bias'. Second, do not include control variables that are totally or in part a consequence of the key causal variable to avoid problems with endogeneity. Determining the order of causation is seen as a problem to be solved by theoretical argument, not by empirical testing (King, Keohane and Verba, 1994, pp.168–82).

Finally, including additional independent variables increases the uncertainty associated with our estimation of causal effects. Therefore, we should avoid 'irrelevant' control variables not correlated with the dependent variable.[7] If such an irrelevant variable is not correlated to the key causal variable either, it will not hurt our findings (beyond a marginal loss in efficiency due to the estimation of an additional parameter). If such a correlation exists, though, including an irrelevant variable will decrease the efficiency with which we can estimate the causal effect of our key causal variable, even though it will not bias the estimate (King, Keohane and Verba, 1994, pp.182–5).

To clarify the verbal argument, let me display these conditions for including control variables graphically (Figure 9.1). The dependent variable is called Y, the key causal variable X. For reasons of simplicity I display only one key causal variable. Control variables are labeled Z. Variables in solid print have to be included whereas variables in italics are excluded. The relationships, denoted by r, between variables to be included are indicated by solid arrows, the other ones by dashed arrows.

We can distinguish between four types of independent variables that might qualify as control variables depending on their relationship with the dependent variable Y, their relationship with the key causal variable X, and their position in the assumed causal process. In a factor-centric design, only one of those should be included as a control variable, because its omission would bias the estimated causal effect of X on Y. This is the case for Z_1, which is correlated (that is, $r > 0$) with both X and Y and is logically prior to X. If we left out Z_1, some of its explanatory power would be falsely attributed to X.[8] In contrast, the other three

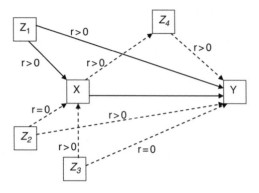

Figure 9.1   Variables to include in a factor-centric approach

types of potential control variables should *not* be included. First, Z_2, while correlated with Y, is not correlated with X. Therefore its omission does not bias the estimate of the effect of X on Y. As Z_2 is not part of the theory to be tested, it is not included in the factor-centric design, even though it would capture additional variance in Y. Second, Z_3 is correlated with X but not with Y. Thus it is an 'irrelevant' control variable. Its inclusion would not bias the estimated causal effect of X on Y but would lead to a loss in efficiency and should thus be avoided. Finally, Z_4 is not included, because it is partly caused by X so that its inclusion would create problems with endogeneity.

For reasons of simplicity I only displayed one key causal variable X. Of course, we can imagine testing a theory with more than one such variable. In this case, several X variables would be included. Still the approach would be factor-centric because other independent variables not covered by the theory and not correlated with the key causal variables would be excluded even if they were correlated with Y. Equally, factor-centric approaches can attempt to test the success of different theories emphasizing different causal variables as long as these theories are compatible with regard to fundamental assumptions (see section below). In this case, X_1, X_2 etc. would refer to causal variables from different theories. Control variables would be included under the same rules, in other words only if they are correlated with both Y and one of the X and are not caused by that X.

Even though control variables are not of substantial interest to factor-centric researchers, one nonetheless has to put effort into their careful selection, operationalization and measurement. Too often, very general variables such as per-capita income, GDP and population size are included in regression models as control variables with little or no argument about why these variables should matter in the first place. Sometimes, the easy availability of data seems to be the main reason why a particular control variable is used. The above discussion makes clear that this kind of 'control' does not in any respect improve the confidence we can have in our estimates. The same is true for variables that are theoretically useful controls but are operationalized and measured inadequately through remote proxies. Of course scarce resources limit our ability to design new measures and collect new data for all relevant control variables; one should nonetheless try to get the best available measures for these variables as well.[9]

Let us now turn to the way outcome-centric designs deal with "control variables". As stated above, the goal of outcome-centric research designs is to account for the variance in the dependent variable the best we can. To achieve this goal, this approach includes all independent variables that improve its ability to account for Y. This is the logic behind path analysis and many structural equation models.

This approach differs from the factor-centric conception in two important ways. First, it would include independent variables correlated with the outcome in order to increase the fit of the model, even if their omission would not bias the other effects in the model. Second, outcome-centric approaches do not distinguish between key causal variables and control variables with a lower status. Instead, all independent variables are of equal logical importance as factors explaining the outcome. Even though some of them may emerge as more powerful predictors and thus as more important in substantive terms, none of them have a superior status in theoretical terms – the very term *control* variables as opposed to *causal* variables is alien to this approach. Again, we can clarify the outcome-centric approach graphically (Figure 9.2).

First of all, you will notice that figure 2 does not distinguish between causal variables denoted by X and control variables denoted by Z, because all independent variables have identical logical status.[10] All of the variables labeled control variables in Figure 1 become causal independent variables in an outcome-centric approach. They are included in the model as long as they are correlated with the dependent variable. Only X_3 is not correlated with Y and is thus not included in the model. The other independent variables are all included, as each makes its own contribution to explaining Y.

Some of the variables in the model (for example, X) are logically prior to other explanatory variables, in this case X_4. Outcome-centric researchers divide the overall causal effect of X into a direct effect and an

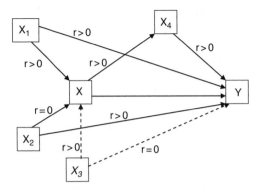

Figure 9.2 Variables to include in an outcome-centric approach

indirect effect mediated via X_4. Therefore, X_4 is also called an intervening variable. Factor-centric scholars would exclude X_4, because it is partly endogenous, that is caused by another variable in the model. Outcome-centric scholars include intervening variables as long as they add explanatory power to the model.[11]

Of course there are also limits on the variables one would include in an outcome-centric design. We would exclude variables that are completely endogenous and variables without theoretical ties to the dependent variable. In addition, the same variable measured at different points in time cannot be included twice in a (not time-series) model, even though this might boost the R^2 of a model. Despite these qualifications, the basic point remains that outcome-centric approaches are much more sympathetic than factor-centric designs to including additional independent variables that contribute to capturing variance in the dependent variable.

Practical guidelines

What practical advice can be given on the question of how to deal with 'control variables'? The following guidelines are derived from the argument in this chapter and, while certainly not exhaustive, should provide some initial guidance. Guidelines 1–5 refer to the role of previous research and theoretical argument in selecting independent variables, whereas Guidelines 6–8 recap advice in the recent methodological literature and emphasize the differences between factor-centric and outcome-centric approaches.

1. Become familiar with the state of research with regard to your research question. You have to know independent variables found to be important in previous studies.
2. Discuss these variables theoretically and place any new variable in this context. Point out what additional insights the new variable can create and which gaps it will fill.
3. Consider which other variables could interfere with the causal effects in which you are interested, even if these variables are not currently discussed in the relevant literature.
4. Spell out the assumed causal mechanisms behind all independent variables. If original authors are not explicit in this respect, try to create as good an argument as possible on why and how their variables should be causal.
5. Spell out the ontological assumptions behind all causal effects you consider. Do not include variables in one model that are based on irreconcilable assumptions, otherwise you cannot sensibly interpret any empirical results. If you want to test theories with such incompatible assumptions, estimate separate models and compare the success of these models in explaining the dependent variable.
6. Make sure your research design is determinate, that is, it does not contain more independent variables than observations and does not contain perfectly collinear independent variables (King, Keohane and Verba, 1994, pp.118–24).
7. Be clear about whether your research design is factor-centric, trying to estimate one or a small number of well-specified, theoretically derived causal effects, or outcome-centric, attempting to capture as much of the variance in the dependent variable as possible.

   7a. If your research design is factor-centric, follow the advice by King, Keohane and Verba, (1994, pp.168–82) and only include those control variables whose omission could bias the estimates with regard to your key causal variable(s). That is, include control variables that are not logically subsequent to your key causal variable and are correlated with it and the dependent variable. Do not include control variables that are not correlated with your key causal variable and do not include control variables that are totally or in part caused by your key causal variable.

   7b. If your research design is outcome-centric, include all theoretically relevant independent variables that allow you to capture additional variance in the dependent variable as long as all of them can be integrated in a consistent theoretical model (see

Guideline 5). Realize that all of these independent variables have the same logical status; none of them is 'merely' a control variable.

8. Put effort into the operationalization and measurement of your control variables. Theoretically and/or operationally flawed control variables do not help substantiate the validity of your causal claims.

Application

After pointing out the importance of theory in the process of selecting independent variables and discussing the different advice given by factor-centric and outcome-centric scholars, I now demonstrate how these general lessons work out in practical research. To illustrate my points, I use research on explaining party unity in legislative voting. Using the same dependent variable and the same large-n analytical tools in both examples demonstrates how the decision on which independent variables to include is affected by the factor-centric versus outcome-centric nature of the research design. After a short discussion of the general relevance of the topic, I illustrate the factor-centric logic in analyzing the relationship between party size and party unity in the US House of Representatives (Cooper and Sieberer, n.d.; Dion, 1997). As an example of an outcome-centric approach, I discuss party unity in Western parliamentary democracies (Sieberer, 2006). I also emphasize the different amount of guidance available from theoretically more or less advanced fields and discuss the importance of ensuring the theoretical consistency of a model.

The state of theory with regard to explaining party unity in legislative voting

Any analysis of legislative decision making has to answer the question of who should be treated as the fundamental actors in these processes. In constitutional theory, the answer is clear: Members of parliament are free in their decision, only responsible to their conscience and ultimately their voters when election-time approaches. In practice, political parties play an important role as actors in parliamentary decision making, especially in parliamentary democracies where we observe high levels of party unity. In fact, the literature often simply assumes that parties behave as unitary actors when analyzing both government formation and legislative decision making (see, for example, Laver and Schofield, 1998; Tsebelis, 2002). Party specialists, on the other hand, emphasize the heterogeneity of interests within modern political parties (Katz and Mair, 1992). Given this heterogeneity, party unity cannot be assumed to develop naturally but the question emerges as to what makes deputies toe the party line in legislative voting.

The state of research on this question varies greatly between legislatures. While legislative voting behavior has been a central topic of research on the US Congress for decades (see overviews in Collie, 1985; Polsby and Schickler, 2002) and has received increased attention in the presidential systems of Latin America (Carey, 2003; Morgenstern, 2004), far less research exists for the parliamentary countries of Europe. Comparative studies of party unity in legislative voting are rare and mainly focus on differences between parliamentary and presidential systems. As the topic received much more attention in the US than in the European context, it is hardly surprising that the state of theoretical argument is far more advanced in the former.

In the American literature, a vivid debate is raging on the question of whether the concept of party is relevant at all for explaining voting behavior in Congress. Krehbiel argues that legislative voting is determined solely by individual preferences of Congressmen and that distinct party effects, if they existed at all, could not be separated from preference effects. Therefore, in Krehbiel's view, it is impossible to assess whether observed levels of party unity result from equal preferences among party members ('cohesion') or from pressure exerted by the party leadership ('discipline'). For Krehbiel, the concept of party thus has no explanatory power (Krehbiel, 2000).

Other scholars do not deny the importance of individual preferences for legislative voting, but insist that parties exert independent influence on how their members behave in Congress. Cox and McCubbins (1993, 2005) as well as Aldrich (1995) conceptualize Congress as being organized in a partisan fashion. This allows members to realize benefits of cooperation, both with regard to policy decisions and to electoral prospects, which would not be available in an unstructured setting. These benefits make it rational for members to give up some freedom in how to vote. The extent to which members of Congress are willing to delegate authority to their parties is not stable, though. Instead, it depends on the degree of policy consensus within the party and on the polarization between parties (Aldrich and Rohde, 2000; Cooper and Brady, 1981; Cooper and Young, 2002).

What unites both sides of the debate is the recognition that the determinants of legislative voting are worth studying and which variables (individual preferences of legislators, organizational resources of party leaders such as agenda control rights, preference homogeneity within parties, polarization between the parties, etc.) could be relevant.

Accordingly, recent studies are not concerned with exploring large numbers of potential causes for party unity, but focus on testing competing theories or investigating the impact of specific, thus far understudied variables. In other words, research mainly proceeds in factor-centric designs.[12] I will discuss the relationship between party size and party unity as one example of such research below.

In parliamentary systems, available research is far less developed. Even though several country studies exist, often focusing on periods of observed disunity, our knowledge on what explains differences in party unity both between countries and within countries over time is very limited. Case studies point to a large number of potentially relevant variables, but we simply do not know whether these claims are valid beyond the context in which they were originally advanced. In addition, the literature is divided with regard to fundamental assumptions on the kind of variables relevant for explaining party unity. The institutional approach claims that party unity should be understood as aggregated individual voting behavior determined mainly by deputies' preferences under given institutional incentives and constraints. The sociological approach, on the other hand, mainly relies on variables such as party culture, socialization of deputies as well as shared norms and values, and argues mostly on the aggregate level (Hazan, 2003).

Research on party unity in European democracies thus varies in two important respects from research on Congress. First, there is little agreement on which independent variables are relevant and should be included in research. Instead, especially comparative work starts out from a rather unconnected and theoretically diverse array of hypotheses. Second, there is no shared overarching theoretical paradigm. Instead, explanations using very different assumptions exist which cannot easily be combined in one theoretical framework. Therefore research on party unity in the parliamentary systems of Europe is currently mainly done in an outcome-centric fashion. This approach seems reasonable because the main challenge is to develop an understanding of which variables are relevant at all, before a more narrow focus on these variables seems fruitful.

Factor-centric design: assessing the impact of party size on party unity in the US House of Representatives

Research on legislative voting in the US Congress today is mainly factor-centric. Surprisingly, party size has been largely ignored as a factor in explaining levels of party unity, even though we may expect a negative relationship because: (1) larger parties are likely to be less cohesive with regard to the preferences of their members and (2) the leadership of larger parties may be more inclined to tolerate a certain amount of defection that will not harm its chances of winning votes. Claims expecting this relationship have only recently been taken up again by Dion (1997) as one step in a more complex argument about the conditions of rules changes in Congress. Dion's goal is to establish a negative relationship between size and party unity during the nineteenth century, not explaining party unity per se. He tests for this relationship using a GLS regression model including several control variables, because he realizes that a simple bivariate test may suffer from omitted variable bias. He finds that the negative effect of party size on unity remains unchanged when controlling for the turnover of legislators and divided government. In addition, Dion introduces several dummy variables for specific Congresses or time periods that are outliers in the original models. The interpretation of these dummy variables is indicative of the factor-centric design: Even though he finds unity to be significantly different in particular Congresses (the thirty-first, the thirty-second) and time periods (the Speakership of Thomas Reed, 1889–91 and 1895–99), Dion does not pay much attention to these findings. All he is interested in is the fact that the negative relationship between party size and party unity remains significant after controlling for these extraordinary periods.

Despite their merits, Dion's tests are limited both in terms of the time period covered and the measures used. It is therefore worthwhile to reanalyze this relationship for the US House of Representatives over an extended period of time ranging from 1869 to 2005 (Cooper and Sieberer, n.d.).[13]

Here the focus is less on our empirical results and more on the variables we included. We calculated separate scores for party unity, our dependent variable, depending on whether majorities of both parties opposed each other ('party vote') or agreed ('bipartisan vote') on a vote. The reason for this distinction is that the causal mechanism behind the expected relationship is based on the ability to win votes and possibly divide a fixed price among as few winners as possible (see Riker, 1962 whose work inspired the early studies on the topic). This logic only applies for votes that divide the parties, that is, for which we can meaningfully speak of winners and losers. Using all votes in calculating unity scores – as Dion does – decreases the value of our evidence for testing a hypothesis based on a specific causal mechanism. For the same reason, we distinguish between the majority party and the minority party, because arguments about winning are mostly relevant for the majority.

Our key causal variable of interest is party size. In line with Dion's purpose, we do not aim at explaining observed levels of unity but want to test whether the size of the majority party has any effect on its unity. Thus our research question is clearly framed in a factor-centric way. A simple bivariate test shows a weak correlation of $r = -0.212$ between majority party size and majority party unity, which is only significant at the 10 percent level. In a simple regression using robust standard errors, the coefficient of majority party size is negative and significant at the 5 percent level.[14] We cannot be sure, though, that the effect is indeed present unless we control for other factors that might bias our results. Two possibilities come to mind.

First, the effect may vary over time and may be present only for certain periods. To test this, we include dummy variables for the different party systems identified in the literature (Aldrich and Niemi, 1996) and interaction terms of these period dummies with majority party size in a multiple regression model. From these models we learn that the negative relationship is only significant during the current party system starting in 1969 ($b = -0.895$, significant at the 1 percent level). During all other periods, the coefficient is statistically indiscernible from zero and even has a positive sign for the periods 1897–1932 and 1933–68. So we have to introduce a first qualification to the bivariate finding: Dion's hypothesis only holds for the period since 1969.

Second, the effect ascribed to majority party size may indeed result from omitted variable bias. As authors like Krehbiel would argue, differences in majority party unity may be better explained by ideological polarization of the parties (higher polarization boosting unity) than by size. Polarization is correlated with both majority party size ($r = -0.14$) and majority party unity ($r = 0.581$) and it is not caused by party size.[15] Therefore it has to be included as a control variable following the rules for factor-centric designs. We can test this claim by controlling for polarization in a multiple regression model.[16] The resulting models reveal that the negative effect of majority party size on majority party unity disappears almost completely when we control for polarization. It becomes statistically insignificant both in the model extending over the entire period and in all four interactive models controlling for differences between party systems. So the weak negative effect we originally found does not hold. As there are some problems with the measure we use for polarization based on the NOMINATE scores (Cooper and Young, 2002), we hesitate to reject Dion's hypothesis completely, but at least we have reasons for serious doubt.

Let me note some general points about the status of control variables in this factor-centric research design. First, we start out from a specific causal hypothesis advanced in the theoretical literature and want to test it empirically.[17] Second, due to this theoretical focus, we are not interested in differences in party unity over time. Thus we do not attach any importance to the finding that the dummy for the fourth party system (1897–1932) is positive and highly significant indicating that party unity was generally higher during this time. This result, well in line with what we know about this era of party government (Cooper and Brady, 1981), would be very interesting for an outcome-centric approach trying to explain levels of party unity in general, but does not concern us here. The only important finding with regard to our argument is that the effect of size on majority unity disappears for three of the four time periods under investigation. Equally, we are not pursuing the role of polarization as an explanation of party unity even though we find a strong and highly significant effect. Our goal is to test whether there is an effect of size on unity, so finding there is none after controlling for a variable whose omission could have biased our results is all we wanted.

Outcome-centric design: explaining party unity in parliamentary democracies

Now consider an outcome-centric approach with regard to the same dependent variable moving from the well-studied US Congress to the parliamentary systems of Western Europe and the Anglo-Saxon countries (Sieberer, 2006). Given the less advanced state of knowledge with regard to this question, my study is framed in a more exploratory style to determine which variables deserve more detailed theoretical and empirical attention. Accordingly, I tried to integrate a larger number of potential causal variables in a consistent model.[18] Nonetheless, I take the requirement to construct internally consistent theories seriously. Therefore I only included independent variables that can be analyzed in a consistent theoretical framework using a unified set of assumptions. As indicated above, there are two main approaches to explaining party unity in parliamentary systems, one sociological, arguing on the basis of socialization and shared norms, the other institutional, looking at incentives and constraints on rational individual actors. Simply combining variables from both approaches would lead to a model in which actions would have to be at the same time determined by normatively driven, rule-abiding behavior and individual utility maximization. Such a model would be internally inconsistent and thus could not be interpreted in a meaningful way even if it was to capture statistically most of the variance in Y.[19] Therefore I choose to limit my exploration to the latter approach, assuming individually rational behavior constrained by a given set of institutional incentives.

Given this restriction, I looked at the (limited) literature available on the topic, mainly studies of individual parliaments (for country studies especially: Depauw, 1999; Rasch, 1999; Saalfeld, 1995; as one of very few comparative studies: Carey, 2007). The various hypotheses advanced in these studies were then combined in a model which explains party unity as the result of individual choices by deputies trying to reach their goals of re-election, and beyond that personal advancement and policy influence. The degree to which deputies toe the party line depends on the ways by which they can reach these goals. If the goals are attainable only via the party leadership, unity should be higher than in situations in which alternative routes are available. The model spells out three groups of variables relevant for the question of whether deputies can reach their goals only through their party. These groups of variables go under the headings: (1) centralized party control on the electoral stage; (2) structural dependencies of deputies with regard to parliamentary business; and (3) situational distribution of time-specific resources in parliament. Under each heading I discuss a rather heterogeneous array of variables.[20]

There are several points to notice with the choice of independent variables. First, all of these variables have the same *a priori* logical status – there is no distinction between causal variables and control variables. Instead, one result of the empirical analysis should be indications on which independent variables are most important and deserve more detailed study. Second, the goal of such an exploratory analysis is moving towards capturing a sizeable amount of the variance in Y by considering all potential explanatory variables in a theoretically consistent model. If I found only non-effects, I would not have stopped there but thought about which additional variables could improve the fit of the model. Keep in mind, though, that theoretical consistency is a *conditio sine qua non*. Therefore we have to spell out the causal mechanisms we assume to be at work behind an observed correlation and ensure their compatibility with each other. Thus an outcome-centric attempt of improving model fit should not be equated with mere data mining.

Third, there are connections between the variables in the model that would be considered problematic from a factor-centric perspective due to endogeneity. For example, the ability of party leadership to discipline a deputy in parliament with the use of sanctions (a variable from the second group) partly depends on central party control over candidate (re-)nomination for future elections (a variable from the first group).

A factor-centric design would probably only include nomination procedures and leave out sanctions by the party leadership as endogenous
results of nomination procedures. In an outcome-centric approach,
though, I use both variables because sanctions in parliament comprise
other elements beyond the threat of not renominating a deputy.

Conclusion

Choosing which independent variables to include in a study is a ubiquitous problem in designing research. It is obvious that only looking at
bivariate relationships and not considering any other variables is likely
to lead to biased findings. Unfortunately, the question of which additional variables must be included to make a study methodologically
good social science is harder to answer. King and colleagues (1994) offer
valuable advice for factor-centric research designs aiming at testing a
well-developed theory (or maybe several such theories) and avoiding
biased inferences with regard to one or several causal effects. Their
advice, though, does not equally apply to outcome-centric studies that
are more exploratory in nature and try to account for the variance in a
dependent variable as well as possible.

In offering some guidance on the selection of 'control variables', I first
emphasized the importance of theory. Second, I suggested that we
should only include variables compatible with regard to the fundamental assumptions behind the assumed causal mechanisms in one single
model. Third, I discussed the different answers which factor-centric and
outcome-centric approaches give to the question of which independent
variables to include. Fourth, I emphasized the different logical status of
'control variables' under factor-centric and outcome-centric designs.
These methodological points and the trade-offs involved in choosing
one approach over another were illustrated by research on the causes of
party unity in legislative voting. The example from the US House of
Representatives represents a factor-centric approach in a theoretically
and empirically well-developed field. The example from parliamentary democracies illustrates the outcome-centric logic in exploratory
research, which tries to provide a first glance at an emerging topic and
to single out variables that deserve more detailed theoretical and empirical attention.

The discussion in this chapter shows that the question of which
independent variables to include in a research project should be made
with an eye on both the theoretical discussion in the field and the fundamental nature of the research question to be answered. While the

process of selecting independent variables is still likely to bring about difficult decisions open to dispute, considering the points raised in this chapter should offer some guidance.

Notes

1. In experimental studies, proper randomization solves this problem, as all other variables except the one that is experimentally manipulated are uncorrelated.
2. In my view, a theoretical argument about causal mechanisms is the best we can do to deal with the ubiquitous problem that correlation between two variables is not the same as causation.
3. 'Irrational' in this context means deliberately acting against their recognized interests whatever those may be. It does not mean acting in the pursuit of strictly egoistic interests; see Scharpf, 1997, pp. 84–9 and Geddes, 2003, pp. 179–82.
4. Predicting future outcomes is a third goal of scientific inquiry, even though many political scientists (election forecasters being a notable exception) tend to be cautious or outright sceptical about their ability to predict future events. Prediction depends on our ability to account for variance in the dependent variable to the highest degree possible. Thus, the points about outcome-centric research designs also apply to research aiming at prediction.
5. This focus has repeatedly been criticized, e.g. McKeown, 2004; Ragin, 2004; Rogowski, 2004.
6. A note on terminology: In their general discussion of causality King, Keohane and Verba use the term 'explanatory variables' instead of independent variables and divide this category into 'key causal variables' (variables whose causal effects are under investigation) and 'control variables' (those variables that are only introduced to avoid bias in estimating key causal effects but are not of any substantive interest for the theory to be tested). In later parts of the book, they sometimes use the terms 'explanatory variable' and 'key causal variable' interchangeably. I stick to the distinction between the two types of explanatory variables throughout the discussion.
7. While King, Keohane and Verba mainly rely on factor-centric designs, they briefly mention that their rules for including control variables do not apply when the goal of a research design is forecasting, which requires capturing as much of the variance in the dependent variable as possible. In this case, additional independent variables correlated with the outcome should be included even if they were irrelevant according to the factor-centric rules (King, Keohane and Verba 1994, p.169 fn.8).
8. The logic of course also applies to relationships with $r < 0$.
9. Often a variable one wants to use as a control is the main variable of interest in another study so that sophisticated measures and good data are actually available in the literature.
10. I still label one variable as X without subscript analogous to Figure 9.1 to show that the arrangement of variables is the same in both figures.

11. In Figure 9.2, for example, X_4 would only be eliminated from the model if X and X_4 were perfectly correlated. Thus, we are back to King, Keohane and Verba warning us not to include perfectly collinear variables.

12. Earlier work in the 1960s and 1970s was more outcome-centric, trying to integrate a larger variety of explanatory variables in one explanatory framework of legislative behavior (see Collie, 1985; Kingdon, 1977).

13. The data we use are party unity scores for each House from 1869 to 2005 which adds up to a total of 69 observations. The factor-centric analysis discussed here is only one part of the original paper which also investigates the importance of party size for explaining legislative victories of the majority party and studies the Senate along with the House. The data was compiled by Garry Young and is available at: http://home.gwu.edu/%7Eyoungg/research/index.html [July 18, 2007].

14. When we follow Dion in including dummy variables for outliers, party size narrowly fails to achieve the 5 percent threshold.

15. Party size and polarization result from the same decisions by voters on Election Day so neither can be caused by the other.

16. Polarization is measured as the distance between the two party medians on the first dimension DW-NOMINATE scores (Poole and Rosenthal, 1997). The data is taken from Keith Poole's homepage at: www.voteview.com [Feb. 27, 2006].

17. In the original paper, we discuss the causal mechanisms behind this hypothesis in greater detail.

18. One could also imagine studying a thus far ill-studied field in a factor-centric fashion focusing on a single factor deemed important. I suggest that this is rarely done in practice, though, because it is often simply not apparent which factor would be of particular theoretical interest.

19. Critics might object that actors are in fact motivated by both rational utility maximization and norms of appropriateness. This is probably true as an ontological statement. Nevertheless, combining variables based on both assumptions in one *model* is problematic if we cannot explicitly model the connection between these motivations or the conditions under which one or the other is dominant.

20. Just to give an example, structural dependencies include the right to initiate bills, staff resources, recall of committee members, influence of the parliamentary party leadership on the selection of cabinet ministers, and the strength of parliamentary committees. While all these variables can be conceptualized as providing incentives for party unity, they are rather diverse compared to the very limited number of well-specified causal variables investigated in a typical factor-centric design.

10
Discriminating among Rival Explanations: Some Tools for Small-n Researchers

Andreas Dür

Introduction

For most real world occurrences, several distinct explanations can be thought of relatively easily.[1] Even for rather understudied events or novel developments, the general social scientific literature, historical accounts and claims by participants can furnish a series of competing hypotheses. Unless one account is privileged by really incontrovertible evidence, such as the often-cited 'smoking gun', discriminating among these potential explanations is tricky. An explanation of an event or series of events, however, will only be convincing to other researchers to the extent that a study manages to establish the superiority of one over all other accounts. The problem for research is thus one of making credible that a specific cause or several causes rather than alternative causes can explain an outcome. In this chapter, I set out some tools that should help researchers achieve just this objective when confronted with rival (middle-range) theories in their research projects.

The solutions suggested in this chapter are relevant for all research of a small-n (and often also of a large-n) nature. They are, however, especially crucial for researchers who seek to explain specific outcomes ('outcome-centric' research design; see Chapter 1) rather than examine the size of causal effects ('factor-centric' research design). Although often neglected in standard treatments of research design in political science (King, Keohane and Verba, 1994), outcome-centric research is extremely widespread and has made significant contributions to the political science literature (Chima, 2005; Mahoney and Goertz, 2006). As compared to cross-case analyses, the main aim of outcome-centric research is not to make inferences from a sample to a universe. Rather, its objective is to establish the causal mechanisms that brought about one or several specific events, and thus to provide internally valid explanations for specific political or social phenomena. Since the causal mechanisms identified are not directly observable, confirming their existence satisfies Imre Lakatos's (1974) criterion for fruitful scientific research: The studies provide insights that go beyond what can be observed directly. Furthermore, context-aware generalizations are also often possible based on such studies, allowing for a contribution to theories that have validity beyond the specific case(s) analyzed (Chima, 2005; George and Bennett, 2005).

As I show in the next section, outcome-centric research confronts similar problems to other types of research, among them omitted variable bias, explanatory overdeterminacy, and indeterminacy. What is particular about this specific type of research is that the number of cases that are looked at generally tends to be small, while the number of variables that possibly have an influence on outcomes is large. In such a situation, the problem of indeterminacy, which arises when several interpretations are consistent with the same data, inhibits inference in cross-case analyses. In addition, since case selection in outcome-centric research is largely predetermined by the substantive interest of specific cases, choosing cases that allow for keeping constant and thus controlling for some variables is hardly possible. To still attain interpretable findings, researchers have to apply specific methods that help them effectively deal with rival theories. Among the tools are: Uncovering logical inconsistencies in alternative explanations, increasing the number of observable implications of their own and rival theories, examining causal mechanisms through process-tracing, and selecting additional 'most likely' or 'least likely' cases. In the central part of this chapter, I elaborate on these recommendations and sketch out their strengths and weaknesses.

I then use studies that aim at explaining trade liberalization to illustrate how the various suggestions can be applied to practical research. This field of research is particularly propitious for my purpose, as a large number of different explanations for liberalization exist. Among the more important explanatory variables mentioned in the literature are (in no specific order) the spread of a liberal ideology (or at least a belief in the dangers of protectionism), domestic institutional changes such as the extension of suffrage and democratization, the establishment of an international institution, changes in the distribution of power in the international system, the political mobilization of exporters, changes in the composition of trade flows, the increasing importance of scale economies, the internationalization of production, an upward swing in the business cycle, macroeconomic crises, and changes in domestic coalitions. This (still not comprehensive) list of variables shows that many explanations of trade liberalization exist that all have some *a priori* plausibility. I show that researchers in this field have applied several of the chapter's suggestions to exclude some of the rival explanations when studying a specific case or a series of cases of trade liberalization. I conclude the chapter with some more general recommendations that may facilitate the work of outcome-centric researchers.

Design problem

Due to the complexity of the social world that we inhabit, in many cases several theories plausibly explain the same outcome. In such a case of equifinality, two (or more) factors, which in the following I denominate a and b, may both bring about a result y ($a{\to}y$ and $b{\to}y$, where $\to$ denotes causality). The existence of rival explanations of an event frequently gives rise to at least one of three related methodological problems, namely omitted variable bias, explanatory overdeterminacy, and indeterminacy.

Omitted variable bias

If a researcher simply disregards rival explanations, arguing that $a{\to}y$, whereby completely ignoring the possibility of $b{\to}y$, the results found can suffer from omitted variable bias. It is possible that a researcher can already provide some plausibility for a theoretical argument by simply mustering empirical observations that support her view (for example, by establishing a correlation). Yet, in many cases the results found are not convincing to other scholars with different *a priori* beliefs. For researchers interested in measuring causal effects, the omission of rival variables is likely to cause an overestimation of the effect of a specific variable on another. The effects of omitted variable bias are even worse for researchers explaining specific outcomes, with the results obtained possibly being completely spurious. In such a case of erroneous inference, a researcher may attribute causal importance to a variable that actually has no impact at all.

Explanatory overdeterminacy

Alternatively, a researcher may opt to include more than one variable into a single model to explain an outcome (e.g., a & $b{\to}y$). The resulting

problem could be denominated as one of 'explanatory overdeterminacy', meaning the superposition of many possibilities in one explanation, without ordering of importance. In such a situation, multiple
(theoretically) sufficient causes are included in a single explanation,
with the researcher failing to determine whether a specific factor did
really contribute to the outcome. This is an unsatisfactory approach for
all researchers accepting the basic premise that the aim of social research
should be to uncover causal relations and *explain* social reality rather
than provide encyclopedic overviews, even if this requires some degree
of simplification.

It could be that a specific event is actually overdetermined in the sense
that it is simultaneously brought about through different causal pathways (alternative causes of an effect are present) and that the various
causal factors are of equal relevance. An example for genuine overdetermination often referred to in the literature is a firing squad that overde-
termines the death of a man (Mackie, 1980: 44). In this example, the
bullets of two soldiers simultaneously hit a deserter in the heart, with
each bullet being sufficient cause for the man's death. Thus $P(Y|ab) =
P(Y|a) = P(Y|b)$; that is, the probability of death does not increase when
both bullets hit the heart as compared to only one bullet doing so. In
such an ideal-typical case, 'even a detailed causal story fails to discriminate between the rival candidates for the role of cause, we cannot say
that one rather than the other was necessary in the circumstances for
the effect *as it came about*' (Mackie, 1980, p. 47; emphasis in original).

It appears to me, however, that in the social world actual overdetermination (in contrast to explanatory overdetermination as set out above) is
hardly relevant.[2] Three arguments support this judgment: First, in many
cases sufficiently precise measurement may allow a researcher to determine which of the different causal pathways was actually completed. It is
hardly plausible, for example, that in the case given above the two bullets hit the heart of the deserter exactly at the same time. If one hit first,
two sufficient causes were present but only one did become causally relevant: the second bullet is only a pre-empted potential cause. The first
bullet was a necessary condition for the event to come about exactly as it
did, although not for the effect as such (Bunzl, 1979, p. 137). The task of
a researcher then is to determine which of several competing causal
chains was completed. When explaining the outbreak of World War I,
the competition over access to resources in Africa may have been a sufficient condition for war. Nevertheless, a study may conclude that the conflict over the Balkans, sparked by the shooting of the Austrian Archduke
Franz Ferdinand in Sarajevo in June 1914, was the actual cause of the war.

Moreover, it may be the case that the supposed second cause is only a consequence of the other explanatory variable ($a{\rightarrow}b{\rightarrow}y$). In this case, as long as we are interested in the 'deep causes' of events, we can neglect b as an explanatory factor. A researcher may argue that both ideas and material conditions brought about a specific event. Yet, policymakers may actually hold a specific set of ideas as a result of being exposed to specific material conditions. In this setting, material conditions cause the event, with ideas only being epiphenomena. A similar logic applies if a simultaneously causes b and y. In the example just mentioned, material conditions may cause certain events directly, and at the same time, independent of this effect, material conditions may also cause the spread of certain ideas among policymakers. In either case, rather than conceding overdetermination, research can uncover the actual causes of an event.

At last, assuming a probabilistic world (and thus going away from the idea of sufficient causes), each of two factors a and b – occurring independently – may bring about a specific event with a certain probability, p_i with $i \in \{a,b\}<1$. When both factors are present at the same time, however, the probability of the event occurring may be higher than if only one factor is present. Take as an example two switches, which switch on a light with probability p_a and p_b respectively. Now moving both switches increases the probability of light being turned on ($P = \Sigma p_i$) as compared to moving only one switch. Thus, $P(Y|ab)>P(Y|a)$ and $P(Y|ab)>P(Y|b)$; that is, the probability of an event occurring is higher if both causes are present than if only one cause is present. Again, the researcher's aim would be to uncover this logic rather than to argue that this is a case of genuine overdeterminacy.

In all these scenarios, the aim of social research should be to limit the explanation of an event to actually relevant variables, excluding spurious ones. By making this statement, I do not want to argue a case for mono-causal explanations, which privilege a single explanatory variable. Multiple causation may actually abound in the social world. I think, however, that large-n researchers are more frequently confronted with a situation in which any specific variable included in a regression only explains a small part of the variance in the sample than small-n researchers. When dealing with a specific case only (or a few cases), it seems less plausible that several (for example, more than five) different causal factors have a genuine and non-negligible impact on the outcome to be explained (although there may be many factors that have some minor impact). I thus stand up for attempts at reducing at least some of the complexity of the world and at avoiding explanatory overdetermination. Some degree of simplification is also necessary to derive more general lessons from the specific case(s) analyzed (Bromley, 1986, pp. 290–1).[3] In short, neither the omission of variables nor the merging of too many variables in one model is an attractive option for researchers.

Indeterminacy

Instead, a researcher should deal with rival explanations by way of what can be called the discriminative approach. Following this approach, the researcher tries to find the few factors that are important for an explanation of an outcome. Yet, when doing so she is likely to encounter the problems of indeterminacy (King, Keohane and Verba, 1994, pp. 118–24) and lack of 'interpretable' findings and inferences (Brady, Collier and Seawright, 2004, p. 238). These problems arise when the number of observations does not provide the researcher with leverage to adjudicate among the many rival hypotheses (King, Keohane and Verba, 1994, p. 119). In this situation, several interpretations are compatible with the data since the researcher lacks enough degrees of freedom to estimate all unknowns. To avoid this problem, the number of observations must be at least as large as the number of unknowns. A determinate research design thus is defined as one with a sufficient number of observations to estimate each parameter of interest (Lehnert, Chapter 4). A researcher can also fail to achieve this objective if two or more explanatory variables are very highly correlated with each other, a problem known as multicollinearity. In this situation, the question whether $a{\to}y$ or $b{\to}y$ cannot be teased out since a and b appear in pairs in all cases under investigation. In both scenarios, little can be learned from the research project. In the words of Gary King, Robert Keohane and Sidney Verba, 'No amount of description, regardless of how thick and detailed; no method, regardless of how clever; and no researcher, regardless of how skilful, can extract much about any of the causal hypotheses with an indeterminate research design' (King, Keohane and Verba, 1994, p. 120).

Summarizing the argument thus far, researchers must consider rival explanations before establishing causal relations. This applies independent of whether large-n researchers try to establish the 'mean effect' of a variable or small-n (Sieberer, Chapter 9) scholars try to explain particular events. Doing so, however, is particularly tricky for outcome-centric researchers because of the combination of two obstacles in their work: Limits on the number of cases included in their analyses and the fact that case selection is often driven by substantive interest rather than the need to keep constant some variables as suggested for example by Mill's methods of comparison (for these methods, see Leuffen; Chapter 8).[4] The following section discusses some strategies that outcome-centric researchers may employ to still come up with interpretable findings.

Practical guidelines

The rejection of alternative explanations is thus an essential step in any attempt at demonstrating the plausibility of a hypothesis. Only by discarding alternative explanations can a researcher establish the internal validity of her research finding, meaning that the postulated cause-effect relationship is really at work in a specific case. But how can this be done in practice? My response to this question starts from the premise that the researcher has already formulated a hypothesis, which she thinks best explains the case(s) under study given the initial evidence collected. In addition, she has clearly established which rival hypotheses are incompatible with her theory (and which may be compatible). This step of theory construction is extremely crucial in the development of a research project, but dealing with it here would exceed the scope of the present chapter. Based on this premise, I propose a series of steps that outcome-centric researchers may consider to achieve interpretable results.[5] I suggest that especially the first three of these suggestions should be considered in all research projects.

Observe as many implications of your own theory and alternative theories as possible. By making additional observations, a researcher may be able to avoid the problems of indeterminacy and multicollinearity as set out above (Campbell, 1975, pp. 181–2). The extra implications looked at may be exogenous to the actual case(s) under study. For example, while predicting y, a theory may also necessarily imply z. Research that demonstrates that z is not present then can cast serious doubt on the explanatory power of the theory. Mostly, however, further observations will be made within the case, by studying subparts of a case. The technique generally used to do so is known as process-tracing (George and Bennett, 2005, chr 10; George and McKeown, 1985, pp. 34–41). Process-tracing 'attempts to uncover what stimuli the actors attend to; the decision process that makes use of these stimuli to arrive at decisions; the actual behavior that then occurs; the effect of various institutional arrangements on attention, processing, and behavior; and the effect of other variables of interest on attention, processing, and behavior' (George and McKeown, 1985, p. 35). Using this technique, even if two theories predict the same result, and the explanatory variables are perfectly correlated, discriminating among them is possible as long as the intermediary steps needed for the two causal arguments are different (a→f→y; b→g→y).

While process-tracing can overcome the degrees-of-freedom problem, and also helps resolve the 'black box' problem from which most studies based on correlations suffer (Goldthorpe, 1997), it is not without drawbacks. For example, since all measurement has a certain probability of error, the more causal steps are distinguished while tracing a process (the more independent measurement operations have to be carried out), the more likely it becomes that a researcher rejects a theory (either her own or an alternative one) as a result of measurement error that arises from misperception or imperfect measurement tools. Consequently, if many small causal steps are analyzed, and on only one of these the researcher manages to reject a rival theory, this rejection is likely to be barely convincing to other scholars. Moreover, there is a resource limit to studying smaller and smaller steps. For empirical scrutiny, therefore, only those steps are interesting on which the predictions of rival theories differ rather starkly.

Even if some evidence is not inconsistent with a rival theory, that theory's plausibility may still suffer if it cannot provide a rationale for the observation of this evidence. Most scholars would agree that the more data a theory explains, the better (*ceteris paribus*). Often, therefore, by listing evidence that is consistent with, and predicted by one's own theory, but unexplainable from the framework of the rival theory, a researcher can undermine the plausibility of that theory. The idea underlying this reasoning is that there is a causal chain that determines most characteristics or features of a specific event. If a theory cannot explain some of these features, it loses some of its plausibility, even in the case that the evidence does not contradict it directly. Carried out this way, process-tracing is likely to reduce the number of alternative theories that may account for a phenomenon; however, it does not necessarily leave only one theory.

Improve your theory.   Improving her own theory gives a researcher more leverage over a research question and helps her tackle alternative theories more effectively. Theories are often underspecified; they do not specify all the steps that are relevant for a causal mechanism. Resolving this problem can help researchers deal with rival theories by outlining multiple observable implications of the theory. As put by King, Keohane and Verba: 'If properly specified ... our theory may have many observable implications and our data, especially if qualitative, may usually contain observations for many of these implications' (King, Keohane and Verba, 1994, pp. 120–1). Especially propitious in this regard appears the drawing out of a causal mechanism of the form a→f→y. In this case, by specifying a theory more precisely a researcher may be able to add a new set of observations measured at a different level of analysis. This then allows for the use of the technique of process-tracing as mentioned above and the search for causal-process observations (Brady, Collier and Seawright, 2004, 256–8).

Nevertheless, this strategy is only successful if two theories differ in their predictions with respect to the intermediary step. Thus, deriving trivial intermediary steps does not help a researcher in the task of discriminating among rival theories. In addition, when adding such intermediary steps to a causal chain, it is important to state whether the earlier events are sufficient or only necessary conditions for the intermediary steps (Goertz and Levy, 2004, 22–7). This makes a big difference: Imagine that *a* is only a necessary condition for *f*. In this case, the link between *a* and *y* becomes conditional upon the presence of *f*. In contrast, if the links between *a, f*, and *y* are of a sufficient kind, *y* should be observable whenever *a* is present. In any case, the suggestion of improving one's theory should not imply a redesign with the sole purpose of making the theory more testable.

Scrutinize and specify rival theories.   A precise analysis of rival theories also often unveils either logical inconsistencies or additional implications of these theories that can be tested. Bruce Bueno de Mesquita (2003, p. 57), for example, provides an interesting example of a logical inconsistency in a widely applied theory. Realist international relations theory as set out by Hans Morgenthau (1978, p. 215–17) argues that all states maximize power and that there are two types of states, those that maximize power, and those that do not. The resulting inconsistency makes it possible to reject Realism as a logical alternative even before engaging in extensive empirical research.

Similarly, a better specification of alternative theories may uncover additional observable implications. Given the dire state of some social science theories, such a specification may even be necessary to allow for a falsification of the rival theory. Hubert M. Blalock (1984, p. 140), for example, points out that in the field of sociology 'many theories are vaguely worded, do not contain any predictive statements, and usually involve a sufficient number of ambiguously defined concepts and implicit assumptions that it is very easy to wriggle out of a set of embarrassing findings by invoking a series of disclaimers.' With better specification at least of 'middle-range' theories, it may turn out that the values on the dependent variable predicted by two rival theories are not the same, and discrimination among theories may be possible by simply affirming the lack of correlation between independent and dependent variables in the rival theory.

Finally, making explicit rival theories' implicit predictions about causal mechanisms can give a researcher leeway to employ process-tracing to tackle them head on. It is, however, important to stress that if in this process the researcher caricatures rival theories, the resulting rejection will not be convincing. Moreover, consider a theory that is consistent with several causal pathways. Demonstrating that one of them does not hold does not even cast doubt on the theory. In short, the process of specifying rival theories is a tricky one that requires substantial sensitivity on behalf of the researcher to forestall allegations of having misinterpreted the target theory with the sole intention of rejecting it.

Increase the number of cases.   Additional case studies increase the number of observations and thus may help avoid indeterminacy. In situations with several cases, and if certain rather strict requirements are given, qualitative methods of covariation (Mill's methods of agreement, of difference, and of concomitant variation) and congruence testing can lead to reliable findings (George and Bennett, 2005, pp. 153–60, 181–204). For this, the cases added to the study must not necessarily be as well elaborated as the key cases of interests; smaller 'exploratory' case studies based on secondary literature may suffice (see Leuffen, Chapter 8).

In addition, it may be possible to add 'most likely' or 'least likely' cases (Eckstein, 1975; Yin, 2002). Such cases are considered essential tests for rival theories, with their underlying logic being that if a hypothesis is (not) valid for this specific case, it will be (not be) valid for all (or nearly all) other cases. Finding such cases, obviously, is a difficult task. Most likely or least likely case studies only convince other researchers if a relatively small number of cases of this phenomenon exist (for example, full-fledged revolutions) and if the distance between the observed and the expected value is large. The reasoning here is that the likelihood that one of a few cases happens to be far away from the predicted value by chance alone is very low.[6] A probabilistic interpretation of the deviant finding thus can be pre-empted. In sum, the principal advantage of adding extra cases derives from the fact that such a step allows a researcher to combine cross-case and within-case analyses. However, the advice to increase the number of cases is not always appropriate. Adding

cases may lead to the inclusion of domains in which 'measurement procedures are invalid, or causal homogeneity is lacking' (Brady, Collier and
Seawright, 2004: 261). Using this tool to tackle rival theories thus comes
with an important trade-off, with a researcher having to estimate
whether he will win or lose more from the addition of a further case
study (see Wonka, Chapter 3; Rathke, Chapter 6).

Privilege a factor-centric analysis. If all other steps fail, and several rival
hypotheses cannot be excluded, a researcher may refocus her study on
analyzing the causal effects of a particular explanatory variable instead
of trying to explain specific outcomes. The question then becomes:
How much does *a* contribute to *y*, keeping all other variables constant?
This may allow her to limit the number of explanatory variables for
which she has to make causal inferences. In particular, the researcher
may be able to control for the effect of other causal factors by keeping
them constant, a technique that cannot be used if a researcher tries to
explain particular cases. The problem of omitted variable bias, however, may still be present. In addition, changing the substantive focus
of a research project only for methodological reasons is a questionable
strategy.

Most of the solutions just presented are compatible with each other.
In fact, I would argue that researchers should always consider at least the
first three suggestions. The fourth already comes with significant trade-
offs, by requiring a broadening of the research to cases that potentially
were not considered of substantive interest at the beginning. The last
solution comes with the largest trade-offs in that it implies a fundamental change in the focus of the research. For this reason, my recommendation is that it be used only in cases in which all other suggestions have
been tried unsuccessfully.

Application

Before World War II, the trade policies of most countries around the
world could easily be classified as protectionist. Scholars convincingly
explained these policies with the distributional effects of trade, namely
the fact that free trade imposes concentrated costs on some interests and
confers diffuse benefits on other interests. With collective action problems inhibiting the organization of the latter, only the former manage to
influence trade policy decisions (Anderson and Baldwin, 1987). In addition, problems of cooperation among states in an anarchic international
system tend to inhibit trade liberalization (Grieco, 1990). Protectionism

thus appears to be a politically reasonable strategy in many circumstances (Milner, 2002).

Just at the time as this finding became widely shared among scholars, however, countries started to agree upon far-reaching steps towards trade liberalization. Initially, this process mainly encompassed the United States and European countries. In the meantime, trade liberalization has spread and practically all countries on the globe participate in this process.[7] A huge variety of explanations have been proposed to explain this development. Whereas some of these explanations are specific to the case of the United States, others, by contrast, can easily be generalized to apply to several cases. Consequently, researchers studying a case of trade liberalization, even if limited either by time or by geographic scope, must take into consideration several rival theories. In the following, I provide a series of examples of how authors (including myself) have managed to deal with rival explanations of trade liberalization to establish internal validity in their studies, employing the scheme set out in the previous section.

Ad 1   Observe as many implications of your own theory and the alternative theories as possible. I have suggested that researchers study as many observations of their own and of rival theories as possible so as to allow for the use of process-tracing and similar techniques. This suggestion has been applied quite frequently in the literature under review, as the following two examples illustrate. Some authors trying to explain US trade liberalization stress that in the aftermath of the Great Depression, members of Congress realized that the highly protectionist Smoot-Hawley Act of 1930 had been a step in the wrong direction. They thus learned that logrolling (a process, in which legislators cooperate to pass each others' pet projects) leads to inefficient trade policies (Goldstein, 1993; Lohmann and O'Halloran, 1994). By delegating trade authority to the President in the Reciprocal Trade Agreements Act (RTAA), according to this view, legislators managed to resolve the problem of logrolling and, by doing so, enabled trade liberalization. Karen E. Schnietz (2000, p. 420), however, rejects this and other similar explanations that see the American trade liberalization starting in 1934 as a direct consequence of a change in beliefs. To do so, she analyses an implication of the 'learning hypothesis,' namely that a large part of the legislators who voted on both the Smoot-Hawley Act of 1930 and the RTAA of 1934 in the House of Representatives, should have changed their vote from one bill to the other. By showing that of 95 legislators who voted for protectionism in 1930, and who also voted on the RTAA, none changed his or her vote, Schnietz effectively manages to refute this explanation.

Schnietz (2000) herself provides an alternative explanation of American trade liberalization suggesting that the Democratic Party, during its period of unified control over Congress and the Presidency in the 1930s and the first half of the 1940s, managed to lock-in lower tariffs in form of the RTAA. The Democratic Party, which favored free trade because of its constituency of Southern landowners, had tried to achieve a lowering of trade barriers in earlier decades. The party finally engineered the RTAA to permanently 'lock-in' lower tariffs, by taking away tariff setting authority from Congress. Again, the observation of a specific implication of this theory allows for its refutation: The explanation implies that the RTAA should be designed to make its reversal as difficult as possible. In fact, however, it contained a time limit after which it expired and had to be renewed by Congress (Dür, 2007). This time limit is inconsistent with Schnietz's explanation.

Ad 2 Improve your theory. Improving one's own theory to draw out additional implications may give researchers more leeway to tackle rival explanations. Attempts at testing the Hegemonic Stability Theory nicely illustrate this point. The claim of this theory is that the existence of a hegemon that dominates the international system can favor international openness (Krasner, 1976). Empirical research thus should uncover a correlation between phases of high concentration of power in the international system and periods of trade liberalization. When employing this approach, however, scholars necessarily encountered the problem that they could only distinguish two cases of hegemony: British hegemony in the nineteenth century and US hegemony after World War II. In the absence of predictions that could be tested by way of process-tracing, empirical support for the theory thus could only be based on a correlation among very few observations.[8] Edward D. Mansfield (1994), by conceptualizing the distribution of power as a continuous variable, resolved this problem without losing much of the parsimony of the original theory. His prediction is that during periods of both high and low concentration of power, trade should be greater than during middle periods. By doing so, he made possible a quantitative analysis of the argument and in fact found empirical support for his argument. An improvement in theory thus enabled Mansfield to counter the challenge of rival theories.

Ad 3 Scrutinize and specify rival theories. A precise analysis of rival theories may uncover logical inconsistencies or new implications that can be tested in empirical research. With regard to uncovering logical inconsistencies, a good example is Michael Hiscox's (1999) attack on the argument that the RTAA made free trade viable, partly by reducing the amount of protectionist lobbying. This argument states that once a country concludes trade agreements, the resulting increase in imports should drive at least some uncompetitive domestic producers out of business and thus make them disappear from the political struggle (Bailey, Goldstein and Weingast, 1997, pp. 328–9). Rejecting this argument, Hiscox argues convincingly that the reduction of trade barriers brought about by the RTAA should actually have increased protectionist lobbying, by exposing more and more sectors to international competition. In face of increased protectionist lobbying, politicians should have had difficulties to sustain the RTAA. Simple deduction thus allowed Hiscox to reject an alternative explanation.

My own work provides an example for an attempt at better specifying a rival theory with the purpose of uncovering additional observable implications (Dür, 2004; see also Dür, 2007). Institutional theories of US trade liberalization argue that the RTAA of 1934 caused the following move towards lower trade barriers. Although not clearly specified in this way by advocates of this approach, it arguably predicts a more or less linear reduction of tariffs after 1934 or at least after World War II. Once further specified in this way, the empirical demonstration of a pattern in which an initial phase of liberalization is followed by a phase of increased protectionism during the 1950s casts substantial doubt on this rival approach. Since my argument predicted such a nonlinear pattern, the evidence not only served to reject alternative theories but also to boost my own explanation.

Ad 4   Increase the number of cases included in the analysis.   Additional case studies, ideally of a 'most likely' or a 'least likely' type, can help solve the problem of an indeterminate research design. As an example for the use of such a case study, several authors suggest that geopolitics was the main driving force behind US trade liberalization after World War II (Eckes, 1995). The argument is that the United States reduced its trade barriers and allowed exporters from European and friendly developing countries to supply to the American market in order to face off challenges from the Soviet Union. Its aim was to keep these countries from siding with the Soviet Union by strengthening their economies. This reasoning leads to a clear cut prediction: American trade liberalization should have been most pronounced in the late 1940s and early 1950s, when the threat from the Soviet Union was highest. In fact, however, the US reversed its prior policy of liberalization and instead became more protectionist during this decade (Dür, 2004 and 2007). The empirical examination thus uncovered a large difference between the rival theory's prediction and the actually observable facts. As a result, the case could be used as a critical one that refuted the geopolitical interpretation more generally.

Ad 5   Privilege a factor-centric analysis.   My final suggestion – if all other remedies outlined above prove unworkable or unsatisfactory – has been to refocus a study from explaining outcomes to analyzing the effects of a particular explanatory variable. Helen Milner's (1988) study provides an illustration of this advice. Her initial interest may have been to explain why the 1970s did not see the protectionist trade policies that characterized the 1930s despite an economic downturn (Milner, 1988, p. 12). Given that directly answering this question is very difficult, her work ended up analyzing the impact of multinationalization on firm preferences instead. Answering this question proved easier than having to consider a multitude of different possible hypotheses explaining developed countries' trade policies in the 1970s. The factor-centric approach also allowed her to control for specific alternative explanations, such as a sector's exposition to foreign competition, by keeping these variables constant.

In sum, this discussion of empirical research in the field of trade liberalization studies suggests the applicability of the tools set out above to tackle rival theories and to avoid indeterminate research designs.

Conclusion

I have suggested a series of methodological steps that can help outcome-centric researchers achieve the aim of establishing internal validity in their studies. The suggestions I have mentioned are to observe as many implications as possible of one's own theory and of rival theories, to improve one's theory to draw out additional implications, to scrutinize and specify rival theories, to add extra cases with specific properties, and to switch to a factor-centric analysis if all other means fail. These tools, I submit, should make it possible for scholars to successfully tackle rival theories in small-n research. Since this chapter's attention has been on how to establish internal validity, a word of caution is due with respect to the possibility of inferring from such studies to a larger population of cases. Even if internal validity is given and a researcher is able to demonstrate that a specific causal mechanism brought about an event, inference to other cases is tricky and necessarily based on the assumption that relatively stable patterns characterize the world. Despite this limitation, the research that I have propagated in this chapter is by no means athe-oretical or idiosyncratic. The whole purpose has been to show how researchers can establish specific causal mechanisms and exclude others. If carried out in this way, outcome-centric research fulfils an important task within the social sciences and is likely to prove a significant contribution to our understanding of the social world.

Some further issues that can facilitate actual small-n research as set out in this chapter are worth mentioning. First, in the main part of this chapter I have highlighted the dangers of omitting alternative explana-tions. Nevertheless, it is hardly ever feasible to deal with all possible rival theories for an outcome in a single publication, which most often is subject to a word limit. Given this constraint, a researcher has to con-sciously select those rival theories that she wants to tackle head on. A first rule in this regard is that theories which already appear very implausible in the light of previous research do not have to be taken up again. When deciding on the relevant rival theories to be dealt with in a study, it is also wise to avoid choosing very broad theories (sometimes euphemistically called 'grand theories') or even meta-theories (for example, examining 'rational-choice theory'). These theories are consis-tent with many different causal pathways, making a rejection close to impossible. Instead, the suggestions made in this chapter best apply to what Robert Merton (1949) has called 'middle-range' theories that are pre-cise enough (or can be made precise enough) for empirical examination.

Second, the prior level of confidence in a theory is an important crite-rion in evaluating the results of a new study. The more supportive research has been for a theory in the past, the more stringent the requirements for a future study that suggests that a novel theory fares even better. As put by Bent Flyvbjerg (2004, p. 428), 'The value of the case study will depend on the validity claims that researchers can place on their study, and the status that these claims obtain in dialogue with other validity claims in the discourse to which the study is a contribu-tion.' Those rivals that are considered most valid in the targeted discourse have to be fought most vigorously to establish the validity claim of the own explanation. Empirical evidence that may easily suffer from measurement error is not then a proper tool to reject such well-established theories. If a lack of data makes it impossible to exclude a specific rival explanation, it is important to mention this caveat and to state which empirical evidence, if it could be found, would help discriminate between the two theories.

Finally, the process of testing may uncover difficulties with one's own theory. Yet, a certain loyalty to your own theory is necessary to allow for scientific progress, even in the face of some evidence that is at odds with it. This is akin to Imre Lakatos's (1974) idea of sticking to research programs even if some evidence seems to contradict them. At the same time, one has to be cautious not to fall into the opposite trap, namely to succumb to a tendency to simply verify one's own beliefs. Rather, a researcher must be conscious of the possibility that a failure of measurement or operationalization (Miller, Chapter 5; Wonka, Chapter 3) rather than a failure of theory may account for unexplained findings. Establishing an explanation thus requires some steadfastness even in the face of messy empirical facts. Keeping these suggestions in mind, outcome-centric researchers may provide important new insights that further our understanding of social processes.

Notes

1. I am grateful to the editors of this volume, the participants of the weekly methods seminar at the Mannheim Centre for European Social Research, and Gemma Mateo for helpful comments on earlier versions of this chapter.
2. For similar scepticism with regard to genuine cases of overdetermination, see Bunzl (1979).
3. This principle can be summarized as '*Pluralitas non est ponenda sine neccesitate* [plurality should not be posited without necessity]' (William of Ockham) or slightly more coarsely as 'KISS: Keep It Simple, Stupid!' In a complex world, this means that a researcher has to find a trade off between simplicity and fit of an explanation.
4. Quantitative researchers, by contrast, have to overcome the problem of finding data for control variables.
5. There are some parallels with D. B. Bromley's (1986, pp. 25–6) ten steps that define his quasi-judicial method to the analysis of singular events or circumstances, but my discussion deals more specifically with the question of how to eliminate rival explanations. Bromley mentions the following steps: (1) clearly state the initial problem and the research question; (2) collect background information; (3) evaluate existing or *prima facie* explanations; (4) set forth a new explanation if a closer observation of the evidence casts doubt on existing explanations; (5) search for evidence that eliminates as many of the explanations under consideration as possible, ideally leaving only one; (6) evaluate the sources of evidence, checking their consistency and accuracy; (7) examine the internal logic and coherence of the argument; (8) reject those arguments that are obviously inadequate and select the 'most likely' interpretation; (9) discuss the implications of the research for comparable cases; and (10) present the findings.
6. Flyvbjerg (2004, p. 423) mentions a critical experiment that only fulfilled the second of these criteria and still was highly influential: a metal and a feather falling at the same speed inside a vacuum tube. Only one experiment was necessary to refute Aristotle's law of gravity.

7. Of 53 countries for which tariff data are available for both 1974–75 and 1994–95, 38 (72 percent) had lower tariff rates in the latter period than in the former. Calculated from data in Rodríguez and Rodrik, 1999, Table VIII.1.

8. In fact, Krasner (1976) drew on six different cases by distinguishing periods of hegemonic ascendance and decline. While increasing the number of observations, this strategy could not resolve the fundamental problem of too few cases for making an empirical test based on a correlation convincing, especially as several cases turned out to run counter his argument.

Part VI
Theoretical Conclusions

11
Falsification in Theory-Guided Empirical Social Research: How to Change a Tire while Riding Your Bicycle

Dirk De Bièvre

> ... And so each venture
> Is a new beginning, a raid on the inarticulate
> With shabby equipment always deteriorating
> In the general mess of imprecision ...
> 'East Coker V', in *Four Quartets* (Eliot, 1943)

Introduction: how to change a tire while riding your bicycle

Changing a tire while riding your bicycle would seem like an impossible task. And indeed it is. In this chapter, however, I intend to show that in the course of empirical social research, it can be extremely useful to change your theory in the middle of the research process. I intend to show that in order to come to insights we did not have before, it is necessary to continue our attempts to reformulate not just some minor hypotheses, but also the central hypotheses of our theory.[1]

When we start research, we first formulate our hunches and precon-ceived ideas and spell out their observable implications. We are, of course, confronted with our own theoretical imprecision and logical inconsistency, as well as the empirical anomalies our theory is unable to explain. What do we do? Do we stop here? No, we attempt to formulate new theoretical explanations for the research question. That is, we refor-mulate our theory in the form of new theoretical statements that refine or completely correct our previous statements. We attempt to formulate *falsifying hypotheses.*

I thus distinguish a theoretical understanding of falsification from an empirical understanding of it. In the case of theoretical falsification, we replace faulty explanatory hypotheses with new, presumably better ones. In the case of empirical falsification, empirical observations stand in contradiction to (some of) the observable implications of our theory. In this contribution, I formulate some guidelines for how we can make the first, theoretical understanding of falsification productive in everyday research, and discuss some of the trade-offs involved in such a choice.

My concern is the final phase of the research process: the reformulation of theory, that is *after* we have defined our research problem, specified our theory for the first time, selected the cases and observations for empirical testing, and after we have tried to maximize leverage through different means (Chapters 2, 7, 8 and 10, in this volume).

I distinguish a merely empirical understanding of falsification from a theoretical one, derive some practical advice on how to go about reformulating theory, and illustrate the usefulness of this approach in a discussion of my own research on the relationship between judicialization and non-trade regulation in the WTO.

The research design problem: almost there, but you might be wrong

The question 'When should I consider my theory falsified?' would seem simple enough. Yet the answer isn't. One possibility is that we consider a theory falsified if we find no or insufficient evidence for seemingly plausible hypotheses. But what is *sufficient* evidence to corroborate a theory? A theory can reject the null hypothesis, but no theory can conclusively exclude *all* possible alternative explanations, nor can it conclusively cover *all* empirical occurrences it should ideally be able to explain. As a pragmatic guideline, the idea of 'sufficient evidence' leaves us in the dark about confirmation and falsification.

The reason for this is that empirical evidence can only speak to the theory's observable implications, and not to the general, abstract statements that make up its theoretical core. The observable implications of a theory are singular, verifiable statements about concrete events (Popper, 1965). In contrast, a theory's core hypotheses take the form of non-verifiable propositions. These are of a high level of abstraction and universality and cannot be observed.[2] We cannot observe the main propositions of the theory of gravity, but we can observe its effects. We observe that the apple falls from the tree, but we do not observe that abstract construct of the mind called gravity. Similarly, concepts in political science such as democracy or legitimacy are unobservable in and of themselves. We conceptualize them (Wonka, Chapter 3), operationalize them, and measure their hypothesized effects (Miller, Chapter 5).

It is therefore a common misunderstanding to view a single empirical observation that is not in accordance with the theory as a statement that proves a theory wrong. Were we to adopt such a static understanding of falsification, we would fail to dynamically generate knowledge. We would only be able to confirm or disconfirm a particular theory, and that would be the end of the story. We would be using 'the theory killer sadism of a rigorous falsificationism', utterly unfruitful for the progress of scientific knowledge (Beyme, 1992). Since the aim of research is to learn, this cannot be a useful route.

What then do we do, knowing we can never attain a perfect fit between the abstract theoretical constructs and the empirical complexities of social reality? This is a question as to how we use theory testing to adapt, develop, and change our existing theory.

Theory testing and the reformulation of hypotheses

When we test a theory, we confront the observable implications of our theory with empirical observations. They can be in accordance with the expectations raised by the theory, or they can be incompatible with them. Empirical testing thus provides information on the plausibility of the theory's observable implications. When we find out they are compatible, we can drive our argument with full force: we have found our hypotheses confirmed or 'corroborated'. When they turn out to be wrong, we have a problem. We may need to once again explore whether we have accurately specified our concepts (Wonka, Chapter 3), or whether we have usefully operationalized and measured them (Miller, Chapter 5). It will also be useful to check our case selection (Leuffen, Chapter 8; Thiem, Chapter 7). Yet, we may also benefit from reformulating the core hypotheses of our theory.

The impetus for the reformulation of theory comes from below, that is at a lower level of abstraction. Some of our empirical observations stand in contradiction to some of the observable implications derived from our theory. These implications have the form of simple basic statements of a low level of generality and with empirically observable content. We consecutively try and formulate ever more general hypotheses changing, the more abstract statements of our theory. The distinction between empirically observable implications and abstract general hypotheses thus constitutes the basis for a theoretical understanding of falsification. In the words of Karl Popper:

> Non-reproducible single occurrences are of no significance to science. Thus a few stray basic statements contradicting a theory will hardly induce us to reject it as falsified. We shall take it as falsified only if we discover a reproducible effect, which refutes the theory. In other words, we only accept the falsification if a low-level empirical hypothesis which describes such an effect is proposed and corroborated. This kind of hypothesis may be called falsifying hypothesis. (Popper, 1965, pp. 86–7)

The level of generality of a theory thus depends on our ability to formulate sentences that claim a systematic ('reproducible') relationship between the *explanandum* of our research question and the *explanans* of our theory, that are our independent variables. Clearly, the establishment of such systematic relationships constitutes the goal of theory-guided empirical research and stands in opposition to erratic, idiosyncratic, or more precisely, hitherto unexplained phenomena. Unexplained single occurrences remain anomalies in light of our theory as long as we have not formulated an alternative, 'falsifying' hypothesis[3]. As a result, the number of such occurrences does not matter; as long as we cannot explain them, they remain exactly that, anomalies. We have not yet generated new theoretical knowledge through the formulation of a new hypothesis able to explain them.

Confronted with disconfirming evidence, we try and formulate hypotheses in such a way as to explain what we could already explain with our existing theory, *plus* those empirical phenomena that had remained puzzling and *un*explained. This gives the new theory that little extra mileage which makes it superior to existing explanations; its empirical content is thereby greater. While concocting these revised hypotheses, we must of course avoid compromising the coherence of the theory. In other words, we must avoid smuggling logical contradictions into it. Parsimony and simplicity can therefore guide us as an end in itself, since they enhance the falsifiability of our hypotheses.[4]

> Simple statements, if knowledge is our object, are to be prized more highly than less simple ones because they tell us more, because their empirical content is greater and because they are better testable. (Popper, 1965, p. 142)

The degree to which a research program is able to generate new general hypotheses is what made Lakatos distinguish between a degenerative and a progressive research program (Lakatos, 1974).[5] The result is that we can consider our theory the best answer we know of, and we accept it *for the time being*. This is the reason why self-critique and intersubjective critique, possibly in the form of peer review, is our main source of reliability and quality control.

If things go well, the logical sequence of how we progress in our research thus consists of a ping-pong movement between deducing empirical implications from our theoretical hypotheses, confronting these with empirical observations, and trying to induct from anomalies by generating a revised theory that in turn allows for new empirical deductions. This continuous attempt to reformulate our theory – sometimes pejoratively called fidgeting with the theory in order for it to fit the data – nevertheless comes at a cost. Bueno de Mesquita and others sound a cautionary note on theory building and falsification, calling their warning 'the 1st principle of wing walking' (Bueno de Mesquita, 2003). When walking on the wings of a flying airplane – but they advise you not to do this – you need to stick to what you've got, rather than to let go and risk falling off the airplane, that is to end up knowing nothing at all. In everyday empirical social research, it may in many instances be advisable to stick to the theory we have, even if we are well aware that there are theoretical inconsistencies and/or single empirical occurrences that do not sit well with the theory. As long as we have not formulated a better version, we keep using it. That is, we trade off deficient theoretical knowledge and no general knowledge at all.

Before deriving some practical guidelines from this simple but fundamental insight into the difference between singular and general statements, I would like to show how some leading textbooks on social scientific methods sometimes mix up the theoretical and the empiricist notion of falsification. This has confusing consequences for clear pragmatic guidelines on how to manage theory reformulation.

Some unclear and differing views in the literature

Invariably, falsifiability is considered an important property of any empirically testable theory. In other words, we should 'choose theories that could be wrong' (King, Keohane and Verba, 1994). To attain this, every researcher is often advised to ask himself the question 'What evidence would convince us that we are wrong?' and is then encouraged to derive as many observable implications from the theory as possible. However, this is not synonymous with confronting our theory with the 'hard facts of empirical reality'. How should we confront our abstract hypotheses with observable phenomena directly? And how will we know something we observe is a fact, if not through the lens of our theory, i.e. rendered observable through the operationalization of concepts and postulated causal mechanisms of our theory? What is actually meant with the requirement to confront theory with reality, is to confront the observable implications of your theory with empirical observations.

Whether the cases covered by our theoretical hypotheses are numerous or limited makes no difference in this respect. Nevertheless, and confusingly so, some authors like Munck, fundamentally set apart qualitative (or small-n) and quantitative (or large-n) research, claiming that one single deviation from an overall pattern in qualitative research allows the analyst to reject a potential explanatory factor (Munck, 2004). He thus confuses an anomaly (something we cannot yet explain) with a refutation (an explanation identifying a systematic causal effect). What he in fact does is to construct two different notions of causality, one large-n, quantitative and probabilistic and another small-n, qualitative and deterministic, claiming they would be grounded in two different ontologies underneath these different research paradigms (Mahoney and Goertz, 2006; see also Chapter 1).

This distinction is an utterly useless guide for pragmatic choices in everyday research for two reasons. First, the most useful starting point for thinking about causality is that we can never definitively know whether the world is causally constituted or not (Popper, 1965). What we can do, however, is to formulate hypotheses *as if* the world were causally constituted: we assume this to be the case, but do not know. Thus, since we can neither be sure, nor conclusively deny, that the physical and social world are constituted of causes and effects, all hypotheses and their potential falsifiers can only be temporarily and conditionally true. As a consequence, there is no reason to construct a fault line between causality in large-n and small-n research. Both merely use different methodologies to examine the plausibility of purely hypothetical and inherently uncertain causal relationships.

Second, it is not useful to construct a contrast between an alleged statistical worldview and a deterministic one (McKeown, 1999; Popper, 1990). Rather than being about different worldviews, the difference at stake is one between two types of statements. Probabilistic statements tell you that there is a certain degree of probability that the dependent variable takes on a particular value within the universe of investigated cases. They do not allow you to derive singular statements about one specific occurrence, since they cannot be stated in terms of an independent variable X *having* or *not having* an impact on dependent variable Y. They therefore merely test the probability that a certain independent variable

X causes Y. In contrast, deterministically formulated causal hypotheses postulate certain states of the world and prohibit others. The observable implications derived from the theory are therefore about a reproducible effect being either *there*, or *not*. For this reason, Popper somewhat provocatively concludes that probable knowledge is no knowledge at all: probabilities do not enhance general knowledge since they do not intend to say anything definitive about a particular case. Hence, the important similarity between probabilistic statements and deterministically causal hypotheses lies in the fact that both formulate propensities (Popper, 1990). They express an expectation – a best guess – of Y given X.

Statistical and non-statistical tests thus perform different functions to evaluate explanations. Probabilistic tests explore the universe of cases, probe the plausibility of a particular theoretical explanation across a wide range of cases, facilitate case selection, and help us to identify possibly relevant causal factors. Deterministically formulated hypotheses force us to make possible causal mechanisms of these propensities traceable, eliminate those causes that could not be of importance, and give us clear guidelines as to what we should be seeing empirically, if they were really true (Lieberman, 2005).

Practical guidelines: how to learn from what is wrong

Be bold: overstate rather than understate your hypotheses. Overstating your hypotheses will make them more simple and general. This renders it easier to find out under which circumstances they hold and under which they do not. It is easier to derive a whole range of observable implications from a somewhat excessively formulated general hypothesis than from a hypothesis with an already narrowly specified empirical scope or lots of complicated qualifications. To find out whether all these nuances are relevant and important, conduct your empirical research. In short: do not be afraid to find out something in your hypothesis must be wrong.

Do not conclude from a single event not in accordance with the empirical implications of your theory that your whole theory must be wrong. A single event in contradiction with the observable implications of your theory is an anomaly, not a falsification. You acknowledge something is clearly not as you expected; yet you are unable to explain it. In that case, find more of these, and then try and formulate a statement about a systematic effect, which can explain both the occurrences your theory correctly explained as well as those that previously were anomalies for your theory. If you succeed in doing that, you have formulated a falsifying hypothesis. Instead of pretending that your theory is absolutely proven, which it will never be, it may well be better to say: This explanation fares better than the ones I know.

Make sure your evidence speaks to the causal mechanisms in your theory. Do not only infer from the relative balance between corroborating and falsifying observations. What you ideally want to achieve is to find systematic causes for specific occurrences. This means that you are likely to find most research satisfaction in understanding why A causes B, not just in factual information that A seems to cause B. It is, of course, important to assess whether you find much support for your explanation across the universe of cases. Yet, since you can never conclusively exclude other potential causal factors (especially those you and others have never thought of), the balance between corroborating and falsifying observations is not enough. You have to process-trace to try and pin down that a particular cause, or several in conjunction, must have caused Y. We learn most about the relevance of our theory from observing the causal chain between A and B.

Do not confuse plausibility with corroboration. By showing that your hypothesis works in many instances, you have added plausibility, you may have rejected other plausible explanations, or you may have facilitated your case selection. In sum, you may have done a very good job. Yet you have not corroborated your theory. If you are able to show that there is no systematic reason (yet) why you should be wrong, you are entitled to consider your theory confirmed. You can only achieve this high aim if you manage to reject all rival explanations you can think of, the topic of the fifth and last piece of advice.

Formulate alternative hypotheses and try to disprove them with your own theory. Constituting the subject of Chapter 10 by Andreas Dür (this volume), this piece of advice is important in order to shield your theory from theory-killing falsificationism and yourselves from frustration and disillusionment – one of our greatest enemies while doing research. If you are able to show that other plausible explanations cannot even possibly be true, you are entitled to defend your explanation as perhaps faulty, but still better than the range of alternative explanations existing in society or in the scholarly literature.

Application: judicialization and non-trade regulation in the WTO

Below, I sketch the broad theoretical lines of a current research project and illustrate some of the pieces of advice just formulated. I only focus on the first two, namely the advantages of bold hypotheses, and the way to deal with single occurrences in contradiction to your theory.

What is the effect of judicialization in the WTO – the presence of binding third party enforcement – on negotiation strategies of WTO member states? To answer this question, I hypothesize that political actors supportive of non-trade regulation try to bring agreements on such issues under the jurisdiction of the WTO rather than to conclude them within other international institutions and organizations such as specialized UN-agencies, whose decisions are not enforceable through binding third party adjudication. With the term non-trade regulation, I denote those agreements that are not directly or exclusively aimed at enhancing or restricting trade. These can be agreements on international technical standards, environmental rules, labor standards, intellectual property protection rules, investment rules, health rules, etc.

The research design is thus factor-centric (see Chapter 1). I analyze the effect of one particular independent variable (judicialization) on the dependent variable, the negotiation strategies of the member states in introducing non-trade regulation into the WTO.

Originally, I had started out from the question why and under which conditions positive integration is possible in the World Trade Organization (De Bièvre, 2004). Positive integration, defined as the correction of negative externalities from market liberalization, is arguably very difficult to achieve in the European Union (Scharpf, 1996). *A fortiori*, so I guessed, this should be the case in an organization with over 140 sovereign states operating under conditions of unanimity. Two observations had thus encouraged me to try out the concept of positive integration in the WTO: First, Scharpf's analysis of why institutions of the EU are geared towards negative integration (liberalization) and are relatively inapt at bringing about positive integration, and second, the fact that the world trading regime was slowly being enlarged with obligations to adopt new regulation in fields such as intellectual property protection, health, technical standards and investment. For reasons I will spell out later, I have currently abandoned the terminology of negative and positive integration.

The three steps in the causal argument which make up the core hypotheses of my theory are the following:

• First, judicialization in the WTO, combined as it is with possible retaliation, facilitates enforcement of previous agreements.
• Second, strengthened enforcement makes commitments more credible.
• And third, strong enforcement leads political actors supportive of non-trade regulation in a particular policy field to bring such agreements under the jurisdiction of the WTO.

As abstract hypotheses, all of these are *un*observable in and of themselves. We can only test their validity against logically derived, empirically testable observations.

I have thus formulated the somewhat excessively powerful and general hypothesis that strong enforcement causes non-trade regulation to be located in the WTO. I attribute great explanatory power to an institution, normally not considered to be very powerful at the international level. The advantage of such an overly bold hypothesis is that it allows us to deduce a set of empirical implications.

A first empirical implication flowing from the theory is that negotiators strive for regulatory agreements on non-trade issues not in specialized international UN agencies, but inside the WTO. That is, I should be able to identify problems for political actors in achieving particular non-trade regulation goals in organizations other than the WTO. Second, negotiators strive for regulatory standards agreed in other agencies to become enforceable through the WTO dispute settlement mechanism. I should find that negotiators explicitly mention the putative strength of the WTO dispute settlement mechanism when motivating their drive to bring new regulatory agreements under WTO jurisdiction. Third, it should be possible to show that the WTO enforcement system is stronger than enforcement mechanisms in other international regimes, both in other policy fields and in the world trading regime before the creation of the WTO in 1995, in other words under the GATT dispute settlement system. This obviously requires the development of a typology of stronger and weaker enforcement mechanisms as well as a theory as to why some would be stronger than others. So far, a comparison of WTO enforcement with GATT enforcement has brought support for this intuitively plausible assertion, but surprisingly enough not with regard to a comparison of WTO adjudication with other international agreements and their institutions (De Bièvre, 2006a; McCall Smith, 2000).

Given the absence of such a theory and an empirical test of it, the assertion that WTO third party adjudication constitutes a 'strong' type of enforcement is a mere assumption, and the value of the independent variable remains to a large extent postulated. I ask readers to accept this assertion for the time being, without being able to rely on empirical validation.

A range of logical inconsistencies have riddled me throughout the formulation of the research question as well as while trying to empirically apply the theory. First and foremost, what if the distinction between negative and positive integration is analytically appealing, yet empirically irrelevant? That is, what if all agreements concluded in the WTO are basically means through which economic actors want to enhance their market access to foreign markets, while trying to protect their own? If export oriented interests want to fix international regulation in their favor in order to conquer foreign markets, their political action is reducible to the twin dimensions of securing market access or protecting domestic markets, a clear trade enhancing or reducing motive for political action in trade policy. In other words, what if I cannot operationalize the abstract and unobservable concepts in my causal theory in order to fill them with empirical meaning? Does this mean the end of the road? No. I have chosen to cling to the wings I have. I stuck to the idea that judicialization might well make the WTO a more attractive locus for international agreements, and I redefined the dependent variable as being non-trade regulation. I thus avoided the thorny issue as to whether actors pursue 'positive integration' for market access goals, which would make it analytically and empirically indistinguishable from 'negative integration'. Thus this change in the theoretical core is certainly related to concept specification (Wonka, Chapter 3), nevertheless having consequences for the formulation of the causal mechanism. I no longer conceived of the motive of political actors as being the correction of market externalities; I rather conceive of their motives as being the introduction of regulation, irrespective of whether this has market enhancing or market correcting effects.

A second problem has been an empirical rather than a theoretical one. During the Doha Round, which started in 2001, some important negotiators like the EU were initially demanding new non-trade regulation in the WTO. However, they have been sidelined or vetoed by others, especially emerging market and developing countries such as India and Brazil. As I am writing, the Doha Round is on a very low fire, if not dead and buried. Were I to adopt a purely empirical understanding of falsification, I should take note of this single occurrence and declare the hypothesized relationship between judicialization and non-trade regulation in the WTO dead, exactly because I already expected from the beginning that if I find a relationship, this would be very astonishing. However, I have stuck to the core hypothesis that judicialization causes non-trade regulation to be included in the WTO, while abandoning success or failure to include new issues in the WTO as the empirical yard stick to test this. Instead, I have reconceptualized the dependent variable in terms of whether political actors strive to set the WTO agenda with non-trade concerns, and not whether they are actually successful in achieving non-trade WTO agreements. I have thus tried to find support for the proposition that the EU, as one of the most prominent proponents of new WTO regulation, has for years tried to push a regulatory agenda in the WTO rather than elsewhere (De Bièvre, 2006a).

Conclusion: uncertainty in research

In this chapter, I have tried to explain why it is useful not to conceive of falsification as a definitive, deadly exercise, but rather as a conscious means to deal with the inherent uncertainty of research.

Having outed myself as a keen reader of Popper's theory of knowledge and its practical value in guiding empirical research, a final note may clarify a common misunderstanding about falsifiability and falsification. I have endorsed the position that single occurrences unexplained by our theory are of no significance for science, since they do not refer to a systematic effect. Noteworthy enough, however, Popper often gets misquoted to make exactly the opposite point: That one empirical observation not in accordance with a theory would be enough to prove the whole theory wrong. Apart from being illogical, this is in no way practical advice. I am of course referring to Popper's example about observing white swans. In that passage, Popper illustrated the problem of induction, in other words that it can be problematic to infer general statements from a single occurrence:

> ... it is far from obvious, from a logical point of view, that we are justified in inferring universal statements from singular ones, no matter how numerous; for any conclusion drawn in this way may always turn out to be false: no matter how many instances of white swans we may have observed, this does not justify the conclusion that all swans are white. (Popper, 1965, p. 27)

The recipe to overcome the problem I have addressed in this contribution therefore does not lie in finding ever more examples of a hypothesized causal relationship, rather in spelling out causal pathways for which this relationship should consist, if it were true. This strategy allows one to derive ever more empirical observations from a theory, enhancing theory testability: A task before me, and a never ending quest with an ever uncertain outcome for all of us.

Notes

1. I would like to thank Andreas Dür, Thomas Gschwend, Bernhard Miller, Cas Mudde, Frank Schimmelfennig, and Arndt Wonka for discussions and comments. Remaining gaps and mistakes are all mine.
2. The core hypotheses of a theory are not identical with its assumptions. Assumptions are statements about cause and effect relations in relation to a question not treated in the research project. The author asks the reader to accept them without elaborately arguing why this may be so and without testing them.
3. The terms 'falsifying' and 'falsification' may well be unattractive words to use. Alternatives to 'falsifying' are 'presumably better', 'rectifying', or 'revised'. The advantage of 'falsifying', though, is that it is a relational concept: a hypothesis stands in relation to another, less valid hypothesis.
4. Though the requirement for parsimony would seem simple and pragmatic enough, many authors insist on calling it into question for unclear reasons and even deliberately misread (or do not read) Popper on the subject. Witness the following approving comment by McKeown on King, Keohane and Verba, 1994, p. 20: '[Like Popper, King, Keohane, and Verba] argue that parsimony as an end is not very important and can often be abandoned as an objective' (McKeown, 1999, p. 162).
5. I thus see no logical contradiction between the Popper and the Lakatos position of what constitutes falsification, although the secondary literature on Lakatos routinely claims such a disjuncture. Like Popper, Lakatos regards hypotheses as inherently uncertain.

12
Conclusion: Lessons for the Dialogue between Theory and Data

Thomas Gschwend and Frank Schimmelfennig

In the introduction, we categorized research designs along two dimensions. One dimension classifies them according to the focus of research as *factor-centric* or *outcome-centric;* on the other dimension, we distinguished *large-n* and *small-n* research designs according to the number of observations. Yet we also claimed that, no matter which research design we use, we all face the same set of core research design issues: Defining the research question and problem, specifying concepts and theory, operationalizing and measuring them, selecting cases and observations, controlling for alternative explanations, and drawing theoretical conclusions from the empirical analysis. Each of the preceding chapters then took on one of these issues and explicated the challenges, and also provided some hands-on advice on how to deal with these challenges.

What are the lessons to be learned from comparing the challenges across all types of research design? The results here seem to be unequivocally clear. It does not matter whether you care about outcomes or causal factors nor whether you can leverage a few or many observations. We do in fact share the very same research design problems. We can identify a set of questions which help to increase the relevance of our research both in the scientific community and beyond (Lehnert, Miller and Wonka, Chapter 2). If your theoretical concepts are fuzzy, your research cannot yield valid inferences – no matter how many observations you can leverage on or the type of inferences in which you are primarily interested (Wonka, Chapter 3). Moreover, measurement as a process of attributing 'values to observations according to pre-defined rules' (Miller, Chapter 5, p. 84) is a challenge irrespective of the number of observations you measure and whether your main theoretical focus is on an independent or a dependent variable. Whether you select a few or many observations, selection bias is always looming large (Thiem, Chapter 7; Leuffen, Chapter 8; Geddes, 1990). Likewise, the decision as to which variables to include in a quest for explanation, and which to control for is tricky in any type of research design (Sieberer, Chapter 9; Dür, Chapter 10). Finally, a potential reformulation of the theory which started a dialogue with the data is an issue in every empirical research process (De Bièvre, Chapter 10).

While all types of research face the same problems and challenges, to what extent do they also lend themselves to common solutions? The answer from comparing the guidelines that are offered in each chapter seems to suggest that we should not expect to find a cookie-cutter approach 'out there' to solve all research design problems for us in the same mechanical way. Surely this does not come as a big surprise. Otherwise our distinction of research designs along two different dimensions would be just one more attempt to clutter the literature with yet another piece of jargon. Rather, the preceding chapters play variations of a common theme: *Different research designs offer and require different solutions to the very same challenges, each of which produces specific trade-offs.* The evaluation of these trade-offs should ideally determine the research design you choose. This fact, we think, has not been appreciated enough in the discussion about unified logics and common standards of good research design.

Relevance

The only exception may be seen at the very beginning of the research process. For one, the social or theoretical relevance of the research question does not appear to be systematically related to the number of observations or factor- versus outcome-centric designs. A single case study can be just as (ir)relevant as a global survey. Both knowledge of the causal effects of a single factor and knowledge of the multiple determinants of a specific outcome can or cannot meet the standards of relevance. At first sight, outcome-centric research – for example, on the conditions of wars, effective institutional reform, or electoral success – may seem more relevant. However, we do not see why this should not be the case for factor-centric research on the causal effects of peacekeeping activities, constitutional designs, or electoral systems.

Concept specification

Clearly specified theories and concepts are indispensable for all types of research design. On the one hand, as Wonka (Chapter 3) notes, the specification of concepts needs to follow the theoretical interests of the researcher or the study rather than the selected research design. On the other hand, however, the extension of a concept must also be commensurate with the object of research. Whereas the 'Cold War' will hardly qualify for a large-n study, 'international rivalry' does. According to Wonka (see also Rathke, Chapter 6), decreasing the intention of a concept to widen its empirical applicability involves raising the level of abstraction and possibly shedding context specificity (for instance from 'Cold War' to 'international rivalry'), which is likely to blur conceptual boundaries and reduce analytical leverage. Hence, the common perception of 'qualitative', small-n researchers that 'quantitative', large-n researchers often work with extremely thin concepts, which neglect important real-world variations and are used out of context. By contrast, large-n researchers may find that many concepts used in small-n research are so 'thick' and overloaded with context-specific attributes that they are not only hard to measure, let alone quantify, but also stand in the way of comparative research and general knowledge. Whereas, in the first case, the analytic leverage of the concept derives from context specificity, in the second case it comes from its general applicability and context independence. This trade-off applies to concept-specification in large-n and small-n studies regardless of whether they are factor-centric or outcome-centric (Table 12.1)

Measurement

Rathke (Chapter 6) brings up a general measurement issue that researchers are confronted with when devising measurement strategies based on secondary data from various sources. Not only may the measures used in different data collection projects be incomparable, but even if the measurement instruments are formulated identically, they may produce

Table 12.1   Research design and concept specification

	Factor-centric	Outcome-centric
Large n	Abstraction, context independence, 'thinness'	
Small n	Concreteness, context specificity, 'thickness'	

Table 12.2 Research design and measurement

	Factor-centric	Outcome-centric
Large n	Variance-based validity and reliability	
Small n	Case-based validity and reliability	

incomparable results because of the different political or cultural context in which they are applied. Researchers must therefore check for and ensure conceptual equivalence of the measures used. Although exemplified based on a large-n research design, the challenge she brings up is neither specific to the number of cases under investigation nor to the focus of research, be it factor-centric or outcome-centric.

Since measurement is intimately linked to concept specification, the conclusions from the book are similar. On the one hand, Miller (Chapter 5) argues that questions of measurement, and the problems of validity and reliability, apply to factors (independent variables) and outcomes (dependent variables) alike. Therefore, it does not make a difference for the choice of solutions to measurement problems whether the research design is factor-specific or outcome-specific. On the other hand, however, the measurement problems in small-n and large-n studies mirror those of the specification of concepts. As Miller points out, large-n studies are 'often said to be reductionist, based on inadequate indicators ... resulting in poor data quality', whereas small-n studies draw criticism for being prone to biases (Miller, Chapter 5, p. 84).

Put positively, small-n designs allow the researcher to become very familiar with the individual cases and to put high emphasis on the refinement of indicators and measures as well as the interpretation of data in order to improve case-based validity and reliability. By contrast, in large-n studies, the researcher is more likely to encounter the full range of variance on the independent and dependent variables, which is equally helpful in refining indicators and measures and improving their variance-based validity and reliability. However, the researcher will not be able to put the same effort into checking the validity and reliability of the measurement in the individual case. Thus, we end up with the familiar trade-off between depth and breadth (Table 12.2).

Case selection

Case selection is the issue on which the four research designs differ most obviously. On the one hand, large-n and small-n studies vary precisely on the number of cases selected for analysis. On the other hand, factor-centric

Table 12.3   Research design and case selection

	Factor-centric	Outcome-centric
Large n	Random selection (or universe of cases)	
Small n	Intentional selection on the independent variable, selection of crucial cases	Intentional selection on the dependent variable plus within-case analysis

research implies the selection of cases on the independent variable, whereas outcome-centric research intentionally selects cases on the dependent, 'outcome' variable. These differences of design translate into different specific problems, solutions and various trade-offs (Table 12.3).

According to Leuffen (Chapter 8) and Thiem (Chapter 7), selection bias potentially plagues all varieties of political science research. This is particularly true of 'real world bias' induced by history and political processes. Yet the extent to which selection bias looms large (and can be detected and corrected) varies across research designs. First, whereas large-n researchers usually select their cases randomly (if not the entire universe of cases), small-n research needs to start from the intentional selection of cases, because random selection would be likely to produce selection bias and thus reduce the validity of inferences (King, Keohane and Verba, 1994, pp. 125–7). Intentional selection is generally more prone to bias than random selection (if it is really random).

Second, if selection is intentional, the inferences drawn from factor-centric research are in general less affected by the selection rule than those drawn from outcome-centric research, because researchers will usually select their cases on the explanatory variable (King, Keohane and Verba, 1994, p. 137). Despite this, a selection that does not cover the full range of the explanatory variables will *a priori* obfuscate their potential impact on the dependent variable, and consequently seriously threatens the generality of the inferences. Leuffen points out that this limit can be addressed if the researcher selects a 'crucial' case study (Eckstein, 1975). A 'theory-confirming' (Lijphart, 1971) or hard case will demonstrate that if the theory holds in this case, it will also hold in most other cases. Conversely a 'theory-infirming or easy case shows that if the theory does not hold in this case, it will also not hold in most other cases (see also Flyvbjerg, 2006, p. 230).

Third, the evaluation of selection bias is easier in large-n than in small-n studies, and large-n studies are more likely to cover the full range of each variable than small-n studies. We can thus conclude that large-n designs are less likely to suffer from selection bias or limited generality, whereas particularly small-n outcome-centric studies are most affected by selection bias and limited generality.

This negative characterization may, however, miss the point of small-n outcome-centric studies, aka case studies (see Table 1.2). Outcome-centric studies often search for explanations of the specific cases they study rather than being inspired by the quest for generalization, and they usually employ within-case designs such as process-tracing to produce causal inferences (George and Bennett, 2005). Limited generality is thus not a major concern, and their case-specific inferences are not affected by selection bias (Collier, Mahoney and Seawright, 2004, pp. 95–7).

To sum up, selection bias is not a threat to your inference if you deliberately limit the scope of your research question. At the same time, however, the limitation in scope does not allow one to draw any generalizations above and beyond the case-specific ones. An intentional selection on the dependent variable does deliberately restrict the range of the dependent variable and, therefore, cannot tell us anything about how well the causal story travels to other cases.

Control

The issues of case selection and control are partially linked via the problem of determinacy. The general rule to avoid indeterminacy is simple. An increase in the number of variables should correspond to an increase in the number of cases. Conversely, as the number of cases decreases, the researcher is forced to be selective with regard to the variables included. This, however, increases the likelihood of an 'omitted variable bias', that is, the lack of control for variables that may be correlated with both the explanatory variable and dependent variable, as well as 'equifinality' (that is, the fit of two and more hypotheses with the evidence and the inability to disentangle them). Again, however, the extent of the problem and the proposed solutions vary across research designs, and both the large/small-n and the factor/outcome-centric dimensions are relevant (Table 12.4).

Table 12.4 Research design and control

	Factor-centric	Outcome-centric
Large n	Add independent variables to avoid omitted variable bias	Add independent variables to maximize explained variance
Small n	Use typologies and matching	Use process-tracing

In general, large-n studies achieve control by adding independent variables to the analysis, because they tend to have high degrees of freedom. By contrast, small-n studies achieve control by carefully delimiting and matching cases and by using within-case evidence. However, there are differences between factor-centric and outcome-centric designs as well. As Sieberer points out for large-n research, factor-centric designs should minimize the addition of those independent variables to what is strictly necessary in order to avoid omitted variable bias. By contrast, outcome-centric studies will include all theoretically relevant and consistent 'independent variables that allow you to capture additional variance in the dependent variable' (Sieberer, Chapter 9, p. 169). The trade-off here is that while maximizing the number of variables included in a multivariate analysis will decrease the likelihood of omitted variable bias, it will also decrease the quality of the inferences the researcher can draw on for any individual variable (Ganghof, 2005a, pp. 79–80; King Keohane and Verba, 1994, pp. 182–4).

For factor-centric small-n research, both Lehnert (Chapter 4) and Leuffen (Chapter 8) emphasize the usefulness of typologies. For Lehnert, 'typologies can serve as a remedy for indeterminacy because they combine several variables into broader concepts, thus reducing the number of variables to be integrated into a causal model' (Chapter 4, p. 67). For Leuffen, theory-guided typologies help the researcher control for alternative explanations and focus research on the theoretically most interesting cells. More generally, factor-centric small-n research relies on the careful matching or controlling of cases. Ideally, if the researcher is able to find cases that vary broadly on the explanatory variable(s) of interest but are constant with regard to all other potentially relevant independent variables, a high degree of control is achieved and the causal impact of factors can be validly assessed without increasing the number of cases.

Dür (Chapter 10) specifically targets the problem of control in outcome-centric small-n research. Just as in outcome-centric large-n research, researchers using this design seek a full explanation of their cases. In contrast with the large-n variety, however, they often combine too little variance on the dependent variable with too many independent variables, thus resulting in indeterminacy or overdeterminacy and, indeed, the inability to decide which explanation *really* works or works *best*. Dür mainly advises the researcher to further specify the causal mechanisms implied by her own and alternative theories and then conduct a process-tracing analysis of these causal mechanisms to discriminate between competing explanations.

Theoretical conclusions

The final issue is the theoretical conclusions which can be drawn from our research. Here it seems that De Bièvre's recommendation not to infer falsification from a single anomalous case indicates that we can draw stronger conclusions from large-n research than from small-n research. In addition, however, it is important to see that falsification follows a different strategy in both designs. In large-n research, the assessment of theories is based on regularity and generality. A theory is corroborated if it is consistent with empirical evidence across many observations, the entire universe of cases or a representative sample, and it is weakened or falsified if it fails to account for the average pattern of outcomes. Single or a few deviant cases or outliers will either 'disappear' in the overall pattern or be consciously disregarded by the researcher. By contrast, small-n research focuses on single, critical cases or observations or conducts intensive within-case analysis to assess theories and explanations (see the discussion of crucial cases above and by Leuffen, Chapter 8). The trade-off is obvious: whereas large-n research tends to 'overlook' and neglect deviant special cases, small-n research is likely to put too much emphasis on them in drawing theoretical conclusions from research. This holds for both factor- and outcome-centric research (Table 12.5).

In addition, the theoretical conclusions one draws obviously have to match the kind of theory addressed in these two kinds of research design. Whereas factor-centric research only tells us something about 'factor-oriented theory', outcome-centric research addresses 'outcome-oriented theory'. To give an example, modernization theory is a typical factor-oriented theory that stipulates socioeconomic development as the cause of various relevant political outcomes such as democracy, political culture, and political cleavages (Lipset, 1959). By contrast, an outcome-oriented theory of democracy might bring together various factors (such as wealth, education, international environment, export dependency, and civil society) to explain the variance in democratic stability as fully as possible. In general, however, De Bièvre's discussion of falsification and the reformulation of hypotheses as well as his practical

Table 12.5 Research design and theoretical conclusions

	Factor-centric	Outcome-centric
Large n	Conclusions based on average pattern of observations	
Small n	Conclusions based on critical observations	

guidelines apply to both factor- and outcome-centric research (De Bièvre, Chapter 11).

Two ways to analytical rigor: the logic of breadth and the logic of depth

In the preceding paragraphs, we have approached the variation of solutions across different types of research design individually for each design problem, from relevance to theoretical conclusions. That leads us to a bigger question: Is there a general logic behind these solutions, which cuts across the individual problems of research design? First, as reflected in the widely perceived cleavage between 'qualitative' and 'quantitative research', it appears from our collection of tables that the number of observations – that is, the divide between large-n and small-n – is the dominant dimension within the universe of research designs. For each design problem, the solutions for large-n research differed clearly from those used in small-n research, whereas the solutions for factor- and outcome-centric research only varied for the problems of control and, partially, for case selection.

In addition, there do seem to be unified logics of both large-n and small-n designs across design problems. In most simple terms, large-n research follows the *logic of breadth*, whereas small-n research follows the *logic of depth*. In the literature, we find other dichotomies that capture a similar distinction. The logic of breadth corresponds to an extensive or generalizing research strategy, whereas the logic of depth resembles an intensive or particularizing research strategy (Dessler, 1999, p. 129). According to the logic of depth, small-n research seeks to maximize leverage by extracting as much information as possible from the analysis of a single or a few cases studied in depth. This includes concrete, context-specific concept specification, the case-based improvement of the validity and reliability of measurement, the intentional selection of the 'right' case or cases, control through within-case analysis or careful matching, and theoretical conclusions based on critical observations. According to the logic of breadth, large-n research seeks to maximize leverage by increasing the number of cases. This entails abstract and context-independent concepts, the variance-based optimization of measurement, random selection, the achievement of control by adding independent variables, and theoretical conclusions based on a lot of observations. Pliny's *'multum non multa'*, cited by Leuffen (Chapter 8, p. 152) as a maxim for case selection in small-n research, can be generalized to small-n research as a whole. Conversely, large-n research acts on the maxim of '*multa non multum*' (many, not much).

In comparison, the distinction of factor-centric and outcome-centric research seems to be second-order and less pervasive. Nevertheless, it is relevant for two crucial problems of research design: The selection of cases (in small-n research) and the control for, and discrimination among, alternative explanatory factors. The common feature of factor-centric research is *a priori selection*. Factor-centric large-n research is highly selective in adding control variables ahead of the analysis. Factor-centric small-n researchers try to find crucial, carefully matched, or typologically categorized cases before conducting empirical research. By contrast, outcome-centric research is characterized by a *posteriori discrimination*. Outcome-centric large-n researchers add all plausible independent variables to their models and see whether they turn out to be significant and relevant in the analysis. Outcome-centric small-n research relies on within-case analysis, in particular the process-tracing of causal mechanisms, to discriminate among alternative explanations (Scharpf, 1997).

In sum, while we have analyzed the different logics and solutions of alternative research designs in this concluding chapter, we do not wish to reify our typology of research designs. Instead we would like to stress two lessons we learned for the dialogue between theory and data that emanates from all this. First, as we have emphasized in the introduction, researchers are free to choose research designs. Nevertheless, *different research designs offer and require different solutions to the very same challenges, each of which produces specific trade-offs*. Second, there is no reason why researchers should not combine research designs or move from one design to the other to compensate for the weaknesses and limits of a particular design and to capitalize on the strengths of the other in a 'nested analysis' (Lieberman, 2005) if time constraints and the scarcity of other resources do not suggest otherwise. But in order to do so, they need to be aware of the logics of different research designs and cognizant of the solutions, guidelines, and trade-offs that any design choice entails. Hence our plea for your dialogue between theory and data: Get in sync with the opposite camps! Understand the conflicts. Make deliberate choices. End the confusion.

References

Aarebrot, F. and Bakka, P. (2003) 'Die vergleichende Methode in der Politikwissenschaft', in *Vergleichende Politikwissenschaft*. 4th edn, ed. D. Berg-Schlosser and F. Müller-Rommel (Opladen: Leske and Budrich), pp. 57–76.

Achen, C. H. (2002) 'Toward a new Political Methodology: Microfoundations and ART', *Annual Review of Political Science* 5: 423–50.

Achen, C. H. and Snidal, D. (1989) 'Rational Deterrence Theory and Comparative Case Studies', *World Politics* 41(2): 143–69.

Alderson, A, Bollen, K. and Entwisle, B. (1993) 'Macrocomparative Research Methods', *Annual Review of Sociology* 19: 321–51

Aldrich, J. H. (1995) *Why Parties?* (Chicago, IL: University of Chicago Press).

Aldrich, J. H. and Niemi, R. (1996) 'The Sixth American Party System', in *Broken Contract?*, ed. S. Craig (Boulder, CO: Westview Press), pp. 97–110.

Aldrich, J. H. and Rohde, D. (2000) 'The Consequences of Party Organization in the House', in *Polarized Politics*, eds. J. Bond and R. Fleischer (Washington, DC: CQ Press), pp. 31–72.

Almond, G. A., Powell, G. B. Jr., Strom, K. and Dalton, R. J. (2001) *Comparative Politics: A Theoretical Framework* (New York: Longman).

Alvarez, M., Cheibub, J. A., Limongi, F. and Przeworski, A. (1996) 'Classifying Political Regimes', *Studies in Comparative International Development*, 31(2): 3–36.

Alwin, D. F., Braun, M., Harkness, J. and Scott, J. (1994) 'Measurement in Multi-National Surveys', in *Trends and Perspectives in Empirical Social Research*, ed. I. Borg and P. Ph. Mohler (Berlin and New York: Walter de Gruyter), pp. 26–39.

Anderson, K. and Baldwin, R. (1987) 'The Political Market for Protection in Industrial Countries', in *Protection, Cooperation, Integration and Development: Essays in Honour of Hiroshi Kitamura*, ed. A. El-Agraa (Basingstoke: Macmillan), pp. 20–37.

Andeweg, R. B. and Thomassen, J. (2005) 'Modes of Political Representation: Toward a New Typology', *Legislative Studies Quarterly* 30(4): 507–28.

Andeweg, R. B. and Timmermans, A. (2007, forthcoming) 'Conflict Management in Coalition Formation', in *Coalition Governance in Western Europe*, ed. K. Strøm, W. C. Müller and T. Bergman (Oxford: Oxford University Press).

Bailey, M., Goldstein, J. and Weingast, B. (1997) 'The Institutional Roots of American Trade Policy: Politics, Coalitions, and International Trade', *World Politics* 49(3): 309–38.

Bartels, L. M and Zaller, J. (2001) 'Presidential Vote Models: A Recount', *PS: Political Science and Politics* 34(1): 9–20.

Barry, B. and Rae, D. (1975) 'Political Evaluation', in *Handbook of Political Science. Vol 1: Political Science, Scope and Theory*, ed. F. I. Greenstein and N. W. Polsby (Reading: Addison-Wesley), pp. 337–401.

Beck, N. (2006) 'Causal Process "Observation": Oxymoron or Old Wine', Manuscript, New York. (Available at: http://www.nyu.edu/gsas/dept/politics/faculty/beck/cponew.pdf)

Bennett, A. (2004) 'Case Study Methods: Design, Use, and Comparative Advantages', in *Models, Numbers & Cases Methods for Studying International*

Relations, ed. D. F. Sprinz and Y. Wolinsky-Nahmias (Ann Arbor: University of Michigan Press), pp. 19–55.

Beyme, K. v. (1992) *Die Politische Theorien der Gegenwart. Eine Einführung* (Opladen: Westdeutscher Verlag).

Binder, Sarah A. (1999) 'The Dynamics of Legislative Gridlock, 1947–1996', *American Political Science Review* 93: 519–33.

Blalock, H. (1984) *Basic Dilemmas in the Social Sciences* (Beverly Hills, CA: Sage).

Bollen, K. A. (1989) *Structural Equations with Latent Variables* (New York: Wiley).

Bollen, K., Entwisle, B. and Alderson, A. S. (1993) 'Macrocomparative Research Methods', *Annual Review of Sociology* 19: 321–51.

Boyer, R. (2005) 'How and Why Capitalisms Differ'. MPIfG Discussion Paper. 05/4. (Cologne: Max Planck Institute for the Study of Societies).

Brady, H. E. (2004) 'Doing Good and Doing Better: How Far Does the Quantitative Template Get Us?', in *Rethinking Social Inquiry: Diverse Tools, Shared Standards*, ed. H. E. Brady and D. Collier (Lanham: Rowman & Littlefield), pp. 53–67.

Brady, H. and Collier, D. (2004) *Rethinking Social Inquiry: Diverse Tools, Shared Standards* (Lanham: Rowman & Littlefield).

Brady, H., Collier, D. and Seawright, J. (2004) 'Refocusing the Discussion of Methodology', in *Rethinking Social Inquiry: Diverse Tools, Shared Standards*, ed. H. Brady and D. Collier (Boulder: Roman & Littlefield), pp. 3–20.

Braumoeller, B. F. (2003) 'Causal Complexity and the Study of Politics', *Political Analysis* 11(3): 209–33.

Braumoeller, B. F. and Goertz, G. (2000) 'The Methodology of Necessary Conditions', *American Journal of Political Science* 44(4): 844–58.

Braun, M. (1998), 'Gender Roles', in *Comparative Politics: The Problem of Equivalence*, ed. J. W. van Deth (London: Routledge), pp. 111–34.

Braun, M. and Mohler, P. Ph. (2003) 'Background Variables', in *Cross-Cultural Survey Methods*, ed. J. A. Harkness, F. J. R. van de Vijver and P. Ph. Mohler (Hoboken: Wiley-Interscience), pp. 101–15.

Breen, R. (1996) *Regression Models – Censored, Sample Selected, or Truncated Data* (Thousand Oaks, CA: Sage).

Brehm, J. (1993) *The Phantom Respondents: Opinion Surveys and Political Representation* (Ann Arbor: Michigan University Press).

Bromley, D. (1986) *The Case-Study Method in Psychology and Related Disciplines* (Chichester: John Wiley & Sons).

Bueno de Mesquita, B. (2003) *Principles of International Politics: People's Power, Preferences, and Perceptions* (Washington, DC: CQ Press).

Bunzl, M. (1979) 'Causal Overdetermination', *The Journal of Philosophy* 76(3): 134–50.

Cameron, Ch. (2000) *Veto Bargaining: Presidents and the Politics of Negative Power* (Cambridge: Cambridge University Press).

Campbell, D. (1975) 'Degrees of Freedom and the Case Study', *Comparative Political Studies* 8(2): 178–93.

Carey, J. M. (2003) 'Discipline, Accountability, and Legislative Voting in Latin America', *Comparative Politics* 35(2): 191–211.

Carey, J. M. (2007, forthcoming) 'Political Institutions, Competing Principals, and Party Unity in Legislative Voting', *American Journal of Political Science*.

Carmines, E. G. and Zeller, R. A. (1994) 'Reliability and Validity Assessment', in *Basic Measurement*, ed. M. S. Lewis-Beck (London: Sage), pp. 1–58.

Carrubba, C. and Gabel, M. (1999) 'Roll-Call Votes and Party Discipline in the European Parliament: Reconsidering MEP Voting Behavior', European Parliament Research Group Working Paper.

Carrubba, C. J., Gabel, M., Murrah, L., Clough, R., Montgomery, E. and Schambach, R. (2006) 'Off the Record: Unrecorded Legislative Votes, Selection Bias and Roll-Call Vote Analysis', *British Journal of Political Science* 36(4): 691–704.

Chima, J. (2005) 'What's the Utility of the Case-Study Method for Social Science Research? A Response to Critiques from the Quantitative/Statistical Perspective', Paper delivered at the 2005 Annual Meeting of the American Political Science Association, Washington, DC, 1–4 September.

Clark, W. R., Gilligan, M. J. and Golder, M. (2006). 'A Simple Multivariate Test for Asymmetric Hypotheses', *Political Analysis* 14(3): 311–31.

Coleman, J. S. (1990) *Foundations of Social Theory* (Cambridge, MA: Harvard University Press).

Collie, M. P. (1985) 'Voting Behavior in Legislatures', in *Handbook of Legislative Research*, ed. G. Loewenberg, Patterson, S. C. and Jewell, M.E. (Cambridge, MA: Harvard University Press), pp. 471–518.

Collier, D. and Adcock, R. (1999) 'Democracy and Dichotomies: A Pragmatic Approach to Choices about Concepts', *Annual Review of Political Science* 2: 537–65.

Collier, D. and Mahon, J. E. (1993) 'Conceptual "Stretching" Revisited: Adapting Categories in Comparative Analysis', *American Political Science Review* 87(4): 845–55.

Collier, D. and Mahoney, J. (1996) 'Insights and Pitfalls: Selection Bias in Qualitative Research', *World Politics* 49(1): 56–91.

Collier, D., Brady, H. E. and Seawright, J. (2004a) 'Critiques, Responses, and Trade-Offs: Drawing Together the Debate', in *Rethinking Social Inquiry: Diverse Tools, Shared Standards*, ed. H. E. Brady and D. Collier (Lanham: Rowman & Littlefield), pp. 195–227.

Collier, D., Brady H. E. and Seawright, J. (2004b) 'Sources of Leverage in Causal Inference: Toward an Alternative View of Methodology?', in *Rethinking Social Inquiry: Diverse Tools, Shared Standards*, ed. H. E. Brady and D. Collier (Lanham: Rowman & Littlefield), pp. 229–66.

Collier, D., Mahoney, J. and Seawright, J. (2004) 'Claiming Too Much: Warnings about Selection Bias', in *Rethinking Social Inquiry: Diverse Tools, Shared Standards*, ed. H. E. Brady and D. Collier (Lanham: Rowman & Littlefield), pp. 85–102.

Collier, D., Seawright, J. and Munck, G. L. (2004) 'The Quest for Standards: King, Keohane and Verba's Designing Social Inquiry', in *Rethinking Social Inquiry: Diverse Tools, Shared Standards*, ed. H. E. Brady and D. Collier (Lanham: Rowman & Littlefield), pp. 21–50.

Cooper, J. and Brady, D. W. (1981) 'Institutional Context and Leadership Style', *American Political Science Review* 75(2): 411–25.

Cooper, J. and Sieberer, U. (n.d.) 'The Importance of Majority Party Size in Congress', Manuscript, Baltimore/Mannheim.

Cooper, J. and Young, G. (2002) 'Party and Preference in Congressional Decision Making', in *Party, Process, and Political Change in Congress*, ed. M. D. McCubbins and D. Brady (Stanford, CA: Stanford University Press), pp. 64–106.

Coppedge, M. (2005) 'Defining and Measuring Democracy', Committee on Concepts and Methods: Working Paper Series, 2.

Conybeare, J. (1984) 'Public Goods, Prisoner's Dilemmas and the International Political Economy', *International Studies Quarterly* 28(1): 5–22.

Cox, G. W. and McCubbins, M. D. (1993) *Legislative Leviathan* (Berkeley, CA: University of California Press).

Cox, G. W. and McCubbins, M. D. (2005) *Setting the Agenda* (Cambridge: Cambridge University Press).

Crepaz, M. M. L. (1996) 'Consensus Versus Majoritarian Democracy. Political Institutions and their Impact on Macroeconomic Performance and Industrial Disputes', *Comparative Political Studies* 29(1): 4–26.

De Bièvre, D. (2004) Governance in international trade: Judicialisation and positive integration in the WTO. Preprint 2004/7 (Bonn: Max Planck Institute for Research on Collective Goods).

De Bièvre, D. (2006) 'The EU Regulatory Trade Agenda and the Quest for WTO Enforcement', *Journal of European Public Policy* 13(6): 105–29.

De Bièvre, P. (2006) 'Counting is Measuring: Learning from the Banks?', *Accreditation and Quality Assurance. Journal for Quality, Comparability and Reliability in Chemical Measurement* 1(1–2): 1–2.

Depauw, S. (1999) 'Parliamentary Party Cohesion and the Scarcity of Sanctions in the Belgian Chamber of Representatives (1991–1995)', *Res Publica* 41(1): 15–39.

Dessler, D. (1999) 'Constructivism Within a Positivist Social Science' *Review of International Studies* 25: 123–38.

De Vaus, D. A. (2001) *Research Design in Social Research* (London: Sage).

Diesing, P. (1972) *Patterns of Discovery in the Social Sciences* (London: Routledge & Kegan Paul).

Dion, D. (1997) *Turning the Legislative Thumbscrew* (Ann Arbor, MI: University of Michigan Press).

Dion, D. (1998) 'Evidence and Inference in the Comparative Case Study', *Comparative Politics* 30(2): 127–45.

Dogan, M. and Pelassy, D. (1990): *How to Compare Nations: Strategies in Comparative Politics*, 2nd edn (Chatham: Chatham House).

Döring, H. (1995) *Parliaments and Majority Rule in Western Europe* (Frankfurt: Campus).

Dreze, J. and Sen, A. (1995) *India. Economic Development and Social Opportunity* (Delhi: Oxford University Press).

Duncan, O. D. (1984) *Notes on Social Measurement: Historical and Critical* (New York: Russel Sage Foundation).

Dunleavy, P. and Rhodes, R.A.W. (1990) 'Core Executive Studies in Britain', *Public Administration* 68(1): 3–28.

Dür, A. (2004) 'Protecting Exporters: Discrimination and Liberalization in Transatlantic Trade Relations, 1932–2003', PhD thesis, Department of Social and Political Sciences (Florence: European University Institute).

Dür, A. (2007) 'Protection for Exporters: Foreign Discrimination and U.S. Trade Liberalization', *International Studies Quarterly* 51(2): 457–80.

Ebbinghaus, B. (2005) 'When Less is More. Selection Problems in Large-*N* and Small-*N* Cross-National Comparisons', *International Sociology* 20(2): 133–52.

Eckes, A. E. (1995) *Opening America's Market: U.S. Foreign Trade Policy since 1776* (Chapel Hill: The University of North Carolina Press).

Eckstein, H. (1975) 'Case Study and Theory in Political Science', in *Handbook of Political Science, Vol. 7: Strategies of Inquiry*, ed. F. Greenstein and N. Polsby (Reading: Addison-Wesley), pp. 79–137.

Eckstein, H. (1992) 'Case Study and Theory in Political Science', in *Regarding Politics. Essays on Political Theory, Stability, and Change*, ed. H. Eckstein (Berkeley: University of California Press), pp. 117–76.

Edwards, George C., III., Barrett, Andrew and Peake, Jeffrey (1997) 'The Legislative Impact of Divided Government', *American Journal of Political Science* 41: 545–63.

Eliot, T. S. (1943) *Four Quartets* (London: Faber & Faber).

Epstein, D. and O'Halloran, S. (1999) *Delegating Powers: A Transaction Cost Politics Approach to Policy Making under Separate Powers* (Cambridge: Cambridge University Press).

Esping-Andersen, G. (1990) *The Three Worlds of Welfare Capitalism* (Cambridge: Polity Press).

Faas, T. (2003) 'To Defect or Not to Defect? National, Institutional and Party Group Pressures on MEPs and their Consequences for Party Group Cohesion in the European Parliament', *European Journal of Political Research* 42(6): 841–66.

Farr, J. (2004) 'Social Capital. A Conceptual History', *Political Theory* 32: 6–33.

Fiorina, M. (1996) *Divided Government*, 2nd edn (Boston: Allyn & Bacon).

Fischer, C. S. (2005) 'Bowling Alone: What's the Score? Book Review', *Social Networks* 27: 155–67.

Flyvbjerg, B. (2004) 'Five Misunderstandings About Case-Study Research', in *Qualitative Research Practice*, ed. C. Seale et al. (London: Sage), pp. 420–34.

Flyvbjerg, B. (2006) 'Five Misunderstandings About Case-Study Research' *Qualitative Inquiry* 12(2): 219–45.

Franchino, F. (2007) *The Powers of the Union: Delegation in the EU* (Cambridge: Cambridge University Press).

Frankfort-Nachmias, C. and Nachmias, D. (1992) *Research Methods in the Social Sciences* (New York: St. Martin's Press).

Fuchs, D. (2000) 'Typen und Indizes demokratischer Systeme', in *Empirische Demokratiemessung*, ed. H.-J. Lauth, G. Pickel and C. Welzel (Wiesbaden: Westdeutscher Verlag), pp. 27–38.

Gabriel, O. W., Kunz, V., Roßteutscher, S. and van Deth, J. W. (2002) *Sozialkapital und Demokratie. Zivilgesellschaftliche Ressourcen im Vergleich* (Wien: WUV Universitätsverlag).

Ganghof, S. (2005a) 'Kausale Perspektiven in der vergleichenden Politikwissenschaft: X-zentrierte und Y-zentrierte Forschungsdesigns', in *Vergleichen in der Politikwissenschaft*, ed. S. Kropp and M. Minkenberg (Wiesbaden: VS Verlag für Sozialwissenschaften), pp. 76–93.

Ganghof, S. (2005b) 'Normative Modelle, institutionelle Typen und beobachtbare Verhaltensmuster: Ein Vorschlag zum Vergleich parlamentarischer Demokratien', *Politische Vierteljahresschrift* 46(3): 406–31.

Geddes, B. (1990) 'How the Cases You Choose Affect the Answers You Get: Selection Bias in Comparative Politics', in *Political Analysis*, 2nd edn, ed. J. A. Stimson (Ann Arbor: University of Michigan Press), pp. 131–50.

Geddes, B. (2003) *Paradigms and Sand Castles: Theory Building and Research Design in Comparative Politics* (Ann Arbor: University of Michigan Press).

George, A. L. and Bennett, A. (1997) 'Process Tracing in Case Study Research'. (Available at: http://web.mit.edu/17.878/www/Bennett/Process%20 Tracing%20in%20CS%20Research.htm)

George, A. L. and Bennett, A. (2005) *Case Studies and Theory Development in the Social Sciences* (Cambridge, MA: MIT Press).

George, A. and McKeown, T. (1985) 'Case Studies and Theories of Organizational Decision Making', in *Advances in Information Processing in Organizations, Vol. 2*, ed. R. Coulam and R. Smith (Greenwich: JAI Press), pp. 21–58.

Gerring, J. (2001) *Social Science Methodology: A Critical Framework* (Cambridge: Cambridge University Press).

Gerring, J. (2004) 'What is a Case Study and What is it Good for?', *American Political Science Review* 98(2): 341–54.

Gerring, J. (2005) 'Causation. A Unified Framework for the Social Sciences', *Journal of Theoretical Politics* 17: 163–98.

Gerring, J. and Barresi, P. A. (2003) 'Putting Ordinary Language to Work: A Min-Max Strategy of Concept Formation in the Social Sciences', *Journal of Theoretical Politics* 15(2): 201–32.

Gerring, J. and Yesnowitz, J. (2006), 'A Normative Turn in Political Science?', *Polity* 38(1): 101–33.

Glover, J. (1996) 'Epistemological and Methodological Considerations in Secondary Analysis', in *Cross-National Research Methods in the Social Sciences*, ed. L. Hantrais and S. Mangen (London and New York: Pinter), pp. 28–38.

Goertz, G. and Levy, J. (2004) 'Causal Explanation, Necessary Conditions, and Case Studies', in *Causal Explanations, Necessary Conditions, and Case Studies: World War I and the End of the Cold War*, ed. G. Goertz and J. Levy (book manuscript), pp. 9–41.

Goertz, G. and Starr, H. (eds) (2003) *Necessary Conditions: Theory, Methodology, and Applications* (Lanham: Rowman & Littlefield).

Goldstein, J. (1993) *Ideas, Interests, and American Trade Policy* (Ithaca, NY: Cornell University Press).

Goldthorpe, J. (1997) 'Current Issues in Comparative Macrosociology: A Debate on Methodological Issues', *Comparative Social Research* 16: 1–26.

Goldthorpe, J. H. (2000) *On Sociology: Numbers, Narratives, and the Integration of Research and Theory* (Oxford: Oxford University Press).

Goldthorpe, J. H. (2001) 'Causation, Statistics, and Sociology', *European Sociological Review* 17(1): 1–20.

Graf Kielmansegg, P. (2001) 'Notizen zu einer anderen Politikwissenschaft. Über Wilhelm Hennis' politikwissenschaftliche Abhandlungen', *Merkur* 55(625): 436–43.

Greene, W. H. (2003) *Econometric Analysis* (Upper Saddle River: Prentice Hall).

Grieco, J. (1990) *Cooperation Among Nations: Europe, America, and Non-Tariff Barriers to Trade* (Ithaca, NY: Cornell University Press).

Gschwend, T. (2005) 'Analyzing Quota Sample Data and the Peer Review Process', *French Politics* 3(1): 88–91.

Gschwend, T. and Leuffen, D. (2005) 'Divided We Stand – Unified We Govern? Cohabitation and Regime Voting in the 2002 French Elections', *British Journal of Political Science* 35(4): 691–712.

Gunther, R. and Diamond, L. (2003) 'Species of Political Parties. A New Typology', *Party Politics* 9(2): 167–99.

Hall, P. A. and Soskice, D. (eds) (2001) *Varieties of Capitalism: The Institutional Foundations of Comparative Advantage* (Oxford: Oxford University Press).

Hatch, J. A. (1985) 'The Quantoids versus the Smooshes: Struggling with Methodological Rapprochement' *Issues in Education* 3(2): 158–67.

Haverland, M. (2000) 'National Adaptation to European Integration: The Importance of Institutional Veto Points', *Journal of Public Policy* 20(1): 83–103.

Hazan, R. Y. (2003) 'Does Cohesion Equal Discipline?', *Journal of Legislative Studies* 9(4): 1–11.

Heckman, J. J. (1976) 'The Common Structure of Statistical Models of Truncation, Sample Selection and Limited Dependent Variables and a Simple Estimator for such Models', *Annals of Economic and Social Measurement* 5(4): 475–92.

Heckman, J. J. (1979) 'Sample Selection Bias as a Specification Error', *Econometrica* 47(1): 153–62.

Hedström, P. and Swedberg, R. (eds.) (1998) *Social Mechanisms: An Analytical Approach to Social Theory* (Cambridge: Cambridge University Press).

Helmke, G. and Levitsky, S. (2004) 'Informal Institutions and Comparative Politics. A Research Agenda', *Perspectives on Politics* 2(4) 725–40.

Hempel, C. G. (1952) *Fundamentals of Concept Formation in Empirical Science* (Chicago: University of Chicago Press).

Hempel, C. G. (1965) *Aspects of Scientific Explanation and Other Essays in the Philosophy of Science* (New York: Free Press).

Henderson, E. A. (2004) 'Mistaken Identity: Testing the Clash of Civilizations Thesis in Light of Democratic Peace Claims', *British Journal of Political Science* 34(3): 539–54.

Hennis, W. (1963) *Politik und praktische Philosophie: eine Studie zur Rekonstruktion der politischen Wissenschaft* (Neuwied am Rhein: Luchterhand).

Hiscox, M. (1999) 'The Magic Bullet? The RTAA, Institutional Reform, and Trade Liberalization', *International Organization* 53(4): 669–98.

Hix, S. (2001) 'Legislative Behaviour and Party Competition in the European Parliament: An Application of Nominate to the EU', *Journal of Common Market Studies* 39(4): 663–88.

Hix, S. (2002) 'Parliamentary Behaviour with Two Principals: Preferences, Parties and Voting in the European Parliament', *American Journal of Political Science* 46(3): 688–98.

Hix, S. (2004) 'Electoral Institutions and Legislative Behavior – Explaining Voting Defection in the European Parliament', *World Politics* 56(2): 194–223.

Hörl, B., Warntjen, A. and Wonka, A. (2005) 'Built on Quicksand? A Decade of Procedural Spatial Models on EU Legislative Decision-Making', *Journal Of European Public Policy* 12(3): 592–606.

Huber, J. D. and Shipan, C. R. (2002) *Deliberate Discretion: The Institutional Foundations of Bureaucratic Autonomy* (Cambridge: Cambridge University Press).

Hug, S. (2003) 'Selection Bias in Comparative Research: The Case of Incomplete Datasets', *Political Analysis* 11(3): 225–74.

Hug, S. (2005) 'Selection Effects in Roll Call Votes', paper presented at the ECPR Joint Sessions of Workshops, Granada, 14–19 April, 2005.

Huntington, S. P. (1996) *The Clash of Civilizations and the Remaking of World Order* (New York: Simon & Schuster).

Jervis, R. (1997) 'Samuel P. Huntington: The Clash of Civilizations and the Remaking of World Order', *Political Science Quarterly* 112(2): 307–8.

Johnson, T. P. (1998) 'Approaches to Equivalence in Cross-Cultural and Cross-National Survey Research', *ZUMA Nachrichten Spezial – Cross-Cultural Survey Equivalence* 3: 1–40.

Jung, S. (2001) *Die Logik Direkter Demokratie*. (Wiesbaden: Westdeutscher Verlag).

Kaeding, M. and Selck, T. (2005) 'Mapping Out the Political Europe: Coalition Patterns in EU Decision-Making', *International Political Science Review* 26(3): 271–90.

Kaiser, A. (1997) 'Types of Democracy. From Classical to New Institutionalism', *Journal of Theoretical Politics* 9(4): 419–44.

Kaiser, A. (2002) *Mehrheitsdemokratie und Institutionenreform: Verfassungspolitischer Wandel in Australien, Großbritannien, Kanada und Neuseeland im Vergleich* (Frankfurt/Main: Campus).

Kaiser, A. (2004) 'Alternanz und Inklusion: Zur Repräsentation politischer Präferenzen in den westeuropäischen Demokratien, 1950–2000', in *Demokratietheorie und Demokratieentwicklung: Festschrift für Peter Graf Kielmansegg* (Wiesbaden: VS Verlag für Sozialwissenschaften), pp. 173–96.

Kaiser, A., Lehnert, M., Miller, B. and Sieberer, U. (2002) 'The Democratic Quality of Institutional Regimes: A Conceptual Framework', *Political Studies* 50(2): 313–31.

Katz, R. S. and Mair, P. (1992) 'Introduction', in *Party Organizations*, ed. R. S. Katz and P. Mair (London: Sage), pp.1–20.

King, C. M. (2004) *Supreme Court Decision-Making in Federal Agency Cases*, unpublished PhD Thesis (New York: Stony Brook University).

King, G. and Zeng, L. (2007) 'When Can History be Our Guide? The Pitfalls of Counterfactual Inference', *International Studies Quarterly*, forthcoming.

King, G., Keohane, R. O. and Verba, S. (1994) *Designing Social Inquiry – Scientific Inference in Qualitative Research* (Princeton, NJ: Princeton University Press).

King, G., Murray, C. J. L., Salomon, J. A. and Tandon, A. (2004) 'Enhancing the Validity and Cross-Cultural Comparability of Measurement in Survey Research', *American Political Science Review* 9): 191–207.

Kingdon, J. W. (1977) 'Models of Legislative Voting', *Journal of Politics* 39(3): 563–95.

Koford, K. (1989) 'Dimensions in Congressional Voting', *American Political Science Review* 83(3): 949–62.

Kohn, M. L. (1987) 'Cross-national research as an analytic strategy', *American Sociological Review* 52(6): 713–31.

Koremenos, B., Lipson, C. and Snidal, D. (2001) 'The Rational Design of International Institutions', *International Organization* 55(4): 761–99.

Krasner, S. (1976) 'State Power and the Structure of International Trade', *World Politics* 28(3): 317–47.

Krehbiel, K. (1993) 'Where's the Party?', *British Journal of Political Science* 23(2): 235–66.

Krehbiel, K. (2000) 'Party Discipline and Measures of Partisanship', *American Journal of Political Science* 44(2): 212–27.

Kreppel, A. and Hix, S. (2003) 'From 'Grand Coalition' to Left-Right Confrontation – Explaining the Shifting Structure of Party Competition in the European Parliament', *Comparative Political Studies* 36(1): 75–96.

Kropp, S. (2004) 'Gerhard Schröder as "Coordination Chancellor"': The Impact of Institutions and Arenas on the Chancellor's Style of Governance', in *Germany On The Road To 'Normalcy': Policies and Politics Of The Red-Green Federal Government (1998–2002)*, 1st edn., ed. W. Reutter (New York: Palgrave Macmillan), pp. 67–88.

Kuhn, T. (1969) *The Structure of Scientific Revolutions* (Chicago: University of Chicago Press).

Laitin, D. D. (2002) 'Comparative Politics', in *Political Science: The State of the Discipline*, ed. I. Katznelson and H. V. Milner (New York: W. W. Norton), pp. 630–59.

Lakatos, I. (1974) 'Falsification and the Methodology of Scientific Research Programmes', in *Criticism and the Growth of Knowledge*, ed. I. Lakatos and A. Musgrave (Cambridge: Cambridge University Press), pp. 91–196.

Lakatos, I. (1979) *The Methodology of Scientific Research Programmes* (Cambridge: Cambridge University Press).

Laver, M. and Shepsle, K. (1994) 'Cabinet Ministers and Government Formation in Parliamentary Democracies', in *Cabinet Ministers and Parliamentary Government*, ed. M. Laver and K. A. Shepsle (Cambridge: Cambridge University Press), pp. 3–12.

Laver, M. and Schofield, N. (1998) *Multiparty Government* (Ann Arbor, MI: University of Michigan Press).

Lehnert, M. (2002) 'Zwischen Wahlsystemforschung und Demokratietheorie. G. Bingham Powells "Elections as Instruments of Democracy"', unpublished manuscript (Mannheim: University of Mannheim).

Lewis-Beck, M. S. and Tom W. Rice (1992) *Forecasting Elections* (Washington, DC: CQ Press).

Lichbach, M. I. (1997) 'Social Theory and Comparative Politics', in *Comparative Politics*, ed. M. I. Lichbach and A. S. Zuckerman (Cambridge: Cambridge University Press), pp. 239–76.

Lieberman, E. S. (2005) 'Nested Analysis as a Mixed-Method Strategy for Comparative Research', *American Political Science Review* 99(3): 435–52.

Lieberson, S. (1992) 'Small Ns and Big Conclusions', in *What is a Case? Exploring the Foundations of Social Inquiry*, ed. C. C. Ragin and H. S. Becker (Cambridge: Cambridge University Press), pp. 105–18.

Lijphart, A. (1968) *The Politics of Accommodation: Pluralism and Democracy in the Netherlands* (Berkeley: University of California Press).

Lijphart, A. (1971) 'Comparative Politics and the Comparative Method', *American Political Science Review* 65(3): 682–93.

Lijphart, A. (1984) *Democracies: Patterns of Majoritarian and Consensus Government in Twenty-One Countries* (New Haven, CT: Yale University Press).

Lijphart, A. (1999) *Patterns of Democracy: Government Forms and Performance in Thirty-Six Countries* (New Haven, CT: Yale University Press).

Lipset, S. M. (1959) 'Some Social Requisites of Democracy: Economic Development and Political Legitimacy', *American Political Science Review* 53(1): 69–105.

Lohmann, S. and O'Halloran, S. (1994) 'Divided Government and US Trade Policy: Theory and Evidence', *International Organization* 48(4): 595–632.

Long, J. S. (1997) *Regression Models for Categorical and Limited Dependent Variables* (Thousand Oaks, CA: Sage).

Luebbert, G. M. (1987) 'Social Foundations of Political Order in Interwar Europe', *World Politics* 39(4): 449–78.

Mackie, J. (1980) *The Cement of the Universe: A Study of Causation* (Oxford: Clarendon Press).

Mahoney, J. (2000) 'Strategies of Causal Inference in Small-N Analysis', *Sociological Methods and Research* 28(4): 387–424.

Mahoney, J. and Goertz, G. (2006) 'A Tale of Two Cultures: Contrasting Quantitative and Qualitative Research', *Political Analysis* 14(3): 227–49.

Mansfield, E. (1994) *Power, Trade, and War* (Princeton, NJ: Princeton University Press).

Mayhew, D. R. (1991) *Divided we Govern: Party Control, Lawmaking, and Investigations, 1946–1990* (New Haven, CT: Yale University Press).

McCall Smith, J. (2000) 'The Politics of Dispute Settlement Design: Explaining Legalism in Regional Trade Pacts', *International Organization* 54(1): 137–80.

McKeown, T. J. (1999) 'Case Studies and the Statistical Worldview: Review of King, Keohane, and Verba's *Designing Social Inquiry: Scientific Inference in Qualitative Research*', *International Organization* 53(1): 161–90.

McKeown, T. J. (2004) 'Case Studies and the Limits of the Quantitative Worldview', in *Rethinking Social Inquiry*, ed. H. E. Brady and D. Collier (Lanham, MD: Rowman & Littlefield), pp.139–67.

McKinney, J. C. (1966) *Constructive Typology and Social Theory* (New York: Appleton-Century-Crofts).

Meckstroth, T. (1975) '"Most Different Systems" and "Most Similar Systems": A Study in the Logic of Comparative Inquiry', *Comparative Political Studies* 8(2): 132–57.

Merton, R. (1949) *Social Theory and Social Structure* (New York: The Free Press).

Miller, B. (2006) *The Traffic Warden Control of Bureaucratic Agents: A Principal-Agent Analysis of Ombudsman Institutions in 25 Democracies*, typescript, Mannheim.

Milner, H. (1988) *Resisting Protectionism: Global Industries and the Politics of International Trade* (Princeton, NJ: Princeton University Press).

Milner, H. (1998) 'Rationalizing Politics: The Emerging Synthesis of International, American and Comparative Politics', *International Organization* 52(4): 759–86.

Milner, H. (2002) 'International Trade', in *Handbook of International Relations*, ed. W. Carlsnaes, T. Risse, B. A. Simons (London: Sage), pp. 448–61.

Moravcsik, A. (1998) *The Choice for Europe: Social Purpose and State Power from Messina to Maastricht* (Ithaca, NY: Cornell University Press).

Morgenstern, S. (2004) *Patterns of Legislative Politics* (Cambridge: Cambridge University Press).

Morgenthau, H. (1987) *Politics among Nations: The Struggle for Power and Peace*, 5th edn (New York: Knopf).

Munck, G. L. (2004) 'Tools for Qualitative Research', in *Rethinking Social Inquiry: Diverse Tools, Shared Standards*, ed. H. E. Brady and D. Collier (Lanham, MD: Rowman & Littlefield), pp. 105–21.

Müller, W. C. and Strøm, K. (2000) *Coalition Governments in Western Europe* (Oxford: Oxford University Press).

Niessen, M. (1982) 'Qualitative Aspects in Cross-National Comparative Research and the Problem of Functional Equivalence', in *International Comparative Research: Problems of Theory, Methodology and Organisation in Eastern and Western Europe*, ed. M. Niessen and J. Peschar (Oxford: Pergamon Press), pp. 83–104.

Norpoth, H. and Gschwend, T. (2003) 'The Red-Green Victory: Against all Odds?', *German Politics and Society* 21: 15–34.

Pennings, P., Keman, H. and Kleinnijenhuis, J. (1999) *Doing Research in Political Science: An Introduction to Comparative Methods andSstatistics* (London: Sage).

Peters, B. G. (1998) *Comparative Politics: Theory and Methods* (New York: New York University Press).

Pierson, P. and Skocpol, T. 2002. 'Historical institutionalism in contemporary political science', in *Political Science: The State of the Discipline*, ed. I. Katznelson and H. Milner (New York: Norton), pp. 693–721.

Plümper, T., Schneider, C. J. and Troeger, V. E. (2006) 'The Politics of EU Eastern Enlargement – Evidence from a Heckman Selection Model', *British Journal of Political Science* 36(1): 17–28.

Pollack, M. A. (2003) *The Engines of Integration: Delegation, Agency and Agenda Setting in the EU* (Oxford: Oxford University Press).

Polsby, N. W. and Schickler, E. (2002) 'Landmarks in the Study of Congress since 1945', *Annual Review of Political Science* 5: 333–67.

Poole, K. T. and Rosenthal, H. (1997) *Congress* (New York: Oxford University Press).

Popper, K. R. (1965) *The Logic of Scientific Discovery* (London: Hutchinson).

Popper, K. R. (1990) *A World of Propensities* (Bristol: Thoemmes).

Powell, G. B., Jr. (2000) *Elections as Instruments of Democracy: Majoritarian and Proportional Visions* (New Haven, CT: Yale University Press).

Przeworski, A. and Teune, H. (1966) 'Equivalence in Cross-National Research', *Public Opinion Quarterly* (30): 551–68.

Przeworski, A. and Teune, H. (1970) *The Logic of Comparative Social Inquiry* (New York: Wiley-Interscience).

Przeworski, A. and Teune, H. (1982) *The Logic of Comparative Social Inquiry* (Malabar: Krieger).

Putnam, R. (1988) 'Diplomacy and Domestic Politics: The logic of two-level games', *International Organization* 42(3): 427–60.

Putnam, R. D., (1993) *Making Democracy Work: Civic Traditions in Modern Italy* (Princeton, NJ: Princeton University Press).

Putnam, R. D., (2000) *Bowling Alone: The Collapse and Revival of American Community* (New York, London, Toronto, Sydney, Singapore: Touchstone).

Ragin, C. C. (1987) *The Comparative Method: Moving beyond Qualitative and Quantitative Strategies* (Berkeley: University of California Press).

Ragin, C. C. (1994) *Constructing Social Research: The Unity and Diversity of Method* (Thousand Oaks, CA: Pine Forge Press).

Ragin, C. C. (2000) *Fuzzy-Set Social Science* (Chicago: University of Chicago Press).

Ragin, C. C. (2004) 'Turning the Tables', in *Rethinking Social Inquiry*, ed. H. E. Brady and D. Collier (Lanham, MD: Rowman & Littlefield), pp.123–38.

Rasch, B. E. (1999) 'Electoral Systems, Parliamentary Committees, and Party Discipline: The Norwegian Storting in Comparative Perspective', in *Party*

Discipline and Parliamentary Government, ed. S. Bowler, D. M. Farrell and R. S. Katz (Columbus, OH: Ohio State University Press), pp.121–40.

Reynal-Querol, M. (2002) 'Ethnicity, Political Systems, and Civil Wars', *Journal of Conflict Resolution* 46(1): 29–54.

Riker, W. H. (1962) *The Theory of Political Coalitions* (New Haven, CT: Yale University Press).

Rodríguez, F. and Rodrik, D. (1999) 'Trade Policy and Economic Growth: A Skeptic's Guide to the Cross-National Evidence', CEPR Discussion Paper, No. 2143.

Rogowski, R. (1995) 'The Role of Theory and Anomaly in Social-Scientific Inference', *American Political Science Review* 89(2): 467–70.

Rogowski, R. (2004) 'How Inference in the Social (but Not the Physical) Science Neglects Theoretical Anomaly', in *Rethinking Social Inquiry*, ed. H. E. Brady and D. Collier (Lanham, MD: Rowman & Littlefield), pp. 75–83.

Rohwer, G. and Pötter, U. (2002) *Methoden sozialwissenschaftlicher Datenkonstruktion* (Weinheim: Juventa).

Rosa, H. and Kaiser, A. (2004) 'The Fine Art of Government: Wilhelm Hennis's Comprehensive Conception of Politics and Practical Insight', *European Journal of Political Theory* 3(1): 99–107.

Rosecrance, R. (1998) 'Samuel P. Huntington: The Clash of Civilizations and the Remaking of World Order', *American Political Science Review* 92(4): 978–80.

Rosenthal, H. (1992) 'The Unidimensional Congress is not the Result of Selective Gatekeeping', *American Journal of Political Science* 36(1): 31–5.

Roßteutscher, S. and van Deth, J. W., (2002) 'Associations between Associations: The Structure of the Voluntary Association Sector'. Mannheim: Mannheimer Zentrum für Europäische Sozialforschung – Working Papers 56.

Rudzio, W. (2005) *Informelles Regieren: Zum Koalitionsmanagement in deutschen und österreichischen Regierungen* (Wiesbaden: VS Verlag für Sozialwissenschaften).

Russett, B. (1993) *Grasping the Democratic Peace: Principles for a Post-Cold War World* (Princeton, NJ: Princeton University Press).

Saalfeld, T. (1995) *Parteisoldaten und Rebellen* (Opladen: Leske & Budrich).

Sartori, G. (1970) 'Concept Misformation in Comparative Politics', *American Journal of Political Science* 64(4): 1033–53.

Sartori, G. (1984) 'Guidelines for Concept Analysis', in *Social Science Concepts: A Systematic Analysis*, ed. G. Sartori (Beverly Hills, CA: Sage), pp. 15–85.

Schäfer, J. (2006) *Sozialkapital und politische Orientierungen von Jugendlichen in Deutschland* (Wiesbaden: VS Verlag).

Scharpf, F. W. (1996) 'Negative and Positive Integration in the Political Economy of European Welfare States', in *Governance in the European Union*, ed. G. Marks, F. Scharpf, P. C. Schmitter and W. Streeck (London: Sage), pp. 15–39.

Scharpf, Fritz W., 1997, *Games Real Actors Play: Actor-Centered Institutionalism in Policy Research*, Boulder, CO: Westview Press.

Schelling, Thomas (1960) *The Strategy of Conflict* (Cambridge, MA: Harvard University Press).

Schmidt, M. G. (1994) 'Messen', *in Lexikon der Politik (2): Polititikwissenschaftliche Methoden*, ed. D. Nohlen (München: C. H. Beck), pp. 257–8.

Schmitter, P. C. (1979) 'Still the Century of Corporatism?', in *Trends Toward Corporatist Intermediation*, ed. P. C. Schmitter and G. Lehmbruch (Beverly Hills, CA: Sage), pp. 7–52.

Schnietz, K. (2000) 'The Institutional Foundation of U.S. Trade Policy: Revisiting Explanations for the 1934 Reciprocal Trade Agreements Act', *Journal of Policy History* 12(4): 417–44.

Schwarz, N. and Hippler, H. J. (1991) 'Response alternatives: The impact of their choice and ordering', in *Measurement error in surveys*, ed. P. Biemer, R. Groves, N. Mathiowetz and S. Sudman (Chichester: Wiley), pp. 41–56.

Schwarz, N., Bless, H., Hippler, H.-J., Strack, F. and Sudman, S. (1994) 'Cognitive and Communicative Aspects of Survey Measurement', in *Trends and Perspectives in Empirical Social Research*, ed. I. Borg and P. Ph. Mohler (Berlin and New York: Walter de Gruyter), pp. 26–39.

Seawright, J. (2002) 'Testing for Necessary and/or Sufficient Causation: Which Cases Are Relevant?' *Political Analysis* 10(2): 178–93.

Shugart, M. S. and Carey, J. M. (1992) *Presidents and Assemblies: Constitutional Design and Electoral Dynamics* (Cambridge: Cambridge University Press).

Siaroff, A. (1999) 'Corporatism in 24 Industrial Democracies: Meaning and Measurement', *European Journal of Political Research* 36(1) 175–205.

Siaroff, A. (2003) 'Varieties of Parliamentarism in the Advanced Industrial Societies', *International Political Science Review* 24(4): 445–64.

Sieberer, U. (2006) 'Party Unity in Parliamentary Democracies', *Journal of Legislative Studies* 12(2): 150–78.

Skocpol, T. (1979) *States and Social Revolutions* (Cambridge: Cambridge University Press).

Snyder, J. M. (1992) 'Gatekeeping or Not, Sample Selection in the Roll Call Agenda Matters', *American Journal of Political Science* 36(1): 36–9.

Spector, P. E. (1981) *Research Designs* (Beverly Hills, CA: Sage).

Spicker, P. (2004) 'Developing Indicators: Issues in the use of quantitative data about poverty', *Policy & Politics* 32: 431–40.

Stevens, S. S. (1946) 'On the Theory of Scales of Measurement', *Science* 103: 677–80.

Stevens, S. S. (1951) *Handbook of Experimental Psychology* (New York: Wiley).

Stokman, F. and Thomson, R. (2004) 'Winners and Losers in the European Union', *European Union Politics* 5(1): 5–23.

Taagepera, R. (2003) 'Arend Lijphart's Dimensions of Democracy: Logical Connections and Institutional Design', *Political Studies* 51(1): 1–19.

Taagepera, R. and Grofman, B. (2003) 'Mapping the Indices of Seats-Votes Disproportionality and Inter-Election Volatility', *Party Politics* 9(6): 659–77.

Thiem, J. (2006) 'Explaining Roll Call Vote Request in the European Parliament', MZES Working Paper No. 90 (Mannheim: Mannheimer Zentrum für Europäische Sozialforschung).

Thomas, G. (2005) 'The Qualitative Foundations of Political Science Methodology', *Perspectives on Politics* 3(4): 855–66.

Thomson, R., Boerefijn, J. and Stokman, F. (2004) 'Actor alignments in European Union decision making', *European Journal of Political Research* 43(2): 237–61.

Thomson, R., Stokman, F., Achen, C. and König, T. (eds) (2006) *The European Union Decides* (Cambridge: Cambridge University Press).

Tobin, J. (1958) 'Estimation of Relationships for Limited Dependent Variables', *Econometrica* 26(1): 24–36.

Tsebelis, G. (1990) *Nested Games: Rational Choice in Comparative Politics* (Berkeley: University of California Press).

Tsebelis, G. (2002) *Veto Players: How Political Institutions Work*. (Princeton, NJ.: Princeton University Press).

Tsebelis, G. and Garrett, G. (2000) 'Legislative Politics in the European Union', *European Union Politics* 1(1): 9–36.

van de Vijver, F. J. R. (2003) 'Bias and Equivalence: Cross-Cultural Perspectives', in *Cross-Cultural Survey Methods*, ed. J. A. Harkness, F. J. R. van de Vijver and P. Ph. Mohler (Hoboken: Wiley-Interscience), pp. 143–55.

van Deth, J. (1998) 'Equivalence in comparative political research', in *Comparative Politics: The Problem of Equivalence*, ed. J. Van Deth (London: Routledge), pp. 1–19.

van Deth, J. W. (2003) 'Using Published Survey Data', in *Cross-Cultural Survey Methods*, ed. J. A. Harkness, F. J. R. van de Vijver and P. Ph. Mohler (Hoboken: Wiley-Interscience) pp. 291–309.

van Deth, J. W. and Kreuter, F. (1998) 'Membership of Voluntary Associations', in *Comparative Politics: The Problem of Equivalence*, ed. J. W. van Deth (London: Routledge), pp. 135–55.

Vandoren, P. M. (1990) 'Can We Learn the Causes of Congressional Decisions From Roll-Call Data?' *Legislative Studies Quarterly* 5(3): 311–40.

Voltmer, K. and Schmitt-Beck, R. (2006) 'New democracies without citizens? Mass media and democratic orientations – a four-country comparison', in *Mass Media and Political Communication in New Democracies*, ed. K. Voltmer (London: Routledge), pp. 228–45.

Walker, H. A. and Cohen, B. P. (1985) 'Scope Statements: Imperatives for Evaluating Theory' *American Sociological Review* 50(3): 288–301.

Weber, M. (1988/1904) 'Die "Objektivität" sozialwissenschaftlicher und sozialpolitischer Erkenntnis', in *Gesammelte Aufsätze zur Wissenschaftslehre*, ed. J. Winckelmann (Tübingen: J. C. B. Mohr), pp. 146–214

Western, B. (1995) 'Concepts and suggestions for robust regression analysis', *American Journal of Political Science* 39(3): 786–817.

Westle, B. (1998) 'Tolerance', in *Comparative Politics: The Problem of Equivalence*, ed. J. W. van Deth (London: Routledge), pp. 20–60.

Whitaker, R. (2005) 'National Parties in the European Parliament – An Influence in the Committee System?' *European Union Politics* 6(1): 5–28.

Winch, R. F. (1947) 'Heuristic and Empirical Typologies: A Job for Factor Analysis', *American Sociological Review* 12(1): 68–75.

Winship, C. and Mare, R. D. (1992) 'Models for Sample Selection Bias', *Annual Review of Sociology* 18: 327–50.

Yin, R. (2002) *Case Study Research: Design and Methods*, 3rd edn (London: Sage).

Index